Learning from Sure Start

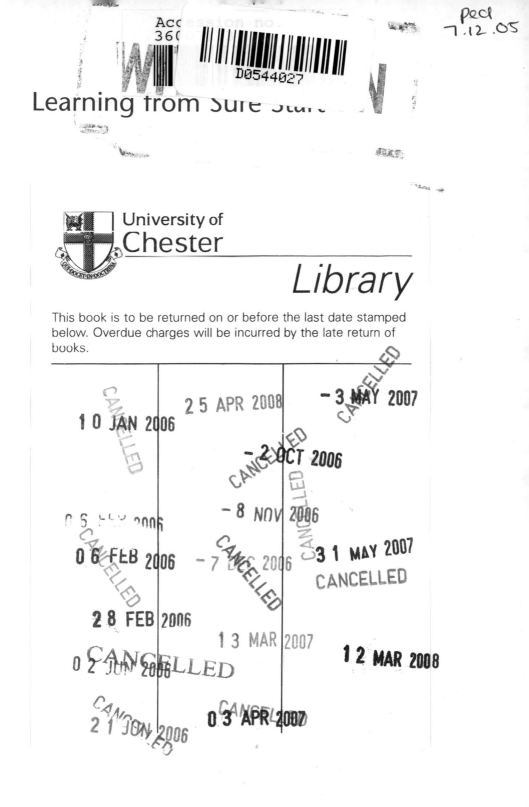

University of
Chester

Library

This book is to be returned on or before the last date stamped
below. Overdue charges will be incurred by the late return of
books.

Learning from Sure Start

Working with young children and their families

Edited by Jo Weinberger, Caroline Pickstone and Peter Hannon

Open University Press

Open University Press
McGraw-Hill Education
McGraw-Hill House
Shoppenhangers Road
Maidenhead, Berkshire
England SL6 2QL

email: enquiries@openup.co.uk
world wide web: www.openup.co.uk

and Two Penn Plaza, New York, NY 1012–2289
USA

First published 2005

A catalogue record of this book is available from the British Library

ISBN 0 335 216382 (pb)   0 335 216390 (hb)

Library of Congress Cataloging-in-Publication Data
CIP data has been applied for

Typeset by BookEns Ltd, Royston, Herts.
Printed in Poland by OZGraf S.A.
www.polskabook.pl

To the children and families of
Foxhill and Parson Cross

Acknowledgements

To all the parents, children, workers and members of the community who have contributed ideas, information and time to turn this book into a reality.

Particular thanks are due to Heather Scott, for the fantastic support and imagination she has contributed throughout to the whole project, extending well beyond the role of research secretary. Our thanks also extend to Greg Brooks, Michele Moore, Cathy Nutbrown, members of the Sure Start Foxhill and Parson Cross *Research, Evaluation and Advisory Committee* and everyone else who has made a contribution to this collective enterprise.

Contents

Foreword

I am delighted to be asked to write this foreword. Foxhill and Parson Cross was a Sure Start 'trailblazer', set up in the very early days of the programme, and has grown from strength to strength. I had the pleasure of attending the launch of the programme in August 1999. It was a cold, wet day on a grim patch of land on a Sheffield estate. Hundreds of people turned out for the event, including the local MP, David Blunkett. Wide community involvement as well as significant political commitment was evident from the start.

This book demonstrates the key strength of Sure Start, its breadth of vision, working on health, education, social welfare and community development. Indeed, my favourite part of the book is the appendix describing the range of services available from Foxhill and Parson Cross Sure Start. It shows not only the range of services, but also that it is possible for the same organization to provide services for all along with services for families with quite complex difficulties. It shows how, with the right effort, statutory and voluntary organizations can work side by side. It also shows how important it is to engage local people in finding solutions, blending professional and community support to strengthen both.

Another asset of the Foxhill and Parson Cross programme was the involvement of academic researchers from the very start of the project. The evaluation strategy was not a second thought after one or two years of operation; it was built in from the beginning, ensuring a complete story told by the researchers, the service providers, and the parents who used the services.

Sure Start has grown enormously since the early days of establishing the trailblazer programmes, but has managed to maintain some key features. Indeed, these features have informed the broader children's agenda set out in *Every Child Matters**, working with parents as well as children, tailoring services to individual family needs, working in interdisciplinary teams, and the need for good information and evaluation. We now have

* Department for Education and Skills (2003) Green Paper, sets out for consultation a framework for improving outcomes for all children and their families, to protect them, to promote their well-being and to support all children to develop their full potential.

the opportunity to make this real for all children, not just under-4s living in poor areas.

Documenting the Sure Start experience is critically important if future investment in children and communities is to be maximized. *Learning from Sure Start* is a significant contribution to the evidence base on what works for young children and families.

Naomi Eisenstadt
Director, Sure Start Unit

Contributors

Sue Battersby
Sue is a Lecturer in Midwifery at the University of Sheffield. She has been the lead researcher for breastfeeding projects within the Sure Start Foxhill and Parson Cross programme. Highly experienced in both hospital and community midwifery posts in England and the Middle East, she has had a personal interest in infant feeding for many years, including involvement in local infant feeding initiatives.

Robin Carlisle
Robin is a Specialist Registrar in Public Health Medicine working across South Yorkshire. He carried out an evaluation of the Sure Start Home Injury Prevention Programme in partnership with Sheffield Health Informatics. Prior to becoming a public health specialist, Robin was a GP, a lecturer at Nottingham University, and led a multi-practice research programme on health inequalities and primary care.

Deborah Crofts
Deborah is a health visitor, currently employed as a public health nurse in Sure Start Foxhill and Parson Cross. She has previously been involved in working on two extensive research projects at the University of Sheffield. As part of her work for Sure Start, she has worked with teenage parents alongside the Sure Start midwife and the safer care worker, and is completing a PhD on the work outlined in her chapter.

Margaret Drake
Margaret was a Parenting Programme Manager of the 'C'mon Everybody' (Connecting with our Kids) team, a partner with Sure Start Foxhill and Parson Cross since it began in 1998. Margaret is a highly experienced teacher with a long-standing interest in children with behavioural problems, and delivered Webster Stratton parenting programmes within Sure Start.

Fiona Ford

Fiona is a Research Dietician in the Centre for Pregnancy Nutrition at the University of Sheffield. She coordinates a group of colleagues whose aim is to reduce inequalities in low birth weight rates across Sheffield. She investigated the nutritional status of pregnant women in the Sure Start Foxhill and Parson Cross area with a view to designing a nutrition intervention to reduce the incidence of low birth weight.

Jan Forde

Jan is currently a Foundation Stage teacher in a large inner-city primary school. She was formerly a community teacher for Sheffield Young Children's Service and Sure Start Foxhill and Parson Cross, working with a wide range of providers for preschool children and local parents. Her previous experience includes family literacy and numeracy, adult literacy, early years teaching, training and journalism.

Linda Fox

Linda is the programme manager for Sure Start Foxhill and Parson Cross. She has a background in nursing and health visiting, and her main interests include maternal depression and issues of social exclusion. She joined Sure Start Foxhill and Parson Cross having had long experience of working with disadvantaged families, and has been at the forefront of developing the programme from its earliest stages.

Imogen Hale

Imogen is currently a welfare adviser (academic) at the University of Sheffield Union of Students Advice Centre, and previously worked as a Young Families Advice Worker (Foxhill and Parson Cross Advice Service), where she was employed to set up and deliver a Sure Start-funded advice service to families with young children. Her main areas of advice were debt, housing, employment and benefits.

Peter Hannon

Peter is a Professor in the School of Education, University of Sheffield. He has directed projects in parental involvement in young children's development, family literacy, early literacy development and research in community-focused programmes. He has been collaborating with the Sure Start Foxhill and Parson Cross trailblazer programme since its inception, and is responsible, with the programme manager, for coordination of research and evaluation.

Helen Lomas

Helen is the Parent Involvement Coordinator at Sure Start Foxhill and Parson Cross, having been involved since the start of the programme as a local parent, a volunteer and a parent involvement worker. She has assisted research and evaluation in the programme and its links with the community. She currently coordinates a team of four parent involvement workers.

Jackie Marsh

Jackie is a Senior Lecturer in the School of Education at the University of Sheffield, where she teaches on the MA Literacy and Language in Education and MA Early Childhood Education. Her research focuses on the role of popular culture and the media in young children's lives and early literacy experiences.

Simon Martinez

Simon is currently Sheffield Citywide Sure Start Manager and was previously the Early Years Manager for Sure Start Foxhill and Parson Cross, a role that he undertook from the early stages of the programme. His previous related professional work was as a health visitor.

Anne Morgan

Anne is currently a Research Fellow in the School of Education, University of Sheffield. Prior to that, she was Literacy Coordinator in a Sheffield primary school and taught across Key Stage 1. At this time, she also worked on an early literacy intervention conducted by the University of Sheffield (the REAL Project) as a programme teacher.

Caroline Pickstone

Caroline is a Research Fellow and also Honorary Clinical Lecturer in the University of Sheffield and has worked with Sure Start Foxhill and Parson Cross on a research study since 2000. She is an experienced speech and language therapist and manager and has long been involved with the development of new working models for child services.

Ann Rowe

Ann is a Research and Development Facilitator within the Institute of General Practice and Primary Care at the University of Sheffield. Her previous experience includes working as a nurse, health visitor and teenage parenting project worker. Ann has led a number of professional and organizational development programmes, and has researched and published widely in the field of public health and health visiting.

Jo Weinberger

Jo is a Senior Research Fellow at Sheffield University and has been working on research and evaluation in the Sheffield Sure Start Foxhill and Parson Cross initiative since 2001. She has previously worked as a lecturer in education, nursery teacher, adult literacy tutor, special needs teacher and community worker focusing on home school literacy development.

List of abbreviations

BIBS	Breastfeeding is Best Support
CCPL	Community Childcare Play and Learning
DoH	Department of Health
ECERS-R	Early Childhood Environment Rating Scale, Revised edition
EPPE	Effective Provision of Preschool Education research project
EYDO	Early Years Development Officer
F&PC SS	Foxhill and Parson Cross Sure Start
FPCAS	Foxhill and Parson Cross Advice Service
FWT	First Words Test
HV	health visitor
LBW	low birth weight
LEA	Local Education Authority
NESS	National Evaluation of Sure Start
PCT	Primary Care Trust
REAC	Research and Evaluation Advisory Committee
RNI	recommended nutritional intake
SGA	small for gestational age
SLT	speech and language therapy
SMP	statutory maternity pay
SSLM	Sure Start Language Measure
SSU	Sure Start Unit
SYCS	Sheffield Young Children's Service
WFTC	Working Families' Tax Credit
YFAS	Young Families' Advice Service

Part One
Introduction

1 Why we should learn from Sure Start

Peter Hannon and Linda Fox

Introduction

It is rare that announcements of government policy concerning young children and their families immediately make practitioners and researchers sit up and take notice. However, one such occasion occurred in England in 1998 when the Government announced an initiative, to be called Sure Start, that was intended to improve support for families with children aged from birth to 4 years. The purpose of the initiative was stated thus.

> The aim of Sure Start is to work with parents and children to promote the physical, intellectual, social and emotional development of children – particularly those who are disadvantaged – to make sure they are ready to thrive when they get to school. (Glass, 1999, p. 258)

The initiative was striking for several reasons. First, there was to be a significant level of funding – many hundreds of millions of pounds – at a time when the new Labour Government was committed elsewhere to no increase in public expenditure. Second, Sure Start was to be focused on relatively small areas of high need, reflecting not only a recognition of the relationships between poverty, family circumstances, health and preschool development but also the desirability of action at the level of communities. Third, in marked contrast to the centralizing tendency of governments for many years previously, there was to be a high degree of local autonomy for Sure Start programmes. Applications were to be welcomed from local communities and, provided they worked to national targets, they were free to develop any reasonable services for their programmes. Fourth, there was the ambitious aim of establishing some 500 local programmes by 2004. It looked as if something quite radical was about to happen that could have a major impact on early childhood health, care and education in England.

This book concerns events and developments in one Sure Start area, in Sheffield, a large industrial city in the north of England. It is written by practitioners and researchers who worked together in the Foxhill and Parson Cross local programme. We hope that our work will be of interest to other practitioners and researchers, whether they work in Sure Start or in other settings, and perhaps to those, including policymakers, concerned more generally with young children and their families.

The local context

The Foxhill and Parson Cross area consists of two linked neighbourhoods some 5 miles to the north of the city centre, with extensive public housing, built from the 1930s to 1970s, when there was high employment in local industry. In the 1980s and 1990s, Sheffield experienced severe economic challenges as steel production, coal mining and engineering contracted. Foxhill and Parson Cross had never been a prosperous area, but by the late 1990s its largely white, working-class community had much higher levels of poverty, experienced poorer health and had lower levels of educational achievement than was the case for the city, or the nation, as a whole. The response to this situation from professionals working in the area and from members of the community was to begin to develop local regeneration and improved services and self-help initiatives in health, care and education.

When news of the Sure Start initiative reached Foxhill and Parson Cross, there was an eager response. Two professionals, one a health visitor based at the Foxhill Medical Centre, and the other, then manager of an NCH Family Centre in the area, were able to draw on close relationships with parents in the community to work on an application for a programme. They and a group of parents were joined by other professionals to design a Sure Start programme to address the community's needs. One of those who contributed to the group was a professor in the School of Education at the University of Sheffield. By early 1999, the group had produced an application for a programme that included ideas for many services wanted by families in the area. Some of the services that were eventually established are described in this book.

From its beginning, the Foxhill and Parson Cross group had a commitment to research and evaluation. The 1999 application stated that it regarded,

> evaluation as absolutely essential for the development of the programme and for sharing lessons learned in Sheffield with Sure Start programmes elsewhere.

After many twists and turns, the application was successful and a delivery plan for the Foxhill and Parson Cross programme was approved in late

1999. It was one of the first programmes in the country to be approved. The delivery plan repeated the commitment to research.

> Research and evaluation will be at the heart of the Foxhill & Parson Cross Sure Start action. Action will be based as far as possible on the circumstances and aspirations of the community. It will also be based wherever possible on evidence about what works in other communities in this country and abroad.

> Evaluation and monitoring will be integral to all initiatives undertaken by the core team and by the Sure Start partners. All accept that some new ways of working may not succeed and will be discontinued. Action will be steered by constant research and evaluation.

This book is one result of the commitment to research and evaluation. In this introductory chapter, we seek to explain why we were committed and how we went about trying to learn from Sure Start. First, however, we need to say more about Sure Start as a national initiative.

Sure Start – the national picture

By mid-2004, there were 524 Sure Start programmes in England; the target set six years previously had been more than met. Most programmes individually served between 500 and 1000 children. The total of children in Sure Start was said to be 400,000. Whatever the exact figure, it was clear that the landscape of services for young children and their families had been changed, particularly in disadvantaged areas of the country.

All Sure Start programmes have shared four main objectives.

Objective 1: Improving social and emotional development
In particular, by supporting early bonding between parents and their children, helping families to function and by enabling the early identification and support of children with emotional and behavioural difficulties.

Objective 2: Improving health
In particular, by supporting parents in caring for their children to promote healthy development before and after birth.

Objective 3: Improving children's ability to learn
In particular, by encouraging high quality environments and childcare that promote early learning, provide stimulating and enjoyable

play, improve language skills and ensure early identification and support of children with special needs.

Objective 4: Strengthening families and communities
In particular, by involving families in building the community's capacity to sustain the programme and thereby create pathways out of poverty.

To realize these objectives, local programmes have had to work towards specific targets, relating, for example, to such matters as making contact with families, reducing the proportions of children requiring statutory child protection registration or specialist speech and language intervention, reducing the proportion of mothers smoking in pregnancy, providing improved play and learning opportunities, reducing the proportion of children in households where no-one is employed, and parent representation on programme management boards. These and other targets are referred to in later chapters in connexion with specific services provided by the programme.

Local programmes are expected to observe certain key principles underlying the whole of Sure Start. Their services must

- co-ordinate, streamline and add value to existing services in the Sure Start area;
- involve parents, grandparents and other carers in ways that build on their existing strengths;
- avoid stigma by ensuring that all local families are able to use Sure Start services;
- ensure lasting support by linking Sure Start to services for older children;
- be culturally appropriate and sensitive to particular needs;
- promote the participation of all local families in the design and working of the programme.

It is recognized that the design and content of local Sure Start programmes vary according to local needs, but there is also an expectation that programmes include a number of core services: outreach and home visiting; support for families and parents; support for good-quality play, learning and childcare experiences for children; primary and community health care, including advice about family health and child health and development; and support for children and parents with special needs, including help getting access to specialist services.

The significance of Sure Start

To appreciate the significance of Sure Start, an historical perspective is helpful. It is not a new policy idea to intervene early in the lives of young children to enable them to do well (or to 'thrive' or 'flourish' in words used by Sure Start) later in life (Tizard, Moss and Perry, 1976). In England, in the field of health, the idea can be traced back to the early 1900s and the establishment of a health visitor service, explicitly focused on improving the care of children after birth. In education, preschool intervention has been a recurrent public policy issue at least since the 1960s. In that decade, in the United States, there began the national initiative of 'Head Start' and also several well-designed and well-researched small-scale projects that showed it was possible to affect children's development (Sylva, 1994). In England, the parallel to Head Start was nursery education (generally a more substantial and earlier intervention than Head Start). Focused on areas of need, it enjoyed increased interest and political support, but there was no research or development of more intensive interventions. In the 1970s, nursery education for 3- and 4-year-olds did expand in England, but there was still no serious commitment to researching the benefits. During the 1980s in England, government support for preschool intervention waned, but that decade in the United States saw some remarkable research findings showing the long-term benefits of the well-designed preschool programmes of 20 years earlier (Lazar and Darlington, 1982). Those findings began to influence policy in England in the 1990s, when there was renewed interest in preschool intervention, by then conceived of not just in educational terms but also including more emphasis on families, parental involvement, inter-agency programmes and having health and social benefits, in addition to educational ones (Ball, 1994). It was in this context that, following a change of government in 1997, the Sure Start policy emerged.

What was new about Sure Start, first, was that it showed a serious commitment to the idea of preschool intervention as a means of reducing educational, social and health inequalities. That commitment could be measured in hundreds of millions of pounds – an investment far exceeding any made in previous eras. Second, there was strong encouragement from government for programmes to think and plan long term, that Sure Start was not another short-term, headline-grabbing novelty but something that would be substantial and sustained. Third, there was its explicit multidisciplinary approach. Preschool teachers, health visitors, social workers and community development workers had an unprecedented opportunity to work together. Fourth, there was an attempt to base the policy on research, chiefly the US research of previous decades (Glass, 1999). Fifth, the intervention period was to be from before birth to 4 years of age. This was earlier than the immediate preschool period (of, say, 3–5 or 4–6), about which findings about programme effectiveness were strongest, but it did have theoretical plausibility and meant that the multidisciplinary work with families could be established earlier.

Those of us contributing to this book were keenly aware that Sure Start may be a once-in-a-lifetime opportunity to try out ways of working with families that we had long wanted to put into practice but never thought the opportunity would arise.

Why we care about local research and evaluation

Most of the workers and members of the community who have become involved in the Foxhill and Parson Cross Sure Start programme have done so because they believed it was the right approach to try with young children and their families, but it does not mean that there they were certain it would succeed. Nothing comparable had ever been attempted before. No-one could be certain that a programme could be devised, implemented, managed and sustained over a period of years. No-one could be certain what would work and what would not. Yet there was a shared determination that if it did work, that story should be told; if it did not work, lessons needed to be learned.

Much of what we need to know about Sure Start can only be discovered at a national level. Fortunately there is a national evaluation of Sure Start. By the standards of social science it is a massive study with a multi-million pound budget, but no more than is justified by the scale of the initiative to be evaluated. At the time of writing, NESS (National Evaluation of Sure Start) is based at Birkbeck College, University of London. The evaluation has four main components: implementation evaluation; impact evaluation; local context analysis; and cost-effectiveness evaluation. It aims to collect data from more than 500 local programmes and directly from families in Sure Start areas whether or not they are involved in local programmes. Although it will have to overcome considerable research challenges, NESS should be able to find out how programmes have been implemented in different local contexts and what impact they have had on children and families. From a national policy perspective, its findings should provide a basis for judging the value of Sure Start.

Why, then, undertake research and evaluation, as we have done, in just one local programme? One reason is that single case studies can sometimes illuminate issues that are bound to occur in many other cases. For example, what we might find in Foxhill and Parson Cross about antenatal and breast-feeding support, parent education, support for teenage mothers, home safety, advice services for families – in fact, all the services to be covered in later chapters – may apply only partially to other cases. We do not pretend that what we find with a white, monolingual community automatically applies, for example, to an ethnically diverse, multilingual community. But the way in which we have had to clarify and reflect upon key issues could be highly relevant to people trying to clarify and reflect upon services in their different contexts. Also, a strength of a group of insiders in one programme reflecting on what they have learned over several years is that they can know a programme much better than any outside researcher visiting from time to time to collect data.

A further motivation, however, for local evaluation stems from our belief that evaluation should be integral to practice, especially in a situation where that practice has to be innovative. If Sure Start is to succeed, it must try new things. Some new things will work; others will not. It is important not to blame those who try new things that do not work as hoped (instead, we should thank them for being prepared to try). A maxim that has been used in the programme is, 'No mistakes, no learning'. Evaluation can be difficult – even conflictual – and it is not the only way to learn from mistakes (common sense and professional judgement have their place too), but it can help show, in a systematic and evidence-based way, what works and what does not.

Establishing evaluation work in the programme

The Foxhill and Parson Cross group recognized from the outset that evaluation needed resources. If it were not adequately resourced, evaluation would become an optional, unimportant activity that would always be likely to be squeezed by other demands within the programme. In 1999 there was no requirement – indeed no encouragement – for local programmes to carry out any evaluation themselves (later, Sure Start did require programmes to have local evaluations), but the delivery plan for Foxhill and Parson Cross budgeted for it. Originally, it was hoped to set aside as much as 10 per cent of the budget for it – not an excessive amount for an initiative that was so new and important – but, in the event, the proportion over the years has averaged under 5 per cent.

Evaluation was also built into the Foxhill and Parson Cross programme by making it a part of all job specifications that staff would be expected to contribute to evaluation work; this could be evaluation of their own area of work or contribution to the evaluation of other areas. The result has been that several workers have completed evaluations, sometimes with the support of the University team. Some of their work is represented in later chapters.

A Research and Evaluation Advisory Committee (REAC) was established within the programme. It has reported directly to the programme management board. REAC has been chaired jointly by the two authors of this chapter – Peter Hannon, responsible for coordination of research and evaluation in the programme; and Linda Fox, programme manager. Other members of REAC have included parent representatives, key members of staff with particular evaluation responsibilities, and outside researchers.

The contribution of outside researchers has been of immense importance and is reflected in this book. Because the programme was seen to take research and evaluation seriously, and because of the involvement of the University of Sheffield School of Education, several other researchers became involved. They have included colleagues in the School of Education and from other University departments such as General Practice, Human Communication Sciences, Public Health, Nursing and Midwifery, and Psychology. There have been four doctoral students who have conducted some or all of their research in collaboration with the programme, including one senior health professional, Caroline Pickstone, who held an NHS Research Fellowship and who is one of the editors of this book. The effect of this additional research capacity has been to double or triple the funds that the programme put into research and evaluation.

Overall, some 40 individuals have been involved, one way or another, in research and evaluation. The University team has been closely involved in much, but certainly not all, of the work. The wider group includes programme staff, staff in partner organizations, University staff, and other professionals in the area. In some instances, the research has been carried out by the 'insiders', usually as practitioners studying their own area of work, thus enhancing professional capacity. Obviously, it has been important in these studies that ways are found of reducing personal bias, being sceptical about evidence and, where necessary, incorporating independent data. In other instances, independence has been of overriding importance. For example, the assessments of 4-year-old children over five successive cohorts of children have been carried out by an entirely independent team of assessors who have no connexion with the programme. Similarly, it was crucial that judgements of the quality of play and learning settings (described in Chapter 10) be carried out by an entirely independent, appropriately trained team. Even in the parent interview surveys (reported in Chapters 2 and 17), carried out by local community interviewers, care was taken that none of the interviewers was involved in delivering the programme.

The range of work undertaken

Research and evaluation has had three main components. First, there have been studies of *community impact*. These include assessments of school readiness (mainly language and literacy-related measures) of 4-year-olds that have been conducted since 2000 and are still ongoing. The idea is to see whether there is any community-wide impact on child development and to relate child development measures to family take-up and other factors. It is too early for this work to be reported in this book. Another indication of community impact can come from what parents say about their experiences of services and of parenting in the area. The preliminary (baseline) stage of this work is described in Chapter 17; the second stage is still in progress. In Chapter 5 there is a description of the baseline stage of a study of support for teenage mothers; again, the second stage will be a future report.

The second, and largest, component of the work has been *evaluation of services*. Up to 25 different services, some small, some large, have been or are being evaluated. Over half the chapters in this book are concerned with such evaluations.

The third component has been *research to support the programme*. This has been work that informs rather than evaluates services. Some of this work has already been published (Pickstone, Hannon and Fox, 2002). Examples in this book are the study of language assessment issues (Chapter 12) and of children's media experiences (Chapter 13).

To address such a wide range of research issues, a wide range of research methods have been adopted. These have included interviewing, qualitative analyses, systematic practitioner reflection, measures of child development, rating scales, baseline-intervention comparisons, and a randomized controlled trial.

It is important to point out that the following chapters reflect only some of the activities undertaken in the Foxhill and Parson Cross programme. There are not enough resources to evaluate everything that goes on, including some work that is widely regarded as of very high quality (for example, the smoking cessation service). There will be future evaluations – more lessons to be learned. It is not even possible to report all the research and evaluation that has been, or is currently being, carried out. The University of Sheffield and the Foxhill and Parson Cross programme have therefore endeavoured to provide reports through their websites, and many of these have been published through the website provided by the National Evaluation of Sure Start.

The work to be described in the following chapters will, we hope, cover key lessons learned so far and will therefore be of some interest to those practitioners and researchers in England who are affected – as almost all now are – by Sure Start, as well as those further afield who are confronting similar issues.

References

Ball, C. (1994) *Start Right: The Importance of Early Learning*. London: Royal Society for the Arts.

Glass, N. (1999) Sure Start: the development of an early intervention programme for young children in the United Kingdom. *Children and Society*, 13: 257–64.

Lazar, I. and Darlington, R. (1982) The lasting effects of early education: a report from the Consortium for Longitudinal Studies. *Monographs of the Society for Research in Child Development*, 47(2–3), Serial no. 195.

Pickstone, C., Hannon, P. and Fox, L. (2002) Surveying and screening pre-school language development in community-focused intervention programmes: a review of instruments. *Child: Care, Health and Development*, 28(3): 251–64.

Sylva, K. (1994) The impact of learning on children's later development. Appendix C in C. Ball, *Start Right: The Importance of Early Learning*. London: Royal Society for the Arts.

Tizard, J., Moss, P. and Perry, J. (1976) *All Our Children: Pre-School Services in a Changing Society*. London: Temple Smith.

Website for information about national Sure Start: www.surestart.gov.uk

Website for information about national evaluation of Sure Start: www.ness.bbk.ac.uk

Website for information and reports concerning research and evaluation in the Foxhill and Parson Cross Sure Start programme: www.shef.ac.uk/surestart

2 Listening to families: a survey of parents' views
Jo Weinberger

Introduction

The whole Sure Start programme is based as far as possible on listening to parents. This chapter is concerned with exploring the questions 'how did we listen?' and 'what did we hear?' In terms of the acceptability and applicability of the work, it is crucial to find out what difference Sure Start makes to families, and what are the parental and community experiences of the work. We decided to do this through an interview survey which systematically attempted to find out about parents' experiences of bringing up young children in the area at the end of the period of Sure Start intervention, that is, once the children were aged 4. This was to be our way of listening to a representative sample of families.

To this end, parents of all 4-year-olds born within a designated period were identified and, where possible, interviewed, by a small team of local people who were recruited as community interviewers, and who used a structured interview schedule (see Appendix 2 for a condensed version of this, listing the questions asked). All the interviewers were independent of Sure Start, in that none of them was involved in delivering Sure Start services (for more on the interviewers' experiences, see Chapter 17). Two cohorts of parents were identified, one whose children were born before the programme began and one whose children were born two years later. This would mean that it would be possible to draw comparisons between the experiences of those families whose children had, on the whole, had limited experience of Sure Start, and a group of families whose children could potentially have had access to Sure Start services throughout their lives. The second cohort survey is still underway and will be reported in due course. This chapter is concerned with the first cohort of families.

The survey itself required detailed and sensitive work in compiling an interview schedule, training the community interviewers, piloting the instrument, contacting families, and conducting the interviews, which has implications relating to evaluating work within community contexts reaching beyond the present programme.

How did we listen? Process of designing a systematic interview schedule

The views of all workers involved in the Sure Start Foxhill and Parson Cross programme shaped the interview schedule that was used. It was compiled by addressing the issues raised by the Public Service Agreement targets and the Service Delivery Agreement targets laid down by the government for Sure Start, alongside what the individual projects within the Foxhill and Parson Cross programme wanted to know and what the programme as a whole wanted to know, both to inform future practice and planning, and to find out about the impact the Sure Start programme was having.

In a fast-changing policy area, documents were constantly being updated, but for consistency, those current at the time of compiling the first interview survey were adhered to. These were the original (1998) Public Service Agreement (PSA) targets between Sure Start and the government, plus the revised (2000) PSA targets and the Service Delivery Agreement targets (2000).

Process of consultation

The process of compiling the interview survey involved extensive consultation with members of each of the projects that contributed to the Sure Start Foxhill and Parson Cross Programme having the opportunity to comment on and revise the questions to be asked. At least one member of each project and each partner organization was contacted, and they cascaded the information about the schedule to the rest of their team, with well over 20 people consulted. As well as the workers, the consultation process involved the steering committee, the research monitoring group (the Research and Evaluation Advisory Committee), and the 'Check It Out group' (a group of local parents who met regularly to provide feedback on new initiatives). The total number of people consulted probably exceeded 50. As part of the process, four drafts were produced and circulated before the final version was agreed upon. This was undertaken as a discrete piece of work, before the interviewers were recruited.

Recruiting, training and supporting community interviewers

The interviews were conducted by a team of community interviewers, who lived in or near the Sure Start area, and who had been given training by the University relating to conducting the survey. Specific training consisted of role-playing using the interview schedule, and discussion with relevant workers, including the midwife on breastfeeding and birth issues and the domestic abuse worker on issues of domestic violence and difficulty in the home. The community interviewers had had previous experience of work within the community, such as conducting a health needs assessment, or undertaking a course concerned with health and community development, or general involvement in community work and activity in the area. Regular meetings were integral to maintaining and monitoring the process. Team members changed over time as other commitments and community work opportunities arose, and change and transition were a distinctive and ongoing feature of this community-focused research. Involvement in the work became a stepping-stone to further work and activities within the community for most of the interviewers, and their childcare and other commitments made regular engagement in the survey work problematic. This meant that flexibility was essential.

Conducting the interviews

Pilot interviews were conducted before embarking on the main survey and the interview schedule was found to be workable, with minor adjustments made as necessary. After the pilot interviews, systematic interviewing began. Interviews, in parents' homes, took on average between 45 minutes to an hour. The aim was to interview parents when their children were around 4, 5 or older.

The work involved contacting families, initially via the nurseries the children attended. Later, as this proved to be time-consuming, and, more importantly, only engaged the most accessible families, contact was made with the families directly, usually after they had given consent to be involved in Sure Start research. On the few occasions when this was not the case, we incorporated asking for consent with the process of asking parents whether they would be prepared to respond to the survey questions.

As time progressed, we streamlined the documentation that each inter-viewer needed to conduct the work efficiently, keeping a record of all work undertaken, and ensuring that none of the families was overlooked. Included in the paperwork were: interview survey forms, letters to set up an interview, pre-prepared letters saying 'sorry you were out' and arranging a subsequent time for an interview, stamps, batteries, blank tapes, Sure Start information packs and consent forms for involvement in the research.

Some key issues that emerged through the course of the work were finding ways to make contact with families to ask if they would be prepared to be interviewed, as parents were frequently hard to contact; identifying and maintaining a group of workers to conduct the interviews; the setting up of structures to point people in the right direction for support if necessary; and creating a mechanism for feeding back childcare issues to influence programmes and facilities.

What did we hear? Findings from the first survey

Findings from the interviews offered general information about the target child and their family and revealed, in detail, parents' views about play and learning, parenting support and information, information about the parent and child together, the child and parents' health, and parents' satisfaction in parenting.

The findings reported here provide the best picture we have of the situation *before* Sure Start (or before Sure Start was fully established). The second survey has yet to be completed. Parents answered 'yes' or 'no' to the majority of questions asked, and the proportions of their responses are reported here. In addition, quotations from parents fill out some of the issues parents raised. We encouraged interviewers to mark those parent comments that were particularly pertinent on the interview schedule. This led to a rich resource of parent contributions. However, as not all parents made comments, this was a way of adding a qualitative dimension to the data we had, offering a sense of the parents' experiences, rather than a systematic elaboration of the entire cohort of parent views. Quotations reproduced here are focused on those comments that had most relevance to Sure Start services.

For the study, 220 families were identified as having children aged 4 within the designated period. As other chapters in this book show, there was high mobility in the area, exacerbated by a housing demolition programme at the time the survey was undertaken. Of 393 visits made by the community interviewers, 115 families were actually interviewed, which highlights the labour-intensive nature of the work. A total of 46 families were found to have moved house while the survey was underway. Of those contacted, 33 families declined to be interviewed, one was not interviewed due to illness, one not interviewed due to bereavement and in 22 cases, the interviewer, despite, in many cases, several attempts, was unable to make contact. Looking at how many families were available to be interviewed, and how many interviews were conducted, this meant we had a response rate of 77 per cent.

In terms of the number of visits made to try and complete the interviews, 64 families were visited once (36 per cent), 47 twice (26 per cent), 42 three times (24 per cent), 14 four times (8 per cent), and a few more frequently than this. From this it is clear that visiting more than three times did not greatly increase the number interviewed and was not especially productive, but it is a testament to the community interviewers' persistence and eagerness to complete the task that they tried to make as many contacts as possible, without appearing intrusive. It was to the advantage of the results of the survey to try and achieve as comprehensive a view of parents' views as possible. (This process is described in more detail in Chapter 17.)

Those interviewed were mostly the mothers (77 per cent) or mother and father together (9 per cent). Interviews were also conducted with fathers on their own (9 per cent), and a small number of other relatives – four grandmothers, one older daughter, one aunt and one foster mother. Of the families with whom interviews were conducted, 33 per cent had lived in the area between four and ten years, and 48 per cent had lived in the area for ten years or more, see Figure 2.1.

Figure 2.1 Responses to the question 'How long have you lived in the area?'

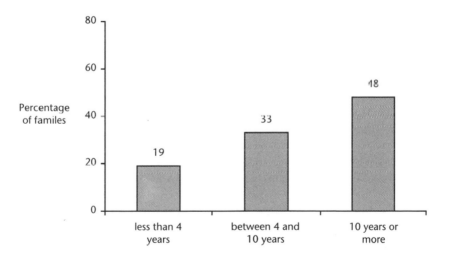

This shows that parts of the neighbourhood were relatively stable and unchanging. However, there was also a sizeable proportion of the population that was more mobile; 19 per cent had moved into the Sure Start area after their child had been born.

Background information about the child and family

In terms of the composition of the families, 39 per cent of the target children (45) had younger siblings, who would subsequently make use of Sure Start services. In addition, 61 per cent of the children had older siblings. And 31 per cent of the target children (32) lived in single-parent households; 36 per cent of the mothers and 48 per cent of the fathers were in employment at the time of the interview, and in addition, 12 per cent of the parents reported being involved in voluntary work of some kind.

There was economic hardship in the area, as evidenced through the information compiled by the Young Families' Advice Service, discussed in Chapter 16. Forty-three per cent of families were in receipt of some type of benefit (excluding Working Family Tax Credit, a tax credit available to working families responsible for at least one child under 16) and 37 per cent of the target children (43) lived in families in which no-one in the household was employed.

Responses to questions on play and learning

Attendance at groups for babies and young children

Parents reported that 36 per cent of the children had attended a baby group, and a larger proportion (46 per cent) had attended a parent and toddler group. These groups were clearly something that many parents felt able to access within the neighbourhood, although, in keeping with childcare concerns voiced elsewhere, one of the fathers mentioned the lack of appropriate facilities for men:

> ... if there's only one man and ten women with kids it doesn't seem to work. They ought to have father and toddler groups.

While parents reported that all the children accessed a nursery place, a smaller proportion (36 per cent) attended a playgroup. Seventeen per cent of parents said their child had attended a crèche, and indeed 10 per cent of parents made use of this facility on a regular basis, indicating that some parents were making use of childcare facilities to support their own activities.

Talking about play and learning with others

Forty-seven per cent of parents responded that they had talked with others about how their child played with other children, and a number offered examples of when talking with others about how their child played had proved helpful. These included talking with relatives, friends and teachers. Sure Start services offered support too, for example, as one parent recalled:

At Connecting with our Kids [see Chapter 4] I spent a lot of time talking about C because they thought he had some behavioural problems. They were going to get [Sure Start outreach worker] to come out and talk about a play course because he were being aggressive towards me, but he's calmed down a lot since I've started playing with him and stuff.

A smaller number of parents (23 per cent) expressed that they had felt concern about their child's behaviour in relation others. For example, one parent reported:

He's bored, no matter what I do. I haven't got money to buy him things every week. I bought him a Playstation, he's fed up with that now ... He wants out all the time, he's an outdoor person. He's just stuck up on front, football and that, playing with big 'uns. It's a bad thing really because he's playing with older ones, they're aged from 2 to 15 on here. Big 'uns ... he like learns too much. When he comes back in, he's coming in with language. ...

Talking about their child's language

Parents were asked if they had had concerns about their child's talking or listening, and 29 per cent said that they had (for more on this, see Chapter 12). Hearing problems and delayed speech were reported, and actions taken made a difference, for instance:

They've actually now referred her to the Children's [hospital] and they've found out that she's slightly deaf, which I wouldn't have found out if it weren't for the Outreach [team] getting speech and language involved.

Responses to questions on parenting support and information

Attendance at parent groups

Thirty per cent of parents interviewed said they had been to antenatal groups (n = 34). This is higher than for groups in general, as these were provided routinely by midwives, as well as through Sure Start services.

Fifteen per cent of parents interviewed (18) said they had taken part in a parenting group. As more groups become available in the area, this is something that we envisage would increase over time.

Nine per cent of parents interviewed said they had been to other groups not yet mentioned (n = 10). These were a swimming group for babies, a group organized for parents and babies by the local surgery, a smoking cessation group, a foster parents' group, breastfeeding workshops and groups focusing on children's learning. This shows that for some of the families, the impact of Sure Start and other local initiatives was starting to provide opportunities, which would hopefully develop to reach more families over time.

Breastfeeding

About half of the parents, 54 per cent (62), were feeding their babies on formula milk. Chapter 7 shows how Sure Start work was having an impact in supporting mothers to breastfeed. At the time of the survey, 24 per cent of parents (28) said their child had been fed on breast milk as a baby, with 21 per cent (24) saying their baby had been fed on breast and formula – see Figure 2.2.

Figure 2.2 Responses to the question 'When your child was a baby, was she or he fed on breast or formula milk, or other, e.g. soya?'

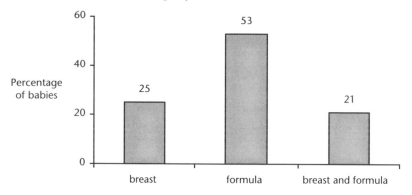

Breastfeeding was clearly an emotive subject, and 15 of the parents talked about the issue during the interviews. Their recollections included:

> Actually I did try and it were midwife who were showing me but I just couldn't do it.

> I did [breastfeed] in the hospital, but he didn't seem to settle as well. He weren't taking to it as well himself, but as soon as he got a bottle, from being a month old, he slept all night …

I had help from doctor, midwife and health visitor but it were my choice – I didn't want to breastfeed her.

I would really like to have gone to a breastfeeding group but it wasn't offered.

This is not a summary of all the comments made but indicates the range of experiences recalled by those who made additional comments to the interviewers. Further information on this subject can be found in Chapter 7.

Smoking whilst pregnant

The majority of mothers (54 per cent) said that they did not smoke while they were pregnant. While 37 per cent reported smoking while pregnant, a number of mothers reduced their smoking, or stopped smoking during pregnancy – see Figure 2.3. Eight parents offered comments, which included:

I did smoke but I stopped when I knew I wanted to have a baby.

As soon as they start playing up the first thing you do is hit a cig. I'd rather hit a cig than hit a kid. People say 'Oh, you smoke when you've got kids'. What should you do, plug hell out of them when they're playing up? I'd rather have a cig.

Just the odd few …

We never smoked indoors. We always smoked outside.

After the pregnancy, 24 per cent of the parents said that they had started smoking again, and 39 per cent said that someone smoked in the home (an additional 4 per cent smoked outside) while the child was under 2 years.

Smoke cessation was an area of considerable input by Sure Start Foxhill and Parson Cross. Although this falls outside the scope of this book, with the input being made, it could be envisaged that increasing numbers of mothers would stop smoking.

Equipment and advice

Nineteen per cent of parents said they had received safety equipment that they needed for their child and mentioned receiving items such as stair gates and smoke alarms. Twenty-eight per cent of parents said they had been given help or advice about either benefits or money matters. See Chapters 9 and 16 for further details of the work Sure Start offered here.

Figure 2.3 Responses to the question 'Did you smoke while you were pregnant?'

Did you smoke while you were pregnant?

❖ 37% yes

❖ 54% no

❖ 9% no response

If yes, did you give up or reduce smoking at all while you were pregnant?

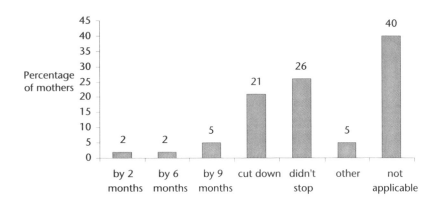

Responses to questions on the parent and child together

Overwhelmingly, 96 per cent of parents said they spent time playing with their child, and indeed also said they sat down and read with their child (95 per cent). To support this, 50 per cent said that their child was a member of the library, and almost as many of the parents (48 per cent) said that they were too. Children also owned their own books. Parents estimated that 29 per cent owned between 20 and 50 books; 27 per cent owned up to 100; with 23 per cent owning more than 100. At the other end of the scale, 8 per cent of children were thought to own fewer than 10 books. Again, a large number of children (76 per cent) were reported by their parents to have a favourite book. We were also interested to know whether the children borrowed toys in the neighbourhood, and 14 per cent of parents said that this was something that their child did. Alongside their play, the children also watched television and videos together with their parents (88 per cent) (see Chapter 13 for more on this). There was a separate question about how much television the children were reported to watch on their own. Here, 41 per cent of parents reported that their child watched between two and four hours of television a day, with 23 per cent watching more, and 33 per cent watching up to two hours. Only four children were thought to watch under an hour a day. These figures were often hard for the parents to estimate when the television may be on in the background, for instance: 'It's on permanently, but he probably watches about an hour in the morning ... up to three hours.'

In terms of other language and literacy activities, a large proportion of parents (86 per cent) said they wrote with their child or helped them with their writing. We were interested to know how many children knew nursery rhymes, or knew other rhymes off by heart, as this can be very helpful for language development. There was a distinct minority of children (5 per cent), whose parents said they thought they did not know any rhymes; 40 per cent said they knew a few; while the majority (58 per cent) said their child knew lots of nursery rhymes. We asked parents whether they had had any problems themselves, since leaving school, with their own reading, writing or spelling. For 15 per cent of the parents, they said this was the case, with 4 per cent saying they had received help for this. Further information was offered in relation to the parents' educational experiences, in accordance with the stage at which the mothers left school. Most of the mothers had left school at the minimum school leaving age of 16 (63 per cent) or before that age (16 per cent). Twelve per cent of mothers left school at age 17 or 18. Seventy per cent of the mothers had received a qualification at school, while 30 per cent left without any qualifications. However, this was not their only opportunity for education, and 21 per cent of those interviewed said they were involved in education or training courses at the time of the interview.

Children's health

While 70 per cent of parents said their child's health had, on the whole, been good, 23 per cent said it had been fairly good and 7 per cent said it had not been good. In addition, 42 per cent of parents reported that their child had been admitted to hospital as an emergency (48). This figure is very high, and one explanation of this was that the question was understood by some parents to mean attendance at the accident and emergency department of the hospital, rather than the child having been admitted to the hospital itself. However, it also indicates that there was a high level of child accident or acute illness in the area (see Chapter 9 for more on this). In terms of preventive measures, the majority of families said that their child was registered with a dentist (84 per cent) (although 8 of these children did not attend appointments regularly).

Parents' health, including postnatal depression

Parents were asked about their own health in the period since they had had their child. While 57 per cent said their health was on the whole good, a third (33 per cent) thought their health was only fairly good, and a sizeable proportion (10 per cent) said their health was not good. Indeed, 25 per cent of the mothers reported that they had suffered from postnatal depression at some point (29). This would obviously impact on their experience of bringing up young children.

Responses to question on parents' views about local services

Parents were asked their views about local services for young children. Most said they were satisfied (37 per cent) or very satisfied (9 per cent). However, as Figure 2.4 shows, a sizeable number said they were dissatisfied (30 per cent) or very dissatisfied (19 per cent). (At a later stage, this will be an area to examine in relation to responses from the second survey.) Responses need to be treated with care, as offering more services can actually increase dissatisfaction, since it gives people a greater awareness of what could be possible. This means that responses to this question will need to be read alongside the range of responses to other questions, and handled in a holistic way, to give a rounded picture of families' experiences and expectations. In particular, it is helpful to read responses here alongside parents' comments about improvements in services.

Figure 2.4 Parents were asked their views about local services for young children

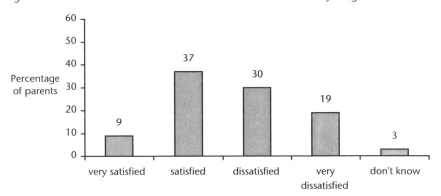

Views about improvements in local services for young children

In response to the question 'Have you noticed any improvements to services for young children and their families in the time that you've lived here?', 31 per cent reported 'yes' (36) and 59 per cent reported 'no' (68) – see Figure 2.5.

Figure 2.5 Responses to the question 'Have you noticed any improvements in what's on offter to young children and their families in the time that you've lived here?'

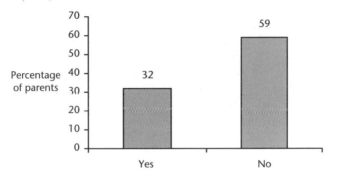

Those parents who commented on the way things had improved pointed to specific examples, such as:

> ... the playgroup I go to – that's been a massive improvement up there. They've got new toys – they are doing things a lot more now ...

> ... I've had information through the door and it sounds like they're trying to make things better and help children along the way – improve their education and things for them to do. I must admit I think they're helping a lot.

> ... When I had T [older child] there were nothing, and nothing advertised. It was just what you got to know through talking to other mums. They put a lot of stuff into that...parent and toddler group. Now they can sit down and draw. It's more organized since Sure Start's got involved.

Typical comments from those who were dissatisfied included:

> Dissatisfied because there's not much for them around here.

Dissatisfied because I've never had no services.

I don't think there is a lot of services for young children. Even if you take them on park they've burnt it or ripped swings off.

Indications from the subsequent survey are that views are changing, as more support and facilities become available in the area. The findings reported here give a flavour of the context in which the Sure Start Foxhill and Parson Cross programme has been developed. The impact of Sure Start varied, with 10 per cent of mothers and 6 out of 15 fathers who responded saying they had not heard of it or had contact, while the others had varying levels of involvement. Parents were asked what Sure Start meant to them, and any other observations they might like to add. Comments they made included:

... My Sure Start worker who used to come out ... used to fetch a big bag of books with her. I used to like them coming round, someone to talk to when I were on me own.

I think Sure Start is a good thing because at least people know there is some help and advice. It's a daunting thing when you become a mother and it's nice to know you've got some backup.

I feel as if they are doing something in the area.

Thank you to Sure Start for being there. If it hadn't been for Sure Start, most of the time I'd have gone out of my head with not knowing what to do with him.

Conclusion

This first survey, in which we have listened to families' views, provides a baseline against which the changes that Sure Start seeks to make can be measured. It focuses on the views of parents of children born before the programme was fully underway. Whilst parents clearly expressed unmet needs in the survey, Sure Start, alongside input offered by statutory services, had begun to make an impact on individuals and their families. Over time, we would hope that Sure Start will make an appreciable difference in relation to many aspects of child and family life. These might include greater access to play and learning opportunities, increased breastfeeding rates, reduction in the incidence of postnatal depression, increased rates of smoking cessation, increased home safety and positive indicators of child health, constructive parent and child interaction, and increased opportunities for parents for self-development and employment – all themes explored within this volume. Meanwhile, what we have learned from listening to families helps to provide a context for work described in the subsequent chapters.

Part Two
Improving social and emotional development

3 Family support
Jo Weinberger

Introduction

It was recognized from the outset that families in particular adversity would need targeted input, so from soon after its inception, the programme devised a Family Support Service. The key aims were to engage families that programmes find hard to reach, prevent children having to be looked after by the Local Authority, work with existing agencies to identify and support vulnerable families in the community and reduce re-registration on the child protection register. This chapter reports a study of the work of the Family Support Service, records views of those involved, summarizes the strengths of the work and offers ideas for further development.

Context for family support

Recent years have seen a dramatic increase in reported child abuse and neglect, which has placed new demands on finding effective preventive measures (Parton and Mathews, 2001). Research has shown that children's emotional well-being can be improved when risk factors, in particular family-based adversities, are reduced, and protective factors, which provide support, are increased (Buchanan, 2002). Pioneering family support work conducted in the United States (for example Seitz, Rosenbaum and Apfel, 1985; Zigler and Black, 1989) developed flexible approaches, based on daily problems experienced by families, that allowed for an indefinite number of changing goals (Hermanns and Leu, 1998). In the United Kingdom, the Children and Young Persons Act (1963), the Seebohm Report (1968), and the Children Act (1989) spelled out the need for comprehensive implementation of family support. The Department of Health's *Working Together to Safeguard Children* (1999) stressed the need for joint responsibility, advocating inter-agency collaboration (Department of Health, 1999). It noted that many of the families with child protection concerns struggled with 'multiple disadvantages'. Offering support to these families may allow parents to address their children's needs before the effect of unrelieved stress leads to abuse (Department of Health, 1999: 2 para 1.9).

Promoting inter-agency working, the *Framework for the Assessment of Children in Need and their Families* (2000) adopted an ecological approach in which 'an understanding of a child must be located within the context of the child's family ... and of the community and culture in which he or she is growing up' (Department of Health, 2000: 11). The Family Support Service documented here operated within this context, had a preventive focus, and was local and flexible in its mode of delivery.

Nature of family support work: gathering information

The questions this chapter seeks to answer are:

- what was the nature of the family support work in the programme?
- what views did users have about the service?
- what appeared to be the main successes of the service?
- how did other workers with whom the service collaborated view it?
- what were the main frustrations experienced by the service team?

Answering these questions involved analysing job descriptions and written records and interviewing the team leader, the other two team members in post at the time of the study, a social work student, the team leader's line manager, and other professionals with whom the team collaborated (health visitors, social worker, project manager with the psychological support service).

In addition, the views of a representative sample of families involved in the work were sought. A dozen parents were selected. The team leader identified six families whom she felt illustrated the range of family support work. These families were selected for interview. A further six were randomly picked from the 129 referrals on the team's books. Eleven of the 12 parents so selected agreed to be interviewed. The team member working with the remaining parent indicated that this was not a suitable time to make contact, due to an extreme domestic crisis. Although 100 per cent response would have been desirable, it was an achievement to obtain the views of such a high proportion of families, since these parents were all vulnerable and hard to reach.

Nature of the family support work

The Family Support Service evolved in response to need, providing crisis intervention and extra support for families experiencing difficulties. There were approximately 30 families receiving regular involvement at any given time. As well as collaborating with other programme workers, the team worked alongside other professionals such as health visitors, social workers, education welfare officers, teachers, the psychological support team, drug and alcohol abuse workers, the youth service, adult education and a voluntary organization for lone parents. Work with families often began with intensive, frequent interventions to start with, followed by less intensive contact. The aim was to leave families with strengthened community networks to support them. Input could lead to a range of possibilities, such as neighbourhood group work, peer support and structured help to attend groups.

The family support team

The team comprised two full-time staff – a social worker and a family support worker – and a part-time family support assistant. At the time of this study, the team also included a social work student. The social worker was responsible for dealing with child protection issues within Sure Start. Her post involved ongoing work with families and acting as a mediator between social services and families. The family support worker undertook case work with an initial targeted focus, with up to eight families, and also made one-off visits as required. The family support assistant offered practical support with housing, furniture and shopping, and was also confident in DIY skills and hairdressing (a new hairstyle can do wonders for raising self-esteem).

Work with individual parents

The list that follows illustrates the range of work conducted by the family support team.

- Work with a depressed mother whose toddler was developmentally delayed, including obtaining furniture and making a referral for financial advice.
- Work with a young mother (who, as a child, had herself been on the child protection register) to assess her parenting capacity and, once the baby was born, to give support in looking after the baby.

- Offering support to a depressed mother with a large family (whose oldest child had a baby of her own on a care order) until she felt able to cope.
- Support to an isolated new-to-area family with four children in which the mother and children had speech problems, including help to attend a parenting group, and help with potty training the youngest child.
- A parent with a child who had fled domestic violence was introduced to parenting groups in the area.

Other work included supporting a socially isolated, drug-using mother of three small children who was not looking after the children in the morning. The oldest child was helped to attend school. The mother was introduced to the Young Families Advice Service (see Chapter 17), helped with a court appearance because of payment arrears and supported to obtain a nursery place for the middle child, including checking the child's special needs. This involvement spanned two years. In the view of the worker, this intervention averted a deeper crisis, because 'there was nobody (else) in there to help take the problems apart one by one'. In addition, a young mother who was worried she might harm her child had worker involvement to set up a meeting with grandparents (with whom the child subsequently lived), and the family support worker and health visitor monitored the situation, which meant the case did not have to be referred to social services; and a mother with older children in care, who received ongoing family support from the time of a pre-birth conference, which led to the baby being de-registered at 3 months. The family took part in the baby massage group, and they were helped to access a programme outreach worker.

Collaboration and group work

Although most of the Family Support Service work was with individual parents, there were also group work initiatives. A group for substance-misusing parents was formed because it was difficult to run a group containing both substance-misusing and other parents. Parents with drug habits tend not to access mainstream facilities such as mother and toddler groups. Many of these parents experienced similar problems such as guidance and boundaries issues, and difficulties in providing stimulation for children. The workers felt that participation in a group was needed prior to parents accessing other community-based services. Since other services were based within the same building, the new services could seem less threatening. For instance, one of the programme outreach workers asked a mother from the substance-misuse group if she could demonstrate baby massage with her baby. She had been severely depressed yet, after involvement with the group, went on a parenting course and started making friends. Her children attended the crèche, where the workers were able to talk about a range of issues, such as the variety of foodstuffs the children might be prepared to try. The group also planned a residential weekend in conjunction with the coordinator of a city drug and alcohol project. Parents worked around issues together and also engaged in outdoor pursuits, supported by crèche provision for children. One of the mothers commented she had not had a holiday for years.

Another group aimed at supporting teenage mothers was organized by the social worker and the programme midwife. The aim was to deliver antenatal education and promote peer support. The work was collaborative, with responsibility split between Sure Start and the youth service. A striking piece of work was planning, making and launching a video about the experiences of teenage parenting from a young mothers' point of view (*Think Twice*, 2001). Using drama and discussion, the video explored complex issues behind teenage pregnancy, including under-age sex, peer pressure, and the influence of drugs and alcohol. It has subsequently been used as an educational tool by young mothers to raise awareness amongst local teenagers.

Users' views about the family support service

In the course of interviews to find out about users' views, parents were asked about what happened during their involvement with the family support work, the nature of their experiences, and to what extent they had been helpful or unhelpful. They were asked what they would tell other parents about Sure Start, and if they continued to have contact with Sure Start.

At the time of interview, families had had contact with family support for differing lengths of time, from one family with contact from the inception of the service two years previously, to one that had had involvement for three months. Eight of the 11 families were still in contact with the programme at the time of the interview, mentioning telephone contact and visits, going to a teenage parents' group and a baby massage group and being accompanied to groups.

Parents' reported experiences with family support included being found a solicitor to help with custody; provision of furniture and safety equipment; attending a teenage parents' group; help in getting a child to school; being offered emotional support; helping with children's behavioural problems; helping with attending the baby massage group; support in reporting a rape to the police; help with obtaining advice and managing money; liaison with other agencies including social services about child protection issues; information about drugs, jobs, college courses and accreditation. A small detail, but significant to the parent concerned, was that the team had given a Christmas present to her child.

As well as detailing their experiences, parents talked about the way the service was delivered. For example, when explaining about attending the teenage parents' group, one mother commented:

> They used to come and pick me up 'cos I were pregnant. It just makes you feel nicer, it makes you feel right wanted like my family hadn't done … They've been there for me.

A parent with considerable contact with social services found the family support work helpful:

> Social services come out with … foreign language basically, it could be to some people… Sure Start's (different) – we'll put that in simple terms – and they are breaking things down and explaining things clearly.

All but one of the 11 families stated clearly that their experience of the family support team had been helpful. They mentioned learning how to play and deal with their child's behaviour; attending groups; telephone contact; obtaining safety equipment; offering support at case conferences and offering emotional support. Comments were: 'We've always seemed to have got a positive attitude from them', 'They do listen to you – they don't judge you'. The couple who said their experience had not been particularly helpful commented on attending a group they had found difficult 'because of the druggies'. However, they also commented positively on being interested in watching videos about how to play with children, attending a baby massage group, and receiving practical help.

Parents were asked what they would tell other parents about Sure Start. They commented that what was offered was helpful and 'there's always people to listen to you if you've got any problems'; that it helps the children; it helps with introductions to other people; it offers help with looking after the children; it helps obtain equipment; it offers support and training for teenage parents; and that workers had information about what was happening locally.

A teenage mother said this is what she would say to parents about Sure Start:

> I'd tell them that I didn't want to listen to nobody at the time. These people aren't here to tell you off … they're just here to help you and show you right way.

And a couple of parents who also had older children said:

> First impressions what we thought of Sure Start, we thought, – Oh, it's just another organization what's going to come prying in and saying, 'Oh you do it this way, you do it that way' – and they haven't.

Finally, one parent made the general comment about Sure Start:

> As a parent, our opinions are very well respected and heard.

Main successes of the service

Central to the work of the Family Support team was preventing children being placed on the child protection register. One can only speculate about what might have happened, but on a number of occasions workers could reasonably point to cases where they felt, without their intervention, the child would have been placed, or would have remained, on the register. For instance, one worker said of a mother with whom she had been working intensively:

> I think the improvements she's made and how well she's managed since she had the baby stopped the situation going quite sour.

A distinctive feature of the service was the ability to offer *practical* solutions to problems, which gave tangible benefits to a family that was struggling and contributed to building working relationships. As one team member said:

> Being trusted is also about being able to offer the practical side. Often when I start working with a family there are some practical things I can do which means for that family, she [mother] is on our side.

The team was able to make links. For example, a team member introduced the Sure Start dietician to a parenting group.

> That's the sort of thing that the family support team can do and a social worker can't do because the family support worker can give a more intensive package of care.

When asked what she noticed as distinctive about the family support work located within Sure Start, the social work student commented:

... the community feel of it. It's less us and them ... Sometimes as a social worker they don't engage with you at all then you can't do your job and you end up having to take drastic measures ...

Views of other workers

The team identified other sectors with which they collaborated, including social services, health, and the voluntary sector. Four workers from these settings, and the team leaders' line manager, were interviewed about the impact of the family support work. Distinctive features mentioned included the intensive nature of the service,

> ... outside the Sure Start catchment area... there's the basic funding for parenting groups, but for people who would find that level of group quite threatening there's nothing at a more appropriate level ... The groups are too big and there's too much of an emphasis on meeting targets.

In terms of family support group work, being based in the programme family centre, which housed many other activities, was important. It made it easier to enter the building and engage in other activities. The localized nature of the service was seen as a clear advantage. For instance, a health visitor commented on the team's accessibility:

> I think because they're more localized they will know the area a lot better and they are based at (the family centre) so families can just call in and see them if they are around and available. Families get to know people who roam around the area and will stop you in the street.

A successful feature noted by a voluntary sector worker about the work was that it was possible to modify a package on offer to parents and 'adapt it to meet the needs of the community'. Another aspect of the service of recognized benefit to the health visitors was the practical element of the work, ranging from contacting the housing department to using links to acquire tins of paint.

The family support interventions impacted on the work of others. For instance, one of the health visitors observed:

> It's probably lessened my work ... I can pass things on to the family support ... Probably the ones from Sure Start may get involved more with the families, they've probably got more time than the social services team.

The worker from social services explained that the family support team could afford to take a more conciliatory approach than social services, which helped minimize social service involvement. From her perspective of statutory work, she commented that:

> We do have a lot of families that don't co operate … you end up taking the hard line and legal advice whereas sometimes it's unnecessary … [Family support] can save families and the state quite a lot in stress and money and eventual outcome.

Another instance offers an illustration of the benefit of the family support work:

> … we needed the parent to come in to discuss the adoption and what the process was. I don't think we would have got her anywhere near coming in without [the worker's] support.

The cumulative views of workers with whom the team collaborated suggested that the work had a valuable contribution to offer.

Main frustrations experienced by the team

One of the team's difficulties was that, as they became known in the area, they uncovered greater levels of need than first envisaged. It was impossible to target all the people eligible for certain services. For instance, there was a group attended by 12 young mothers, which represented a fraction of the young mothers who were actually in the neighbourhood.

There were structural problems with local housing and little employment in the neighbourhood. The workers believed some areas were very difficult to live in. In addition, even when family support workers had raised aspirations, for instance introducing young mothers into mainstream college courses, it transpired that they were unsuitable because of insufficient flexibility to meet the young women's needs.

There was a shortage of resources in other agencies, particularly social work but also education. Even where additional resources had been introduced, there were occasions when links made with other agencies had not worked out.

The geographical boundary of the Sure Start programme, limiting who was eligible for services, was also a problem. This issue goes beyond this particular work; it concerns any service delivered within targeted neighbourhood contexts.

Whilst recognizing successes with the work, it is also necessary to acknowledge its limitations. As one of the Family Support Service team expressed it:

> At the end of the day we can do so much, but we can't be there 24 hours a day and we can't be that missing family person ... You feel you can change the world when you start and you can't.

In addition, to maintain worker morale it was important to recognize the nature of the work and that family responses can be slow and incremental, without immediate results:

> working with people that are hard to engage with ... there's very little response. But you just have to see things long term, in terms of have you made improvements that will ultimately help develop the child's welfare?

> Because we work with a lot of ... hard to reach families it does take a lot more time ... You've always got to have a team there working with the hard to reach because they are the children that would just slip through the net.

The greatest difficulty of all arose from the paucity of input into the area in the past, meaning problems built up over time, leading to 'generations of difficulty'. The family support team formed an important resource for helping to alleviate some of the needs of families within this context.

What are we learning?

Key findings

The Family Support Service has been able to work in a preventive capacity to identify and support vulnerable families, and work with existing agencies. As well as individual work, the team carried out group work with teenage parents and substance-misusing parents, ran a baby massage group, and facilitated access to other services. Findings from interviews with the team, service users and workers with whom the team collaborated revealed that the work was complex, imaginative, flexible and highly valued by those who came into contact with it.

Areas to be developed and strengths of the work

The study pointed to areas to develop. Communication systems could be strengthened, within the team, within Sure Start and with other agencies. Informal systems work well, but consistency through more formal arrangements would be beneficial. It would have been useful for the Family Support Service to have had a central summary of when a family was taken on for family support work, the level of intervention and when it finished. An awareness of the needs of fathers and possible ways of engaging with them could be developed more fully. Where feasible, it would be beneficial to try to expand group work to target *all* teenage parents and *all* drug-abusing parents in the area. A major group with whom it was seen to be important to develop work was families with mental health problems. Innovative work in relation to contacting new-to-area families could be expanded. Since this study was first reported to the programme, the above issues have been tackled as part of the programme's continuing cycle of action-research-action.

The work of the family support team involved creating new ways of working, exploring new professional roles and finding ways of working with para-professionals that required flexibility and imagination. While increasing levels of communication would be helpful, multi-agency and joint working proved possible. The family support team have been able to help with some of the child protection cases that over-stretched health visitors have had responsibility for, in ways it is not always possible for social workers to do. The team was able to put in long-term support if necessary, and also to resume work with a family if the need arose. Overall, the service was shown to be of benefit for some of the most vulnerable members of a community.

References

Buchanan, A. (2002) Family support, in D. McNeish, T. Newman and H. Roberts (eds) *What Works for Children?* Buckingham: Open University Press.

Department of Health (1989) *Children Act.* London: HMSO.

Department of Health (1999) *Working Together to Safeguard Children.* London: HMSO.

Department of Health (2000) *Framework for the Assessment of Children in Need and their Families.* London: HMSO.

Hermanns, J. and Leu, H. (eds) (1998) *Family Risks and Family Support: Theory, Research and Practice in the Netherlands.* Delft: Eburon.

Parton, N. and Mathews, R. (2001) New directions in child protection and family support in Western Australia: a policy initiative to re-focus child welfare practice. *Child and Family Social Work,* 6(2): 97–116.

Seebohm, F. (Chairman) (1968) *Report of the Committee on Local Authority and Allied Personal Social Services*. Lincoln: HMSO.

Seitz, V., Rosenbaum, L. and Apfel, N. (1985) Effects of family support intervention: a ten-year follow-up. *Child Development*, 56: 376–91.

Think Twice (2001) Video. Sheffield: Foxhill and Parson Cross/NCH Sure Start. [Enquiries to programme]

Zigler, E. and Black, K. (1989) America's family support movement: strength and limitations. *American Journal of Orthopsychiatry*, 59: 6–9.

4 'Connecting with our Kids' parenting programme
Margaret Drake with
Jo Weinberger and Peter Hannon

Introduction

'Connecting with our Kids' is a parenting education service provided for the programme by one of its partners, C'mon Everybody, a Sheffield organization created some years ago by Geoff Evans (a teacher) and John Rylance (a social worker) who researched personal and social education in relation to children's behavioural problems. They visited a clinic in Seattle directed by Carolyn Webster-Stratton, and, impressed by her approach, brought it back to Sheffield. C'mon Everybody was the first organization in the UK to take up the Webster-Stratton approach, since taken up by many others.

The approach is based on behaviour/social learning principles about how behaviours are learned and how they might be modified. A core idea is that people change as a result of their daily interactions with others. This suggests that when children 'misbehave' and families become disrupted, it is necessary to change the parent's behaviour as well as the child's. The emphasis is on helping parents' interactions with their children become more positive. Courses for parents mix videotape modelling and therapist-led group discussion in a collaborative process. Sessions are intended to be relaxed, enabling therapists and parents to develop close and meaningful relationships (Webster-Stratton, 1992, 1999; Webster-Stratton and Herbert, 1994). Week by week parents build up skills and strategies, practising them during 'homework' sessions. The course includes the following:

- how to play with your child;
- how to use praise and rewards to promote good behaviour;
- how to communicate effectively with your child;
- how to cope with specific problems, such as disobedience, lying, TV addiction, bed-wetting, stealing and temper tantrums;
- how to manage your own anger and frustrations.

At the beginning of each session, parents discuss 'homework' and share experiences. Basic evaluations of the course are completed weekly, with a more in-depth evaluation at the end. Future weeks are planned according to the needs of individual parents. A crèche is always provided.

'Connecting with our Kids' and Sure Start

Adapting the Webster-Stratton approach for Sure Start meant devising new ways of working that would be suitable for parents of younger children (under 4) and that would provide a suitable programme for *all* families in the Sure Start area, rather than only for parents experiencing acute problems. This marked a shift from a 'clinical' programme to a 'community' programme.

In this way, Connecting with our Kids aimed to provide open access to all families with children aged up to 4. Other aims included:

- to improve the quality of child/parent relationships and equip parents with strategies for coping with a range of early childhood behaviours;
- to raise parents'/carers' confidence in themselves;
- to increase parents' awareness of, and access to, other services and activities within the Sure Start programme.

Initially, it was felt that vulnerable families might feel less threatened if what they were offered was both short and practical. As a result, a five-week course was designed, called 'Gimme Five'. This was based around practical activities, extending the parents' knowledge of the nursery curriculum, with local nurseries helping to engage parents of 3-year-olds. Later, however, as the reputation of the Connecting with our Kids service became better established, there was no need for Gimme Five, and parents enlisted for the 12-week Connecting with our Kids programme from the outset.

There were few suitable venues in the Sure Start area within pram-pushing distance for families, and the need for crèche facilities made matters even more difficult. Initially, spare space in schools, nurseries, community halls, churches, park pavilions, family centres, a youth centre and the entrance hall of a community centre were used. Later, the building of a Sure Start nursery eased the situation. The importance of the 'within pram-pushing' distance is that regular participation on a course is seen to wane if a bus journey is involved.

The Connecting with our Kids team received referrals from a broad range of professionals, including health visitors, Sure Start family support workers, local nurseries and schools, social workers and also, once the service had become established, self referrals. Initially, parents were often lacking in confidence and the service sought to recruit them, for example when they took their children to nursery. One of the team engaged each parent in conversation, welcomed them to a course and also expressed hopes that they would attend. Mid-week phone calls were also important to ensure attendance at the next session. A pre-course visit was considered essential to build trust between parents and the course facilitator.

Evaluation of the programme

During the first year of Connecting with our Kids, 53 Sure Start parents took up the opportunity to join the basic 12-week course. At the time, there were between 150 and 200 families in the area with children aged 3 to 4. Therefore the take-up for the new service was of the order of 20–30 per cent. This was quite high bearing in mind that the course was being offered for the first time in the area, that Sure Start itself was new, and that the idea of such a course would be unfamiliar to most parents. In addition, the drop-out rate was small (17 per cent). Thus one of the first lessons learned was that many parents were ready to make use of the new service.

Most of the parents were in their early twenties (teenage parents attended their own less formal group) and came from a broad range of backgrounds, but a significant number lived on their own or had relationship problems. Most were unemployed and on low incomes. Some had had drug/alcohol problems in the past. Several were specifically interested in learning how to manage child behaviours. Usually, groups became well bonded and strong friendships were formed.

Views of parents

The course has run for a further three years. To establish their views of the course, parents were asked to complete questionnaires at the beginning and then again at the end of the course. Questionnaires were returned by a total of 85 parents.

Parents were asked how often they had played with their child over the previous few weeks. At the beginning of the course, 40 out of 85 reported that they either played with their child hardly ever or sometimes, whereas at the end 76 played either often or very often (see Figure 4.1).

Even greater change was recorded in relation to the question of how parents felt about the way they got on with their child/children: 34 reported very negative feelings about this at the beginning, whereas at the end of the course none reported this, and 84 said that they either felt good or very good about it (see Figure 4.2).

Figure 4.1 Over the past few weeks', how often have you played with your child?

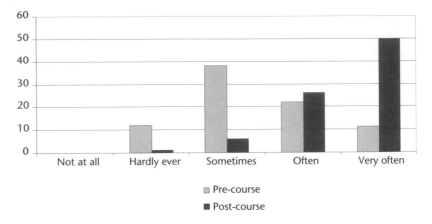

Figure 4.2 How do you feel about the way you get on with your child/children?

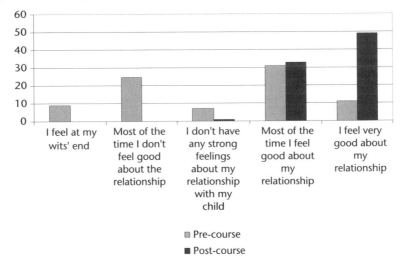

Coping with their children's behaviour was another key issue. Before the course, 56 said they felt unable to cope either most or some of the time, but post-course only 3 reported this; 82 reported that they could cope either most or all of the time (see Figure 4.3).

Figure 4.3 Over the past few weeks', how have you coped with your child/chidren's behaviour?

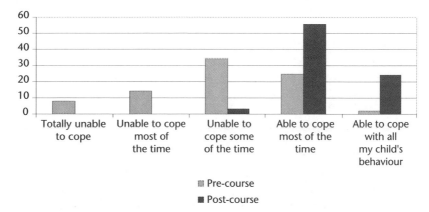

Confidence as a parent/carer is an important dimension. Pre-course, 38 reported lack of confidence some or all of the time, but none post-course; 84 felt quite or very confident post-course (see Figure 4.4).

Figure 4.4 How confident do you feel about yourself as a parent/carer?

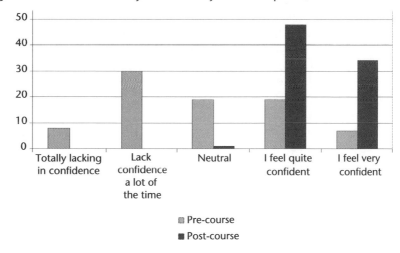

Key learning points for the Connecting with our Kids team

When the team reflected upon their experience, they identified the following key issues.

- The course had developed simple behaviour management strategies which most parents could implement in a structured way.
- The nature of the course (group discussion of videos showing children interacting with their parents, role plays, homework, celebration of successes and so on) helped to raise self-esteem and extend skills in group participation.
- Parents realized they were not alone and that they shared common problems, for example relating to mealtimes, supermarket checkouts, sibling rivalry, temper tantrums, bedtimes.
- The basic course that had been developed was not appropriate for those parents who had only one child under the age of 2 or for teenage parents.
- In cases where there were multiple problems (such as substance abuse or debt), it was sometimes necessary to work with other agencies to address difficulties before parents could commit to the course. The time was not always right for a parent to attend, and course facilitators needed to be sensitive to this. 'Befriending' periodically, by lending a listening ear, was sometimes necessary until the time came when parents were ready to join a course.
- Some parents needed to repeat a course to maximize the benefits as, initially, concentration and listening skills needed to be developed.
- Fathers were difficult to engage. A group was trialled for fathers, at times to accommodate their work schedules, set in a local public house, supported by home visits and telephone calls. It did not prove possible to establish a functioning group. Families in which the father was the only carer very often moved from the area. This may have been due to employment opportunities or returning to an extended family.
- Couples attending together led to the most successful outcomes. When fathers did not attend, mothers were encouraged to pass on information in a 'leading by example' manner.

With experience, it was found that parents needed help with transitions at the beginning and end of courses. Therefore the first week was an introductory coffee morning, followed by ten weeks on the course. The penultimate week was a personal development day (with speakers invited from local adult education organizations, colleges and careers services). As the area of personal development became a more established part of the programme, links with other professionals and agencies were developed. The final session was set aside as a 'nurturing day', which included activities of the parents' choice, such as massage, nail care, hair care.

Long-term parent evaluation of the programme

The long-term benefits of the course can only be judged over time. To explore this, 20 parents who had attended the course between two and three years previously were interviewed. Initially, selection was random. One parent in every five was chosen from a list of participants, but this proved to be more difficult than anticipated due to the demolition of many houses in the area. The sample was, therefore, supplemented by contacting other known parents. (Thus, out of the 20 parents, 16 were randomly selected and 4 were a sample of convenience.) Interviewing was carried out by the author, one of the course facilitators.

There were a variety of reasons why parents had agreed to attend the course. Five said they needed help and guidance, five had problems with their child's behaviour and five felt it was something different. Two parents wanted to meet other mothers, and the others talked about personal development and supporting their child's education. One said she came in order that her child could attend the crèche. For 15 out of 20 this was the first course of any kind they had attended as adults.

Learning from the course

Parents were asked about the use of strategies they learned on the course. Seven reported that they had incorporated most of them into their everyday dealings with their children. Eleven said they still used many of the strategies as well as the book which accompanied the course (all parents had been given a copy of *The Incredible Years* by Carolyn Webster-Stratton). No parents had forgotten all the strategies but two only used a few. Comments made by parents, reporting on their strategies, included:

> Praise works for us and asking them to do one thing at a time. I don't raise my voice as much – I suppose we just talk about it. Five minute warnings definitely work, especially in the bath – it's just part of our house now, even my husband does it.

> I also use the strategy of explaining things more clearly. For example, if my child is pestering to do something but I'm having a busy day doing the housework, I'll explain, 'today I need you to behave so that I can get all my jobs done and then tomorrow we have the day to go to the park, swimming, etc'. Usually it works.

Strategies specifically mentioned as having a significant impact were: praise, rewards, offering choices, ignoring, clear explanations, the five-minute warning, divert and distract and time out.

The value of giving parents a copy of the book was confirmed by the following comments:

> I still refer to the book because I now have a younger child and the problems I have with him are different from those with my older child.

> I still use the book – in fact I turned to it about a month ago for bed-wetting. It's at the side of my bed.

In response to a question about their child's behaviour as a result of the course, nine felt proud of their child's behaviour and felt confident as a parent, five felt they were good at managing their child's behaviour and a further four felt they managed their child's behaviour most of the time. Only two said they still struggled and none reported that their child was still out of control. Typical illustrations of what parents said in response to this question included:

> I struggle a bit but I find it easier now.

> This morning I didn't feel in control of the situation. We all got up late, he wasn't having any breakfast, but we got there eventually. But I did actually put in some of the strategies – like I said to go upstairs and get yourself ready and when he made an attempt to get up I praised him and then he ran upstairs.

> It's better because before I went on the course I couldn't go out of the house because he showed me up that much with his tantrums.

> It has made me think a lot more about why they are behaving badly. I have seen a change because, for instance, when you go to the swimming baths and you see other parents, you think, 'I used to say and do things like that'.

Impact of the course

When asked about the long-term value of the course, 8 of the 20 said that it had helped them a lot and had helped them to move forward with their lives, 9 reported that it had helped a lot and had had valuable long-term effects. None said that it had not helped at all or that they were struggling with their child's behaviour and still were. The rest concluded that it had helped a little. The following comments illustrate how far-reaching some of the effects were for individuals:

I respect my children. If I get it wrong when one of 'ums misbehaved I apologize to them. It has made me have more respect for them and probably them for me now. It has built my confidence which I think shows in the kids. I think it's making everyone happier.

It was like a weekly dose of therapy where I could go and moan and listen to others in similar situations. It calmed me down for the rest of the week.

At the time I had just left my husband. He was violent and it helped me to handle situations which would have caused me even more stress.

I feel that ever since doing the course I have realized how important it is not to snap and shout. I try to stay calm.

The team was interested in the impact the course had on the family situation, particularly in relation to older/younger siblings and also to adult relationships. The general view was that, although the strategies worked to some extent on older children, starting the programme from the age of 2 maximized the results. In relation to partners, six parents said it had brought them closer. Four reported no change. Three split up and said the parenting approach had created friction in the household. Six parents had no partner.

The following comments are illustrative of the effects on couples:

We teamed up together which made life a lot easier.

My children's father and I were having problems, but it took a long time to admit it to myself and we eventually split up.

Yes I think it was a bad effect. Him and his mum thought the things I was doing were silly. They (the children) were doing things for me because I was fair. It took two months for them to start listening to me.

As far as involving partners in the principles of the course was concerned, 9 said they had done so. For others it was not applicable, but 5 for whom it was had not managed this. The following comments were indicative of those who had not managed to involve partners:

He was supportive, but I think he thought it was mumbo-jumbo until he could see certain things working and at times it caused problems because I think he felt that he couldn't handle the situations but I could. I was the expert.

No because he was an idle toe-rag.

Parents were asked what was the most difficult thing about the course. Four said there was nothing difficult. Four said entering a new group was hard and other parents mentioned learning to praise, ignoring, role-plays, descriptive commenting (where parents comment on the child's play rather than asking questions), homework and leaving a child in the crèche. Admitting that you are the one with the problem and refraining from eating the biscuits were two further issues that parents had found difficult.

A clear outcome of the course was the extent of personal development for the parents: 19 out of 20 said it had given them more confidence; 14 that they were more outgoing and assertive; 16 that it had helped with other activities; and 7 that it had helped sort out personal relationships. A further 18 said that it had made them feel more in control of themselves and that it had calmed them down; 17 felt less isolated; 17 had become involved with Sure Start; and 13 had made friends whom they still saw socially.

Since attending the course, parents had gone on to attend a wide range of other courses, including vocational courses, such as IT, sign language and first aid, and non-vocational courses such as line dancing, aromatherapy and healthy eating. Several parents had attended courses to support their child's education. There was also involvement in community activities, many run by Sure Start. Two became voluntary members of Sure Start advisory boards. Seven parents returned to paid employment (including three within Sure Start, one a manager in a charity shop and one an accredited play worker) and another was planning to become a foster parent. Others formed their own group called 'Women Together' and sought funding to set up their own courses (for instance keep fit and karate). Others became leaders in local mother and toddler groups.

It is known that in some cases the bad behaviour of the children can be the result of the poor quality of the adult relationships in the home. It is also known that when two parent carers are using the strategies it maximizes the effect (Webster-Stratton, 1999). The course seemed to achieve one of two outcomes. Very often it highlighted differences in attitudes within the family, either between partners or, in some cases, with grandparents, and these issues needed to be addressed. When this was tackled, communication became easier and, as a result, relationships improved to the benefit of the child. The team saw cases in which the whole family had been turned round as a result of the course and had become a happy, positive unit. However, in other cases it seemed that the course had confirmed the feelings of one parent that there were irreconcilable differences, resulting in a family split. This was sometimes facilitated by the fact that the parent had access to a closely bonded friendship group in which painful and intimate experiences had been shared and where support and caring from others was available.

For many parents in this follow-up sample, Connecting with our Kids was the first course they had attended, and for many it led to involvement with Sure Start and other community activities. Over the years, the service team acquired new skills in how to respond to parents' needs. Parents reported favourite strategies which they used regularly and others that were no longer used. However, this does not seem to have affected their success as parent managers. Indeed, it shows that parents do not need to be proficient in all areas or use all the strategies in order to succeed. The book *The Incredible Years*, given to all parents to accompany the course, proved a valuable support: 18 out of 20 parents still had the book and referred to it regularly for reference as their children grew up and exhibited different problems. The favourite strategies included praise, rewards and choices, rather than the more negative ones such as time-out and ignore. The majority felt that they were good at managing their child's behaviour and were proud and confident as parents. It is possibly because of this that such high numbers reported that the course had had long-term effects or had enabled them to move on with their lives.

The responses to the question about how the course had affected the parent personally were revealing, with only one mother reporting that it had not helped to improve her confidence. There were also positive responses to the development of social skills which this new-found confidence had given them, for instance becoming more out-going, making friends, feeling more calm and in control. In the small number of cases when parents did not report this, it was usually because they felt they already had these qualities.

As far as difficulties associated with the course are concerned, it was encouraging that most parents reported none, although more research needs to be done in order to ascertain the reasons why it was not possible to engage some parents, including fathers, on the courses.

Conclusion

From difficult beginnings when the team was making initial contacts, finding venues and setting up crèches, successful working systems have been established across the Sure Start area. The work described here shows how the Webster-Stratton parenting programme can be transferred from a clinical setting into a community context, with the strategies and principles employed proving viable and valid for both children and their families.

There is evidence that the Connecting with our Kids intervention has had long-term positive effects on a significant number of families within the Sure Start area.

References

Webster-Stratton, C. (1992) *The Incredible Years*. Toronto: Umbrella Press.

Webster-Stratton, C. (1999) *How to Promote Children's Social and Educational Competence*. London: Paul Chapman/SAGE.

Webster-Stratton, C. and Herbert, M. (1994) *Troubled Families – Problem Children*. Ontario: John Wiley and Sons.

5 Meeting the needs of teenage parents
Deborah Crofts

Introduction

This study aimed to evaluate the long-term effects of a community-based social support programme on the social, health and educational outcomes of teenage mothers and their children. It aimed to understand the experiences of teenage mothers in the first one to two years of their child's life, their parenting, the nature of the support needed and the impact, if any, of new forms of support being developed within the local area. Its main concern is not with reducing teenage pregnancy rates (for example through contraceptive and sex education), which has been the topic of many previous studies, but on improving the outcomes for the mother and child in the first few years of the child's life.

Reports and research papers often identify teenage parents as being in need and suggest that they should be targeted to receive extra support from statutory and other services. How much of the support is wanted by these mothers, and does it reach them when they most need it?

Foxhill and Parson Cross is characterized by low levels of educational achievement, high levels of poverty, ill health, and avoidable early death. Prior to Sure Start, there was little provision of family support services outside the Primary Health Care Team, and the local culture discouraged group activities. Children in the area lacked access to good-quality and affordable childcare and play facilities. This, no doubt, has contributed to the poor educational achievement locally. The area also has above average numbers of low birth weight babies (see Chapter 6), and high levels of teenage pregnancy. Approximately one birth in six is to a mother in her teenage years.

Sure Start has worked with this vulnerable group to meet their needs in the form of one to one and group work in collaboration with Connexions, an organization that offers information, advice and practical help to young people. The researcher is a health visitor who has worked in the research field for ten years, researching mainly in the field of public health.

Background

The United Kingdom has teenage birth rates that are twice as high as Germany, three times as high as in France and six times as high as in the Netherlands (Social Exclusion Unit, 1999). In England there are nearly 90,000 conceptions a year to teenagers: around 7700 to girls under 16 and 2200 to girls aged 14 or under. The Social Exclusion report published in June 1999 revealed the scale of the problem and contained a package of measures to tackle social exclusion among young parents and their families.

Teenage pregnancy is associated with increased risk of poor social, economic and health outcomes for both the mother and child. Samuels et al. (1994) found self-esteem to be positively correlated with mother's adjustment to parenting, and importantly, mothers with higher self-esteem perceived their babies to be less troublesome. In a study of factors related to adjustment of children born to teenage mothers, Dubow and Luster (1990) found that low maternal self-esteem was related to behaviour problems in children. Teenage pregnancies may also result in significant public costs (Burt, 1986). Pregnancy rates are higher in more socially deprived areas, possibly making the associated risks of teenage pregnancy even greater (Smith, 1993).

Methods

The researcher completed face-to-face semi-structured interviews with all teenage mothers aged 18 years and under in the Sure Start area. The survey commenced in February 2001 and continued until July 2001, when the majority of the teenagers had been interviewed and all attempts at contacting the remainder had failed. The target population was teenage mothers, that is aged 18 or less who had not had the benefit of the Sure Start programme because the programme was new and services were just beginning.

The target sample chosen to be representative of that population were all those living in the Sure Start area whose babies were born between September 1998 and December 2000. Those children born before September 1998 were in nursery and those born after December 2000 may have been contacted by Sure Start as the programme had started seeing new births routinely at this point.

A list of these mothers was obtained from the Sure Start database. This database holds the demographic details of all the children and their mothers who live within the geographical parameters of the Foxhill and Parson Cross Sure Start area.

Mothers were contacted in a variety of ways. Those attending the Sure Start antenatal group were contacted first, and the results of these interviews were used to amend the questionnaire. When the researcher had a telephone number, the mothers were contacted to arrange a home visit for the interview. Alternatively, a postal appointment was sent to the mother giving a time and date for a home visit. If the mothers were out at this visit, a card was left giving a new time and date and contact number if this appointment was inconvenient. Additionally, all existing groups within the local area were contacted to increase the chance of contacting teenage mothers who attended. In this case, the mother was contacted at the group and an appointment for a home visit arranged. When all other methods had been exhausted, the researcher called at the home unexpectedly.

Initially, 96 mothers were identified from the programme database. Nearly a third of the mothers and children (26 mothers) had moved out of area prior to the visit. The researcher was unable to contact a further six mothers, and two mothers whose children lived with another family member. One child was cared for by the maternal grandmother, and the other by the child's father. Interviews with these mothers may have highlighted the difficult decisions that teenagers have to make after becoming pregnant, as these girls had decided they could not continue with their own lives in the same way and support a child. One interview was conducted with a mother whose children were both in foster care, one child because of physical abuse and the other because she decided she could not cope with the child.

Face-to-face semi-structured interviews were completed with 62 mothers in their homes, representing a response rate of 91 per cent. This represents an excellent response rate. These interviews were recorded and transcribed, and brief written notes were taken during the interview. All replies were themed and coded following the completion of the survey. No pre-coded replies were included in the semi-structured interviews. All notes were entered onto a database and longer responses to specific questions were transcribed.

The questions

The interview schedule initially asked about the teen mothers' living arrangements, whether she had the support of a partner and if that partner was the baby's father. The questions then moved on to their child or children and asked about their health, their eating habits, reading and library attendance, watching television and activities that the mother did with the child on a regular basis, for example whether they went swimming, to the park, or to any groups or structured activities.

The mother was then asked about her own health and about her pregnancy. Questions included whether she considered a termination, how she and her partner felt about her being pregnant, whether she had been using contraception, and if she smoked during her pregnancy. The researcher then went on to ask about the support she received from the baby's father, her family and professional support, if the mother was still at school and whether the school staff were supportive. Finally, the mother was asked about her plans for the future. Where did she see herself in a years' time and had she made any plans for the future?

Main findings

The pregnancy

A sixth of the teenage pregnancies (11 mothers) were planned, although judging by the number of women using contraception at the time of conception, a few more of the teenagers should have been expecting to become pregnant. Some felt that it wouldn't happen to them, sometimes for unusual reasons; some were secretly happy when it happened, although they hadn't consciously been planning a pregnancy.

> No, cause I was taking speed and I was told it lessens your chances to get pregnant. I assumed I wasn't going to get caught. I did.

A third of the mothers (22 women) reported they were happy when they found out they were pregnant.

> I wanted to be a young mum. You can grow up with them really. I were right pleased. I'd got responsibilities and someone to look after.

Several of the women reported that they never thought they would be able to have children, even though there had been no medical evidence to support this belief.

When they became pregnant, only 37 of the young women were using any form of contraception. When women were, many reasons were given why the contraception didn't work. One woman said her boyfriend threw all the pills down the rubbish chute so she didn't take them. One woman was on the injection Depo-Provera, but because she wasn't going out with anyone for a long time she failed to keep up the injections, and got pregnant on a one-night stand. Antibiotic use and not taking the oral contraceptive pill correctly were the other main reasons for contraceptive failure.

Even though a large number of the women reported that they did not wish to get pregnant again for a long time, only half of the sample was using contraception at the time of interview.

School

Nearly a third of the mothers were still at school when they found out they were pregnant. A large proportion of these mothers reported being 'kicked out' of school or had just stopped attending school even before becoming pregnant. Only four of the mothers took any exams at school-leaving age.

Relationships with the fathers

A large number of the fathers were reportedly 'over the moon' when they found out their partners were pregnant, although this quickly wore off, and seven of these men denied they were the fathers. A quarter of the fathers were no longer in contact with the mother or saw their child. One father committed suicide and four were in prison at the time of the interview. One father did not know he had a child. This was upsetting for the mother, who would have liked her child's father to take a more active role in the child's upbringing.

> It bothers me in a way cause at the end of the day it's J whose going without a dad. I grew up without a dad and I know what it's like. You get picked on and stuff. He's not going without owt (anything) though.

Nearly two-thirds of the fathers (39) were reported to be good with their children, although this did not necessarily mean they did much for them. The amount of interaction ranged from being the primary carer (one father) to offering financial help only (six fathers). A quarter of fathers (16) were reported to be only 'good for the occasional hour's baby-sitting'. A further quarter (18 fathers) were reported to be generally good with their children and took an active part in their upbringing.

Relationship with parents

After the partner, the girl's parents were usually the next to be informed of the pregnancy. Only a small number of the mothers reported that their own mothers were upset they were pregnant, with most saying they didn't seem bothered, or they expected it.

> My mum said we can't get a new carpet now.

Teenage pregnancy is the norm in the local area, and therefore it becomes socially acceptable to become pregnant at such a young age. There appeared to be a feeling amongst the girls' mothers that it was a *fait accompli* and there was now nothing they could do. Their daughter was pregnant and so they should support them whatever.

The majority of the mothers received some help and support from their parents. This was usually the girl's parents, although some of the girls did say both sets of grandparents helped. This help was invaluable to the young mothers.

> If it weren't for our parents, I don't think we'd have food in our fridge. They support us 100 per cent. I go to my mum's every day.

Seven young mothers received no help or support from their parents. This was due to a serious breakdown in the relationship due to violence, alcoholism or death. When asked to whom they would turn for support, the majority of the teenage girls (49) said it would be to their own mother, and five said their mother-in-law. Occasionally, the grandmother lived a long distance away and so accessing that support was particularly difficult. One mother reported she would have no-one to turn to. Being a young mother is especially hard, but without the support of family it becomes even harder.

Support from professionals

Nearly all the mothers felt their midwife had been supportive during their pregnancy. However, when asked to say in more detail how she had been of support, the mothers went on to describe routine antenatal support, for example being available at clinic when they wanted to ask questions, or giving routine health advice during an antenatal visit.

> She were brilliant when I were pregnant. Towards the end of it, it were really hard. I got pre-eclampsia [a dangerous condition involving high blood pressure and fluid retention]. She were always coming to the house. Helped a lot as well when I'd just had her.

A sixth of mothers (12) felt their midwife had given them no support, and three mothers went further to say their midwife was not very good and they were not happy with her care during their pregnancy.

The health visitor was not seen as any more supportive unless she had supplied the mother with baby equipment or applied to a charity for money. The seven mothers who had received such equipment or money which they may have perceived as a gift from the health visitor, all thought their health visitor was very good, although only two mothers described their health visitor as supportive.

The mothers and their children

Over half the mothers had lived in the Parson Cross and Foxhill area all their life. Just under half of the mothers (25) had moved into the area since the birth of their babies. Housing in the area is relatively easy to access and so these young mothers were given their first properties in the area.

Half of the mothers (31) lived alone with their child or children. A further 20 lived with their partners and children. One mother lived alone with her partner as her children were in care. The remainder (10 mothers) lived with family, of whom seven lived with their mother and father, two with their sisters and one mother lived with her step-grandfather.

Well over half of the mothers (46) reported themselves to be in a relationship, although some of these relationships were unstable. Of these relationships, half (33 mothers) reported they were still with the father of their children, and 13 mothers were now in new relationships.

The child's behaviour was generally reported to be good, although some admitted their children were only good for others such as grandparents. A small number of mothers (7) admitted their child was not particularly well behaved.

> He screams all the time. He's started fighting, he bites and head butts her.

Several of the mothers admitted that looking after their child was hard. They recognized they needed help in managing their child's behaviour but didn't know where to turn.

> He does naughty things so he'll get more attention and I just don't know what to do. I've got no help at all.

Nearly half the mothers (28) breastfed their child after birth, although six mothers breastfed for fewer than seven days. The average here was three days, within a range of one to seven days. Reasons given for stopping were the baby wasn't getting enough milk (9 mothers); it was too much trouble or the baby was too demanding (7 mothers); or the mother wasn't enjoying it (2 mothers). The numbers of mothers breastfeeding their child is below the national average for feeding at birth and 4 weeks of age. A sixth of mothers (10) who breastfed said they received no support for breastfeeding, but only one felt this was a problem.

The mothers were asked where they took their children and what they did with them on a regular basis, to identify the types of experiences the children were having. Overwhelmingly, the most common activity was going to their mother's home (24) or going shopping (21). Only 4 mothers out of 62 described the groups they attended or the constructive play activities they engaged in. A third of mothers (24) reported they did not tend to go out with their children, although some did describe how they played with their children in the home.

> I never go out. I stop in all the time. Just to my mums for Sunday dinner. Occasionally I go to town with my mum.

Over a third of mothers (25) reported going to the park regularly. A further third (21) said they had been once or twice, or went to the park only when the weather was nice.

A third of families (23) had been swimming at some point, although half of these (11 children) did not go on a regular basis. Nine mothers reported they had not taken their child swimming because they could not swim themselves. The main reason for the remainder of mothers was their own fear of the water.

> We do, but it's not really warm so when you put her in she looks cold and horrible so I don't really like taking her.

Two-thirds of the mothers (40) reported they read to their child. However, this was often on an irregular basis. A quarter of these (7 mothers) reported reading less often than once a week. More worrying is that a further third of the mothers (22) reported never reading to their child. Some reasons given were that their child was too young to understand (2 mothers), they just could not be bothered (2 mothers) or they had no books (4 mothers).

A quarter (14 mothers) of the mothers reported attending a mother and toddler group at some time since the birth of their child, although 12 of these mothers had either stopped going or only went once or twice. Cost was given as a reason for not attending groups, although confidence and the welcome they received were also mentioned.

When asked about their children's health, all the mothers described it as good or alright. A third of the children (22 families) were reported to have had 'lots of illnesses', although over half the illnesses reported were minor ear, nose and throat infections, which are common in young children. The more serious illnesses included Kawasaki disease, heart murmur, gastroenteritis and bronchiolitis, and six mothers reported their child having breathing difficulties requiring medical attention.

The mothers themselves

Three-quarters (45) of the mothers described their own health as alright or good, although 4 of these mothers were on antidepressants. Two-thirds of the mothers were smokers (44), smoking on average 10 cigarettes a day, ranging from 4 to 40 cigarettes a day. Just over half this number (27 mothers) reported they smoked throughout their pregnancy.

> Yes I smoked a lot. I didn't drink, I wouldn't drink. They always said don't smoke but she were nearly ten pounds when she were born. Otherwise she could have been twenty!

The mothers were asked to say how they felt they were managing at the time of the interview. Two-thirds of mothers (43) felt they were managing 'alright' although half of these (19) also said it was both hard and tiring being a young mum.

> Alright but not perfect. I get stressed out and tired because of him.

> I wouldn't manage at all if I didn't have my mum and dad behind me, but I think I'm managing alright.

This mother was referred to a Sure Start parenting programme with her agreement. Another mother felt she was not coping with her son and needed some extra help.

> I feel like my head's going to explode, just not being able to cope with him. I know it's evil but I feel like just taking him to my mum's and saying 'Mum, just have him for a bit, please for gods sake.'

Parents reported various things that would help, including more money, a new house, to have their partners' home from prison and more childcare provision for their child, in the form of a babysitter so they could either go out themselves socially or to get their child into the local nursery earlier than planned.

> To tidy my bedroom up. With just moving in over the weekend and I'm at school, everything just gets chucked all over.

> To take their voice boxes out now and then. And then I don't think I'd want anything.

> My boyfriend to come home, for B's dad never to see him and to

hope my baby calms down.

All but 10 mothers (52) reported becoming down or fed up at least some of the time. Reasons given were mainly that they could not go out for lack of childcare, or do the things they wanted to do as teenagers (14 mothers). Three mothers blamed their families for interfering, or partners for not being supportive.

> [I get fed up] a lot. I think it's because of all the cleaning I have to do. I wish I had never got my own house. If I'd have lived at my mum's I wouldn't have two kids.

Plans for the future

When asked if they had made any plans for the future, it was found that 21 mothers had made no plans at all, with a further 4 mothers deciding to take each day at a time. For 12 women, their living arrangement was the main priority for the future and they wanted a larger or better house, preferably outside of the Parson Cross and Foxhill area, or to own their own property. A number of the women talked about going to college at some point in the near future, but hadn't thought what they wished to study or when they would actually make that move.

Employment was a difficult issue for many of the women. Some did wish to go out and get a job, but not until their child was at school. A third of the women had no plans for a job as either they didn't feel they would get a 'decent' job with their experience and qualifications, or they planned to have more children and so wouldn't have the time for a job.

Finally, when the mothers were asked where they saw themselves in a year's time, 28 women felt nothing would have changed and they would still be in the same house with the same problems. A further 10 women had not thought that far in advance and didn't know where they would be in a year.

On a positive note, 21 women did feel that something would change and they would be doing other things within a year. This included getting a job, going to college or getting their children into nursery. However, some of the changes did seem to be unrealistic.

> If it's a dream, my own house and car and everything. Millionaire!!!

Discussion

Within the interviews, the researcher was trying to get an understanding: first, of what it is like to be a teenage mother and how these girls came to be pregnant in the first place; second, to look at the how these girls manage bringing up a small child whilst still only a child themselves; and third, how much help they both receive and need in that quest.

Support, in particular family support, is clearly important to teenage mothers, with the person they rely on for practical and childcare support usually being their own mother. Initial observation shows that the professional support does not reach those who need it the most, but the majority of the teenagers report they do not want help from professionals and local services. They prefer to call on their mothers or other family members, with 54 of the mothers all saying they would call on their mother or mother-in-law first. This is understandable to a degree. Their mothers live close by, are often available 24 hours a day, and have only recently stopped being a full-time mother to these girls. The teenagers have not done what many women do – moving out of the family home, getting married or living with a partner for a period of time. Many of these girls had been living in the family home until they had their babies, only then going on to get a home of their own with their baby.

The relationship between mother and daughter is often not a straightforward one, however. Conflict between the teenage mother and her own mother, and in some cases with other members of the family, has been found to diminish some of the positive impact of family support and has been associated with less optimal parenting behaviours (Bunting and McAuley, 2004). Studies have highlighted, however, that grandmothers themselves are aware of the potential for conflict and struggle to maintain a balance between helping their own child and recognizing that she is a mother in her own right (Dennison and Coleman, 1998). This conflict in mother and daughter relationships was an issue for the women in the study. Several mothers moved out of the family home to reduce conflict. Those who were too young to live alone found themselves in conflict with their mothers on a regular basis. Having said that, mothers were the main source of support, physical, emotional and financial, and a number of young mothers reported they couldn't have coped without their own mother.

Seven mothers received no help or support from their families. These mothers did struggle to care for their children, experiencing behavioural difficulties, sleep and feeding problems, and problems relating to their own self-esteem and self-confidence. These mothers were in need of more targeted support but didn't know where to turn to for that extra help.

The women did not seem to recognize when their own health, in particular their mental health, was poor. Several mothers, although they were on antidepressants, described their health as alright or good. Self-esteem appeared to be low for many of the women. Several described how they felt that the general public reacted negatively to them being mothers at such a young age and some members of the general public had actually commented to them about their situation.

At least two mother and child dyads seen during this interview survey were referred to a parenting course, as the mothers reported that their child's behaviour was unmanageable.

The adolescent mothers interviewed would have greatly benefited from courses on money management, teen support groups, managing finances, career workshops and other such services to help them to deal with the stresses of everyday life and parenting. Providing a solid foundation will greatly increase the likelihood that these young adolescent girls will be successful in life at whatever they choose.

Finally, many of these young mothers cope very well with a small child and feel they bring their child up as well as, if not better than, an older mother. They do not see themselves as in need or any different to any other mother having a baby. They do recognize that they missed out on the social scene that some of their friends are experiencing, of partying into the small hours, but several of the women say that wouldn't have been their scene and they did not like drinking in pubs anyway.

The Sure Start Foxhill and Parson Cross programme has developed a support programme for teenage mothers in collaboration with the youth service and Connexions. Teenagers are offered support on a one-to-one basis, with particular emphasis on support to access training and employment and group support with crèche facilities. The teenage mothers are encouraged to access training in parenting. Alternative courses are offered in arts, computer skills, first aid and other relevant issues.

References

Bunting, L. and McAuley, C. (2004) Research review: teenage pregnancy and motherhood: the contribution of support. *Child and Family Social Work*, 9: 207–15.

Burt, M.R. (1986) Estimating the public costs of teenage childbearing. *Family Planning Perspectives*, 18: 221–6.

Dennison, C. and Coleman, J. (1998) *Adolescent Motherhood: The Relation between a Young Mother and Her Mother*. Research report, Trust for the Study of Adolescence, Brighton.

Dubow, E. and Luster, T. (1990) Adjustment of children born to teenage mothers: the contribution of risk and protective factors. *Journal of Marriage and Family*, 52: 393–404.

Samuels, V.J., Stockdale, D.F. and Crase, S.J. (1994) Adolescent mothers' adjustment to parenting. *Journal of Adolescence*, 17: 427–43.

Smith, T. (1993) Influence of socio-economic factors on attaining targets for reducing teenage pregnancies. *British Medical Journal*, 306: 1232–5.

Social Exclusion Unit (1999) *Teenage Pregnancy*. London: HMSO.

Part Three
Improving health

6 Low birth weight – exploring the contribution of nutrition
Fiona Ford

Introduction

In February 2001, Sure Start programmes were extended to cover pregnant women and their partners for the first time, to enable them to access a wide range of advice and support services and help tackle problems such as poor nutrition, low birth weight (LBW), smoking and access to benefits.

Prior to any nutrition intervention, it is advisable to collect baseline data so that any dietary deficiencies can be documented. Researchers from the University of Sheffield, Centre for Pregnancy Nutrition have been working with the Foxhill and Parson Cross Sure Start Project (F&PC SS) in order to connect the increasing body of evidence for effective interventions to reduce the incidence of LBW, and improve maternal nutrition overall. Two aspects of this local work are explored in this chapter: an analysis of the diet of local mothers and building capacity in maternal nutrition. The work reported here is still at an early stage.

Definition of low birth weight

The commonest cause of infant death is LBW, that is babies born weighing less than 2500 grams, and very low birth weight (VLBW), babies weighing less than 1500 grams. Birth weight has been related to both neonatal and adult health and reflects fetal growth. An infant may have a sub-optimum birth weight because of impaired fetal growth and/or because of reduced gestation length. LBW reflects prenatal, periconceptional and genetic factors, including ethnicity, maternal smoking, maternal age, gestational weight gain, poverty and parity (birth order) (Kramer, 1987). Average birth weight in the UK after a normal length pregnancy is 3400 grams. Ten per cent of all births result in babies who are small for gestational age (SGA). Overall, about two-thirds of LBW babies are mature but SGA. The rest are premature, which is defined as a baby born before 37 completed weeks of gestation.

Relationship between socioeconomic status and low birth weight

In the UK there are marked social classes differences in rates of LBW. Pregnant women who have a low income and low level of education are more likely to be undernourished, to smoke and to live in poor housing. Intertwined with the effects of low income are stress and anxiety from many sources, including increased physical work, isolation, lack of social support, illness, close birth intervals and ambivalence about pregnancy outcomes. The prevalence of undernourishment among low-income women increases the risk of them having a baby with a LBW and/or a premature baby, although non-nutritional factors such as smoking modulate this relationship and cannot be removed from the equation. In addition, the mother's own birth weight, childhood environment and present stature and weight may be indicators for LBW (Kramer et al., 2000).

Taking Sheffield as an example, where over 6000 babies are delivered per annum, the incidence of LBW has been rising gradually over the years from 7.7 per cent in 1993 to 8.9 per cent in the year 2000. However, the rate of LBW varies considerably across the city, from a rate of 4.5 per cent in the more affluent areas to 13.5 per cent in the more deprived areas (Richardson, 2002). Within the Foxhill and Parson Cross Sure Start locality, the majority of mothers are Caucasian, 50 per cent of them smoke and the average maternal age is 19 years. There are about 200 births per annum and full-term infants consistently weigh on average 400 grams less than the local and national average for infant birth weights.

The overall infant mortality rate for England and Wales fell to 5.6 deaths per 1000 live births in 2000, from 5.8 in 1999. The infant mortality rate for Sheffield for 1998–2001 was 6.3 per 1000 births, which was slightly above the national average figure. This average figure reflects wide disparity across the city; the rate varies from 3.8 to 12.9, with the higher rate occurring in areas of high deprivation and/or where there are high concentrations of asylum seekers or women from the Indian subcontinent. Nationally, the infant mortality rate disparity between social classes I (professional) and V (unskilled manual) widened by 9.3 per cent between the years 1997–99 and 1998–2000. The infant mortality rate for the Southey Green electoral ward that encompasses the F&PC SS locality is almost double, at 11.1 per 1000 births.

Relationship between nutritional status and low birth weight

Poor maternal nutritional status at conception and a number of dietary factors have an influence on LBW, including pre-pregnancy maternal weight, gestational weight gain, and dietary energy, iron and calcium intake. The prevalence of undernourishment among low-income women increases the risk of LBW and prematurity. Inadequate nutrition in the pregnant mother has repercussions for fetal and child growth, and for pregnancies in the next generation. In addition, their own birth weight, childhood environment and present stature and weight may be indicators for LBW. For teenage mothers, whose own physical maturation is incomplete, nutritional demands in pregnancy may lead to additional health problems (Kramer et al., 2000).

Relationship between nutritional status and socioeconomic status

It has been reported that the poorest 10 per cent of households spend 29 per cent of their income on food, compared to 18 per cent in the richest. A typical basket of goods purchased in local shops can cost 24 per cent more than those same goods bought from a large supermarket (Darmon et al., 2004). This difference can rise to 60 per cent if the supermarket economy lines are compared. It also costs more to shop because of the physical inaccessibility of large retail food outlets, necessitating expenditure on transport or the higher prices in small local shops. People in low socioeconomic groups spend more on foods richer in energy and high in fat and sugar, which are cheaper per unit of energy than food rich in protective nutrients, such as fruit and vegetables. Current recommendations are that everyone should eat at least five portions of a variety fruit and vegetables each day. Average fruit and vegetable consumption among the population in England is less than three portions a day, and consumption tends to be lower among children and people on low incomes.

Foxhill/Parson Cross Sure Start Nutrition Project

Methods

A study was undertaken to determine the dietary intake of local pregnant women living in the F&PC SS, recruited from the antenatal clinic at the city maternity hospital.

Retrospective methods to obtain qualitative and descriptive data were used to assess average typical daily intake using a combination of 24-hour recall and diet history of 'usual' intake. The method is relatively quick and easy to administer, inexpensive, without use of equipment, has high subject motivation and low respondent burden (Nelson et al., 1997). Measuring dietary intake in this way currently requires the skills of an experienced dietician/nutritionist. The limitations of this method depend on the skills and persistence of the interviewer, subject motivation, and rely on accurate recall of participants. The interviewer sought information on the type of food eaten, a description of the food, including method of cooking and brand names, quantified by the use of household measures and average portions and the frequency of consumption. Food data was analysed using a commercial dietary analysis package to determine energy, macro- and micronutrient intake.

Data recorded included:

- age
- ethnic origin
- height
- weight
- body mass index
- number of existing children
- smoking status
- educational attainment
- socioeconomic status
- periconceptional nutritional supplementation.

Dietary data was obtained from 89 pregnant women in the F&PC SS area and is displayed in Table 6.1 which appears on p. 76.

Comparisons were made between pregnant women in the F&PC SS area (SS) and:

- women from less deprived areas of Sheffield (Shef)
- UK recommended nutrient intakes (RNI) (Department of Health, 1991)
- Results from a dietary survey of 12,000 pregnant women in the UK (ALSPAC) (Rogers and Emmett, 1998).

Results

Results for nutrients that are particularly important for pregnancy or of which there was found to be a deficiency are discussed below.

Dietary energy (calorie) intake

As can be seen in Figure 6.1, women from the F&PC SS area consumed fewer calories than recommended but almost the same as the ALSPAC survey of pregnant women. This is reassuring and a good quality assurance factor about the research.

Dietary fibre intake

As can be seen from Figure 6.2, the dietary fibre intake of the women from F&P SS area was only 11 grams per day, considerably less than recommended and the amount eaten by other pregnant women in the UK.

Figure 6.1 Dietary energy intake per day (Kcals)

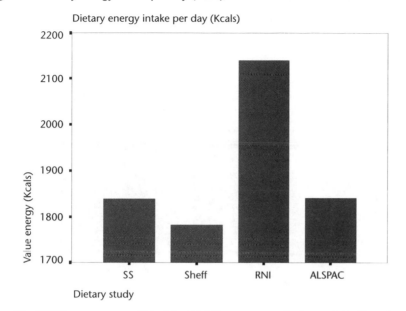

The UK Department of Health (1991)recommends that adult diets should contain on average 18 grams per day (individual needs range from 12 to 24 grams per day). Dietary fibre, or 'roughage', is only found in foods derived from plants, such as cereals, grains, seeds, pulses, fruit and vegetables.

Dietary fibre is provided from carbohydrate sources and is essential for the body to function properly. Apart from being a valuable source of many micronutrients, fibre provides bulk to stools, which makes them easier to pass and is therefore essential to reduce constipation – a common pregnancy problem.

Previous research undertaken at the Centre for Pregnancy Nutrition showed that women eating low-fibre diets had disordered glucose and insulin metabolism, making them more prone to develop impaired glucose tolerance and/or diabetes in pregnancy.

Dietary calcium intake

As shown in Figure 6.3, the dietary calcium intake of women in the F&PC SS area was satisfactory. However, one of the major reasons for this is because a high proportion of the women were in receipt of benefits and therefore eligible for free milk – an excellent source of calcium. About 99 per cent of the calcium in the body is found in bones and teeth, and a plentiful supply of dietary calcium is necessary to maintain adequate levels in these tissues. Calcium is also essential for blood clotting, muscle contraction

Figure 6.2 Dietary fibre intake per day (g)

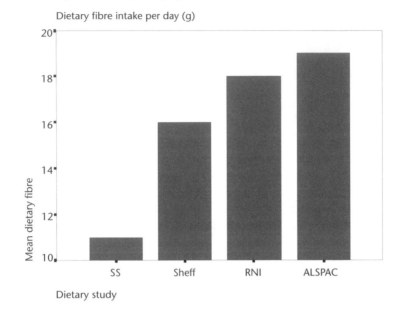

and nerve signalling. There is evidence to support the effectiveness of calcium supplementation for a reduction in preterm birth and the incidence of LBW in pregnant women, especially those at risk of hypertensive disorders (Atallah et al., 2001). It is important to note that dietary calcium intakes in the UK female population are usually low, with 27 per cent of 16–18 year olds and 10 per cent of 19–50 year olds consuming an intake below the lower reference nutrient intake (400 milligrams a day) (Gregory et al., 1990).

The recommended intake of calcium for women over 18 years is 700 milligrams per day. For 15–18 years, it is 800 milligrams per day. During pregnancy the body's efficiency at taking calcium from the diet is improved and therefore no increase in calcium intake has been recommended. Dairy products are the richest sources of calcium. Leafy green vegetables, especially spinach, contain calcium, but the body is less efficient at absorbing it from these particular foods. There is no evidence that high intakes of calcium are harmful. Calcium supplementation may be necessary for those avoiding or unable to consume dairy products.

Dietary iron intake

As shown in Figure 6.4 the mean dietary iron intake of women in the F&PC SS area was worryingly low at 10.3 milligrams a day, especially as some

Figure 6.3 Dietary calcium intake per day (mg)

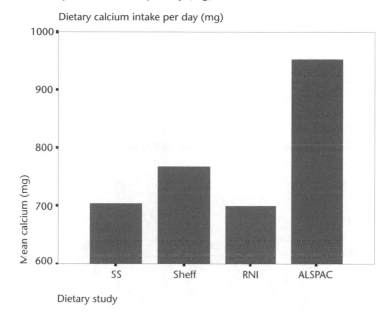

Dietary calcium intake per day (mg)

intakes were less than 6 milligrams a day. It has been shown in many previous studies that low dietary iron intakes are more common in low-income women. Many women have very low stores of iron pre-pregnancy, due either to heavy blood loss during menstruation or inadequate iron intake, and supplemental iron is necessary during pregnancy to prevent anaemia. To ensure that appropriate levels of iron are stored in the body, the recommended intake for women has been set at 14.8 milligrams a day.

No increase is necessary during pregnancy because menstruation ceases, absorption of iron from the diet becomes more efficient and some of the body's stores of iron are brought into use. Iron is primarily needed for the formation of the protein haemoglobin in the red blood cells, which transport oxygen in the bloodstream. In pregnancy the number of red blood cells increases, which means that iron is a nutrient that is in great demand. Good stores of iron are essential for a healthy pregnancy.

Iron is present in many foods, from both animal and plant sources. The iron that is found in red meat is absorbed more efficiently than iron from other foods, so vegetarian and vegan women need to take special care that their diet contains enough iron. There are steps that can be taken to increase the amount of iron absorbed from food:

- Drinking tea with meals and snacks, and taking iron tablets that contain non-animal (known as haem) iron should be avoided.

• Drinks or foods containing vitamin C should be consumed with non-animal sources of iron.

Figure 6.4 Dietary iron intake per day (mg)

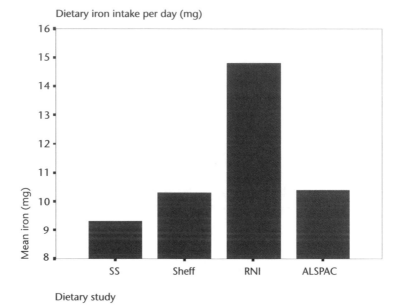

Dietary folate intake

The mean dietary folate intake for the women from the F&P SS area was only about two-thirds of that recommended for pregnancy. Folic acid is essential for the creation of new body proteins, and if the body is deficient in this nutrient, macrocytic anaemia can develop.

Rich food sources of folate include leafy green vegetables, orange juice, yeast extract (Marmite), meat extract (Bovril) and pulses such as black-eyed beans. Inappropriate food preparation and cooking can reduce the folate content of foods. Some breads and breakfast cereals are fortified with folic acid, but these tend to be the more expensive varieties and therefore not usually an option for low-income women.

Periconceptional folic acid and neural tube defects

The incidence of neural tube defects such as spina bifida can be reduced if women increase their folate intake before conception and during the first three months of pregnancy. It is now recommended that in this period folic

Figure 6.5 Dietary folate intake per day (µg)

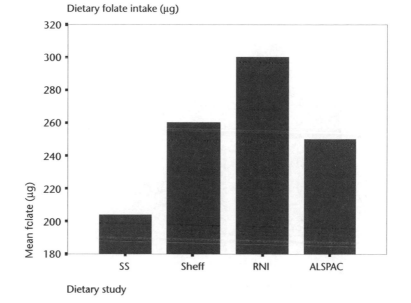

Dietary folate intake (µg)

acid supplements are taken (400 micrograms per day) and dietary intake is increased to 300 micrograms per day.

As can be seen in Figure 6.6, the number of women taking periconceptional folic acid in Sheffield was low, at just over 55 per cent, but reflects the national trends. However, the percentage of women in the F&PC SS area taking the supplements was considerably lower at 23 per cent.

These results are surprising because 45 per cent of the women in the F&PC SS area claimed to have planned their pregnancies. Therefore it can be concluded that low-income women in Sheffield planning pregnancies do not appreciate the importance of periconceptional folic acid in reducing the risk of neural tube defects.

Figure 6.6 Periconceptional folic acid supplementation

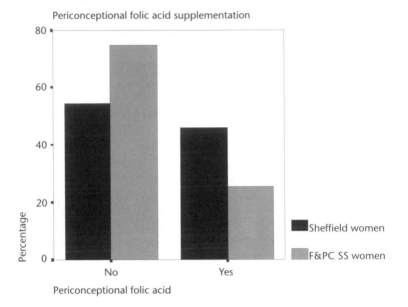

Periconceptional folic acid supplementation

Discussion

This study has demonstrated that the nutritional status of low-income women from the F&PC SS area is sub-optimal, with dietary intakes of fibre, iron and folate causing particular concern. Possible remedies include:

1   Encouraging the consumption of high-fibre, fortified breakfast cereals such as Bran Flakes at least once per day. This would greatly improve their dietary intake of fibre, iron and folate.
2   Encouraging the consumption of orange juice or other foods/ drinks high in vitamin C with the breakfast cereal to improve dietary iron absorption.
3   Reinforcing to all women of childbearing age the importance of periconceptional folic acid in reducing the risk of neural tube defects.

Many questions remain about the appropriate timing and dosage of interventions, considering that long-standing social and nutritional deprivation are difficult to overcome by a nutritional intervention during a few months in the course of a pregnancy. Fetal growth may be more strongly influenced by a woman's nutritional status around the time of conception. In an ideal world, the nutritional status of women would be improved when they were planning a pregnancy. It is estimated that only about 50 per cent of women in the UK plan pregnancies, and this figure is lower in younger and low-income women. Although clearer knowledge is emerging about the causal pathways between low social class and birth weight, there is much less evidence on effective preventive interventions. The UK Health Development Agency has advised against further UK research on nutrient supplementation as a means of preventing LBW (Bull et al., 2003). However, it believes research into other ways of improving the general diet of pregnant women at risk is more of a priority and that a longer-term, more preventive approach clearly has advantages over any attempted 'quick fixes'. That is the thinking behind two programmes that have been running in the United States for over 30 years: the Special Supplemental Nutrition Program for Women, Infants and Children (WIC), and the Expanded Food and Nutrition Education Program (EFNEP).

Special Supplemental Nutrition Program for Women, Infants and Children (WIC)

WIC is a country-wide programme, which has operated in the United States since 1972. WIC programmes are directed towards low-income pregnant and postpartum women, breastfeeding mothers and children from birth to 5 years. Elements of the programme include:

1   Food supplements of dairy products, juice, eggs, cereals and formula provided via market vouchers or home delivery.
2   One-to-one nutritional counselling.
3   Referral to health services which are usually available on site.

Evaluation of the WIC programme (Owen et al., 1997) has shown that fetal deaths, infant mortality and rates of LBW were reduced; dietary intake and gestational weight gain of pregnant women was improved; duration of pregnancy was increased; and women participating in WIC received prenatal care earlier. In addition, breastfeeding initiation and duration rates were substantially increased; the growth of nutritionally at-risk infants improved; the incidence of iron deficiency anaemia in children was reduced; immunizations were more likely to be up to date; and dietary intake and intellectual development improved. It was the highest-risk populations that derived most benefit. It is uncertain whether this was due mainly to the food supplementation, since there were also enhanced medical care and education components.

Expanded Food and Nutrition Education Program (EFNEP)

The EFNEP programme currently operates in nearly 800 counties through-out the 50 states in the USA. EFNEP is designed to assist low-income members of the population in acquiring the knowledge, skills, attitudes and behaviour necessary for nutritionally sound diets, and to contribute to their personal development and the improvement of the total family diet and nutritional well-being. One of EFNEP's primary audiences is the low-income family with young children. Practitioners and volunteers (many of whom are indigenous to the target population) deliver EFNEP as a series of lessons, often over several months. This hands-on, learn-by-doing approach allows the participants to gain the practical skills necessary to make positive behavioural changes (Rajgopal et al., 2002).

The vision for the future

Building capacity in maternal nutrition

The findings of nutrition research are often misrepresented in the media, and the conflicting and negative nature of nutrition claims are confusing and frustrating for practitioners as well as the general public. Nutrition and diet fill a large amount of media space and time, with food-related stories guaranteed to make the headlines. Practitioners must communicate clear and consistent messages about food, health and the concept of a healthy, balanced diet to a wide range of people. In theory, this should be simple, because the underlying messages relating to public health nutrition are fairly consistent. Simply improving people's knowledge about a healthier diet is not enough. Healthy foods need to be available, affordable and acces-sible, and people need to learn how to make the right choices and develop their own budgeting, planning and cooking skills. This means any compre-hensive attempt to improve diet and nutrition within the population must look at interventions across a range of levels, settings and groups of people (Speller et al., 2003). Therefore a capacity-building project for maternal and infant nutrition for the F&P SS needs to be developed, including the use of community food workers who have specialist nutrition training and can undertake much of the dietary education work required to improve the nutritional status of low-income women, in particular 'cook and eat' ses-sions, shopping advice and how to eat more healthily on a low income.

Development of nutrition screening tools for pregnancy

The objective will be to develop a nutrition-screening tool that could be used by personnel with little or no nutrition training, such as peer support and family workers, as well as health professionals such as midwives and health visitors. The tool must be valid, reliable, easy to administer, and measure food intake and dietary patterns in pregnant women. This would help practitioners to work through the screening and care planning process in a systematic and logical way, enabling them to identify those individuals who require further specialist dietary advice.

The next steps

The F&PC SS in Sheffield will deliver a programme for action in maternal nutrition, which will engage and empower the local community to achieve the health equality targets relating to LBW and infant mortality. This will result in sustainable change, connecting the support, enthusiasm and commitment of local people working in partnership with a wide range of local organizations and statutory and voluntary agencies. The partnership between the Centre for Pregnancy Nutrition and the Sheffield Sure Start projects will generate evidence regarding the effectiveness of maternal nutrition interventions targeting specific socioeconomic, ethnic or vulnerable groups and those who have multiple risk factors, such as poor dietary intake and/or smoking, or negative psychosocial factors.

References

Atallah, A. N., Hofmeyr, G. J. and Duley, L. (2001) Calcium supplementation during pregnancy for preventing hypertensive disorders and related problems (Cochrane Review), in *The Cochrane Library*, issue 3. Oxford: Update Software.

Bull, J., Mulvihill, C. and Quigley, R. (2003) Prevention of low birth weight: assessing the effectiveness of smoking cessation and nutritional interventions. Health Development Agency.

Darmon, N., Briend, A. and Drewnowski, A. (2004) Energy-dense diets are associated with lower diet costs: a community study of French adults. *Public Health Nutrition*, 7(1): 21–8.

Department of Health (1991): *Dietary Reference Values for Food Energy and Nutrients for the United Kingdom*. Report on Health and Social Subjects No. 41. London: HSMO.

Gregory, J., Foster, K., Tyler, H. and Wiseman, M. (1990). *The Dietary and Nutritional Survey of British Adults*. London: HMSO.

Kramer, M. S. (1987) Determinants of low birth weight: methodological assessment and meta-analysis. *Bulletin of the World Health Organization*, 65: 663–737.

Kramer, M. S., Sèguin, L., Lydon, J. and Goulet, L. (2000) Socio-economic disparities in pregnancy outcome: why do the poor fare so poorly? *Paediatric and Perinatal Epidemiology*, 14: 194–210.

Nelson, M. and Bingham, S. A. (1997) Assessment of food consumption and nutrient intake, in B.M. Margetts and M. Nelson (eds) *Design Concepts in Nutritional Epidemiology*, (2nd edn). New York: Oxford University Press.

Owen, A. L. and Owen, G. M. (1997) Twenty years of WIC: a review of some effects of the program. *Journal of the American Dietetic Association*, 97: 777–82.

Rajgopal, R., Cox, R. H., Lambur, M. and Lewis, E. C. (2002) Cost-benefit analysis indicates the positive economic benefits of the EFNEP related to chronic disease prevention. *Journal of Nutrition Education and Behavior*, 34: 26–37.

Richardson, A. (2002) *Low birth weight in Sheffield: report by Health Informatics Service*. Sheffield: Trent Regional Health.

Rogers, I. and Emmett, P. (1998) Diet during pregnancy in a population of pregnant women in South West England. ALSPAC Study Team. Avon Longitudinal Study of Pregnancy and Childhood. *European Journal of Clinical Nutrition*, 52(4): 246–50.

Speller, V. and Kelly, M. (2003) *Getting Evidence into Practice to Reduce Health Inequalities*. Health Development Agency.

Table 6.1 Approximate daily intakes for 89 women in the Foxhill and Parson Cross Sure Start area in comparison to the RNIs for pregnancy and results from the ALSPAC study

Daily Intakes‡		SS	RNIs	ALSPAC
Energy	(Kcals)	1839	2140*	1840
Protein	(g)	61.8	51*	66.3
Fat	(g)	74.6	NA	70.4
CHO	(g)	244.1	NA	–
Fibre	(g)	10.86	18	19.4
Sugar	(g)	106.5	NA	105
Calcium	(mg)	704.1	700	953
Magnesium	(mg)	234.8	270	253
Sodium	(mg)	2769	NA	–
Iron	(mg)	9.3	14.8	10.4
Zinc	(mg)	6.7	7.0	8.3
Copper	(mg)	1.1	1.2	–
Selenium	(µg)	35.5	60	–
Potassium	(mg)	2936	3500	2588
Iodine	(µg)	91.1	NA	–
Thiamine	(mg)	1.3	0.9*	1.42
Riboflavin	(mg)	1.3	1.4*	1.73
Niacin	(mg)	22.9	NA	15.8
Vitamin B6	(mg)	1.8	1.2	1.83
Vitamin B12	(mg)	3.4	1.5	–
Folate	(µg)	203	300*	250
Vitamin C	(mg)	122.7	50*	80.3
Retinol	(µg)	443	700*	855
Vitamin D	(µg)	1.6	NA	–
Vitamin E	(mg)	6.1	NA	8.4

‡ The Reference Nutrient Intake shown in the table is the figure for women aged 19–50 with the addition where appropriate of an increment for pregnancy (*).

7 Supporting breastfeeding mothers
Sue Battersby

Introduction

A clear way to improve the health and well-being of families and children before and from birth is through the promotion of breastfeeding with all its actual and potential benefits. The Government has recognized that the promotion of breastfeeding is an important issue, especially in areas of social deprivation where health outcomes are poorer than in more advantaged areas (Mulhall, 2001). This chapter will review the benefits of breastfeeding and consider the importance of recognizing social and cultural factors when promoting breastfeeding. It details the background, management, findings and the recommendations from the 'Breastfeeding is Best Supporter' (BIBS) and the 'Spreading the Word' projects, two specific breast-feeding initiatives within Sure Start Foxhill and Parson Cross.

Breastfeeding is a key public health issue because it confers not only short-term benefits but also long-term effects to both infant and mother. For the infant, the most important short-term benefit is the protection against infections, including gastroenteritis, respiratory infections, urinary tract infections and middle ear infection (Heinig and Dewey, 1996). This results in reduced hospital admissions, and for gastroenteritis alone the rate of admissions in bottle-fed babies, or babies breastfed for a short period only, is just over five times that for babies breastfed for 13 weeks or more (Department of Health, 1995). Further long-term benefits for infants include the enhancement of the value of immunization through an increased active immune response (Pabst and Spady, 1990), a reduced risk of insulin-dependent diabetes in susceptible infants, a reduced risk of childhood obesity (Diezt, 2001) and enhanced cognitive development (Horwood and Fergusson, 1998).

Research now suggests that certain diseases in adulthood may be linked to either the lack of breast milk or exposure to artificial feeds in the first few weeks or months of life, and these include Crohn's disease (inflammatory bowel condition), rheumatoid arthritis, adult food allergy and food intolerance (Minchin, 1998). As well as health benefits, there are also potential adverse effects from artificial feeding including contamination and inaccurate preparation of feeds, which may lead to the over- or under-concentration of nutrients (NHS CRD, 2000).

Recognized benefits for the mother of breastfeeding her infant include a reduction in pre-menopausal cancers of the ovaries, breasts and endometrium as well as the bone disease osteoporosis and hip fractures in later life (Heinig and Dewey, 1997).

Summary

Compared with a fully breastfed baby, a baby who is fed artificially from birth is:

- five times more likely to be hospitalized with gastroenteritis in the first three months of life;
- five times more likely to contract urinary tract infections in the first six months of life;
- twice as likely to have chest infections in the first seven years of life;
- twice as likely to suffer ear infections in the first year of life;
- twice as likely to develop atopic disease where there is a family history;
- up to twenty times more likely to develop necrotizing enterocolitis if born prematurely.

Source: Inch and Fisher (1999: 2)

Alongside the considerable health benefits of breastfeeding, there are also social, psychological and environmental benefits of breastfeeding, although these are rarely cited in health professionals' educational texts. The psychological benefits of breastfeeding are mainly based on extrapolation from animal studies. Minchin (1998) argues that because there are inadequate mother and baby studies it is inappropriate to use psychological benefits to promote breastfeeding. This aside, there is no doubt that the emotional power of breastfeeding can have both positive and negative consequences for mother and child. When breastfeeding goes well and the baby is content and thriving, breastfeeding has the potential for enhancing the mother–child relationship. Sadly, for those mothers who 'fail' at breastfeeding and the baby is fractious and does not thrive, there is the potential for breastfeeding to upset the mother–child relationship. Many of the problems that mothers encounter along their breastfeeding journey could be prevented or reduced if they had good social support.

The importance of the social environment and social support for breastfeeding

Bailey and Pain (2001) argue that health promotion information tends to divorce infant feeding from its sociocultural context and fails to address how infant feeding is perceived and judged by society. Breastfeeding is a complex process that is affected by many factors. The history of infant feeding over the last fifty years, especially in areas of economic and social deprivation, has been a story of the loss of a breastfeeding culture and of the loss of traditional knowledge about how breastfeeding mothers and babies behave, and what kind of support they need.

The importance of how social and cultural factors impinge on breastfeeding initiation and continuation were highlighted by Dykes and Griffith (1998), who described how attitudes and behaviours in relation to infant feeding do not occur in a social vacuum. In order that women can feel uninhibited and empowered to breastfeed, there are many social barriers that need to be broken down and support mechanisms, both formal and informal, re-established. The importance of developing breastfeeding awareness within a society to break down these barriers cannot be understated. To create a culture of breastfeeding as normal and 'first choice' requires a community to be socialized into thinking of breastfeeding when they think of infant feeding. Providing information that is socially and culturally acceptable, whilst at the same time also being sound and up to date, will lay the foundations for meaningful support mechanisms for breastfeeding mothers. Bergman et al. (1993) state that the divide between successful and unsuccessful breastfeeding is very narrow for the individual, and it has been shown that by increasing social support for breastfeeding women the duration of breastfeeding can be increased (Wright, 1996; Thompson, 1998; Morrow et al., 1999). The introduction of breastfeeding peer support and awareness programmes, which are based on an empowerment model, is one method by which this can be facilitated.

The background to BIBS and 'Spreading the Word' projects

The Sure Start Foxhill and Parson Cross and the local hospital received government funding to initiate two peer support projects. The area had one of the lowest breastfeeding rates in the city, and there had been a culture of not breastfeeding for many generations. These projects were well received by breastfeeding mothers and the main recommendations from each project were that the existing programme of breastfeeding support should continue and be expanded. Further funding was obtained which enabled the projects to merge and to incorporate a further area of social and economic deprivation, becoming the Breastfeeding is Best Supporters (BIBS) project. Alongside this project a further government-funded project was initiated, called 'Spreading the Word', which was a breastfeeding awareness programme for the local community.

The combined objectives of the BIBS and Spreading the Word projects were:

- To encourage local women to initiate and sustain natural feeding methods, through the provision of high-quality and consistent information giving and peer support.
- To develop support networks that would provide social and leisure activities for breastfeeding mothers.
- To develop a network of role models which would in the long term influence and enable cultural change to a point when breastfeeding was accepted as normal and 'first choice'.
- To develop breastfeeding awareness days within the community for school nurses, crèche workers, nurseries, playgroups and volunteer groups within the area.
- To introduce a multi-professional breastfeeding training programme for each health centre within the project area.

Project findings

The two projects were evaluated independently to determine if their objectives were achieved. The key areas that were evaluated in the BIBS project included:

- the analysis of the breastfeeding rates;
- the activities of the support workers;
- the activities of the volunteers;
- the mothers' experiences of breastfeeding and their views of the service.

The purpose of the 'Spreading the Word' evaluation was to appraise the different events that the BIBS team undertook to increase the breastfeeding awareness within the area. The main events that were undertaken included:

- community breastfeeding awareness days;
- planned awareness days;
- visits to local schools and nurseries;
- health professionals training sessions.

Table 7.1 Differences between the two projects

Project	BIBS	Spreading the Word
Aim	To increase the initiation and duration rates for breastfeeding	To develop breastfeeding awareness within the local community
Focus	The individual	The community
Areas evaluated	• Breastfeeding rates • Activities of the support workers • Activities of the volunteers • Mothers' experiences • Mothers' views of the service	• Community breastfeeding awareness days • Planned awareness days • Visits to local schools and nurseries • Health professional training sessions

The analysis of breastfeeding rates

Analysis of the breastfeeding statistics proved to be one of the major obstacles in the evaluation process. The analysis of the breastfeeding initiation and continuation rates was perceived as one of the major ways in which the effectiveness of the two projects could be judged. However, difficulty was encountered obtaining accurate breastfeeding statistics. This type of problem is not confined to Sheffield but is prevalent throughout England as was highlighted at the National Conference, Barriers to Breastfeeding (Carson and Thompson, 2000).

Breastfeeding statistics are compiled in Sheffield from two main sources, the maternity unit and the health visitors. The data are not, however, collected using a coordinated approach. The information collected by the maternity unit included the intended method of infant feeding and the method of feeding at transfer to the community and on discharge from the maternity services. The midwives report this information, but one in five records were incomplete. Once collected, the data is entered onto the hospital database using the mother's postcode.

Health visitors and GPs record the infant feeding method at the 6–8 week medical examination, and this is then entered onto the child health system using the child's health number. The collation of the data between the two different systems is problematic because of the two different methods of recording the data. Further difficulties were experienced when the hospital maternity units were amalgamated and data was lost in the transfer process. A comprehensive analysis of the whole of the BIBS area was impossible as a consequence of these difficulties. Fortunately, Sure Start Foxhill and Parson Cross had compiled independent data records. 'Before' data was obtained from an audit of two health visitor caseloads. The 'after' data was obtained from the Sure Start database and a manual trawl of infant health records held by the health visitors. Although the data had been collected at different time intervals, it was possible to identify a marked increase in the initiation rate for breastfeeding from 22 per cent to 49.05 per cent and the continuation rate increased from 2.5 per cent at four months to 11 per cent at six months within the Sure Start area (see Tables 7.2 and 7.3, and Figure 7.1).

Table 7.2 Data from the Health Visitor Audit 1999

Breastfeeding rates	
Breastfeeding at birth	22%
Breastfeeding at 6 weeks	10%
Breastfeeding at 4 months	2.5%

Source: Fox (1999). Foxhill and Parson Cross Sure Start Application Document.

Table 7.3 Sure Start data 2001–2002: Breastfeeding rates
Total births: 210

	Breastfeeding rates	
Initiated breastfeeding	103	49.05%
Initiated formula feeding	92	43.80%
No data	15	7.15%
Total	210	100%
Still breastfeeding at 4 weeks	66	31.50%
Still breastfeeding at 3 months	39	18.60%
Still breastfeeding at 6 months	23	11.00%

Source: BIBS database and Sure Start database.

Figure 7.1 Comparison of the breastfeeding rates for 1999 and 2002

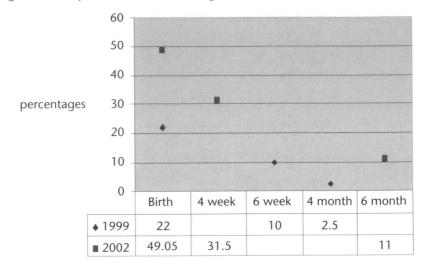

	Birth	4 week	6 week	4 month	6 month
♦ 1999	22		10	2.5	
■ 2002	49.05	31.5			11

Support workers

Twenty-three women completed the La Léche League Breastfeeding Peer Support Training Programme (La Léche League, 2001). The training programme consisted of 24 hours' instruction over four weeks. The aim of the training was:

- to debrief the women regarding their own personal experiences;
- to provide breastfeeding information;
- to assist the development of listening and supporting skills;
- to practice breastfeeding skills in a safe environment.

Thirteen of these women went on to actively support other mothers, seven were in post as paid peer support workers and six were active volunteers. The role of the paid support workers was defined in their job description, but volunteers had offered to undertake their role without payment because they were unable to commit themselves to regular hours and/or their Social Security benefits would have been affected.

Activities of paid peer support workers

The activities of the peer support workers were identified from activity sheets, which they completed on a weekly basis. The highest percentage of their time was spent involved with breastfeeding support groups (17 per cent). The number of support groups in the area had increased from one to six during the year of the evaluation. Seventeen per cent of their time was also taken up with administration, but this included clerical duties and audit, as well as planning and organization time. They spent 11 per cent of their time involved in publicity events to promote breastfeeding and the project. These events included Health Days, a 'Picnic in the Park' for National Breastfeeding Week, and stalls at local festivals, in the shopping precinct and at fun days. Other activities included antenatal home visits, attending antenatal clinics, postnatal home visits, telephone support and training and personal development (see Figure 7.2). There had been changes from previous evaluations, with the biggest changes being an increased involvement in support groups and a decrease in time spent making home visits (Battersby, 2001; Battersby, 2002).

Figure 7.2 Activities undertaken by the support workers

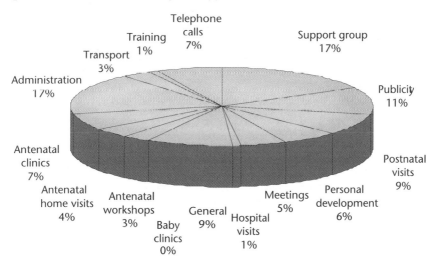

Activities of volunteers

The activities of the paid peer supporters were quickly established within the project, but difficulties were encountered with the volunteers. There were strict protocols and a clearance process that had to be adhered to for volunteers within the NCH (the lead and accountable body for Foxhill and Parson Cross Sure Start). As a result, the role of the volunteers was slow to develop and therefore their activities were not monitored in depth. However, a volunteer worked alongside a support worker in each of the support groups and they participated in antenatal workshops. One volunteer undertook home visiting and another attended a GP antenatal/baby clinic on a weekly basis. The volunteers were keen helpers at publicity events and went into schools to bathe and breastfeed their infants.

Mothers' experiences of breastfeeding and their views of the service

The evaluation was conducted over a year, and during this time 173 mothers initiated breastfeeding within the BIBS area, including 103 within the Sure Start area. At the time of the evaluation there were 140 mothers for whom contact with the BIBS team had ended. They were asked to complete an audit questionnaire, and 90 responded, giving a response rate of 64 per cent. All the mothers who completed the questionnaire had initiated breastfeeding for their current child. There were 30 mothers who had attended breastfeeding workshops undertaken by the project midwives and the support workers. Twenty-four of those who attended the workshops rated the information that had been provided as very informative and six stated it was informative, none gave a ranking lower than this.

There were 55 mothers who had met a support worker during the antenatal period and a large majority had found her helpful, informative and supportive. Not all the mothers who returned the questionnaires required help and support with breastfeeding in the postnatal period. However, there were 53 who did and the number of visits they received from the support worker depended upon their individual needs. Mothers also found telephone calls from the support workers very reassuring, but a change in the way mothers were contacting the support workers was noted. Text messaging was becoming the norm. This was perhaps a consequence of texting being cheaper than a telephone call.

The mothers evaluated the support worker's role very positively. This was especially so when mothers encountered difficulties. When mothers who were still breastfeeding were asked what had helped them to continue, the comments were divided into two categories. The first category was related to the mothers' own determination to breastfeed because of the knowledge that it was the best for the baby and the enjoyment that was felt when breastfeeding.

> I have persevered through all the problems because she enjoys it and I enjoy the closeness it gives us.

Patience, determination, my baby is growing and developing lovely and has never caught a cold or other disease.

Determined to give my child best start. I enjoy breastfeeding. Closeness to my child and cheapness.

The second category related to the support that the mother had received, and although partners, mothers and midwives were frequently mentioned, the support worker was mentioned in 19 instances. The following quotes are just a few given by the mothers.

Support worker and help.

Support from Sure Start workers and family and friends. The health benefits to my baby and myself. Because it's much easier than making up bottles every day.

The help my support worker and Sure Start have given me have enabled me to continue enjoying feeding L all this time. D (the support worker) understands me and manages to say the right things at the right time to get me through the difficult patches. Having up to date facts to hand helped too as peer advice is mostly based on horror stories.

I knew more and I got a lot more help and support off my midwife and breastfeeding peer support worker. I was also a lot more relaxed and I'm really enjoying it! Could I also say that I don't and didn't (with my first child) get any support off my family (only my husband) by family I mean mum, dad, nan-nan, granddad or sister so I felt the help of the support worker and my midwife have been really vital. I know if I've had a bad week or month or even just a bad night, I can go to Sure Start and there is always someone there to give help and support. I love breastfeeding my baby and she seems a lot more content than my first child. Thanks to everyone that has helped.

'Spreading the Word' evaluation

The development of the 'Spreading the Word' project was tortuous and the evaluation was not as comprehensive as anticipated. Although all the aims of the project were achieved, this was not as it was initially envisaged.

The BIBS team developed breastfeeding awareness within the community by employing different strategies in a variety of venues. They distributed breastfeeding information at planned Breastfeeding Awareness Days, attended and promoted breastfeeding at community health fairs and events, as well as by developing educational displays and posters for areas frequented by the target population. This is in line with the recommendations made by Humphreys et al. (1998), who stressed the importance of expanding breastfeeding promotion into the community to reach women's influential social contacts.

The introduction of future parents to breastfeeding was also a successful area of the project. UNICEF (1999) recommends that 'ideally' future parents should receive accurate information as part of their school education, and boys as well as girls should be given this information, as this will enable them to make informed choices in the future. This project commenced this process within the project area and made valuable contacts. Teachers and children welcomed the planned visits to schools and nurseries. The approaches to increasing the awareness of breastfeeding were adapted to the ages of the children and more than 380 children accessed information on breastfeeding. Invitations to participate in further educational sessions followed and were to be responded to.

The introduction of breastfeeding training programmes in health centres and the attendance of health professionals at planned Breastfeeding Awareness Days were disappointing. It was also understandable, in an area that has had low breastfeeding initiation rates for many decades, that health professionals do not perceive breastfeeding updates as essential, and as a consequence their skills and knowledge may decline. This can result in conflicting and inappropriate advice being given to breastfeeding mothers. Whelan and Lupton (1998) state midwifery services need to provide low-income breastfeeding women with better-quality professional support, but until the health professionals themselves recognize the importance of updating this will be difficult. However, by focusing upon the development of breastfeeding awareness within the community and with the increasing number of mothers who were initiating breastfeeding (that is, one in every two mothers) and the increased number of women undertaking the La Léche League peer support programme, it was hoped that the health professionals would recognize the need to professionally update their skills and knowledge. Knowledgeable women will expect knowledgeable health professionals.

The increase in the breastfeeding support network did not develop in line with the project proposal in that there were no newly trained health centre staff to be encouraged to provide breastfeeding forums. Although the support networks for breastfeeding mothers in health centres did not materialize, it did not deter the BIBS workers and volunteers assisting breastfeeding mothers to develop and fund their own breastfeeding forums. There is limited evidence, because only one session had been evaluated, that the mothers who attended will breastfeed for a longer duration or that they valued the social support they received at these groups. A fuller evaluation of all the groups needs to be undertaken.

The empowerment of women through breastfeeding was demonstrated by the increased self-esteem and confidence of mothers within the breast-feeding support groups and also by the challenges that the women who completed the La Léche League peer support programme have undertaken. This was especially evident in the BIBS worker who felt able to question the members of the Primary Care Trust and the young mother who was able to answer the questions of the children at the senior school.

The cost-effectiveness of the breastfeeding peer support programme

Following an evaluation of the above programmes, the opportunity arose to explore whether paid peer support workers are a cost-effective means of pro-moting and supporting breastfeeding in a socially deprived area. However, despite the increase of breastfeeding peer support programmes over the last ten years, evaluating the cost-effectiveness of such programmes is difficult. Although there is a plethora of literature related to the benefits of breastfeed-ing, there is a paucity of literature that relates to the cost-effectiveness of interventions to promote breastfeeding. Despite this, a review of the limited data demonstrated that breastfeeding peer support programmes can, by increasing the number of babies who are breastfed, make significant savings to the NHS. By using the proposed savings, as advocated by Ball and Wright (1999) and the Department of Health (1995), it was possible to calculate that a saving of £16,872 per year to the NHS could have resulted from the increase in the breastfeeding initiation rate within the project area. This saving would be just as a result of the potential reduction of gastroenteritis, respiratory infections and otitis media (see Table 7.4).

Table 7.4 Summary of the benefits of breastfeeding in the Sure Start area

Study	Diseases	Estimated savings to the NHS for all babies breastfed in Sure Start n=103	Estimated saving to the NHS for 57 extra babies breastfed in Sure Start
Department of Health (1995)	Gastroenteritis	£5,885.42 per annum	£3,257.14 per annum
Ball and Wright (1999)	Gastroenteritis	£21,218–£30,488 per annum	£11,742–£16,872 per annum
	Respiratory infections		
	Otitis media		

Further savings could also result from other health benefits that have not been analysed but would give added cost-effectiveness to the project. These include the potential reductions in pre-menopausal cancers of the breast, ovaries and endometrium in mothers who have breastfed; for the infant the potential reduction in childhood obesity, urinary tract infections, and for pre-term babies breastfeeding promotes optimal neurological development and reduces the risk of necrotizing enterocolitis. These are not immediate but long-term savings, with costs associated with treatments, surgery and care not becoming apparent until well after the initial breastfeeding episodes.

Health benefits from breastfeeding also need to be considered, as these would be in addition to the cost savings. The health gains would include the improved quality of life and increased life expectancy that would result from the reduction of illnesses and diseases. These would be particularly relevant when considering pre-menopausal cancers, and ill health and cardiac disease due to obesity.

As well as the cost-effectiveness and health gains of breastfeeding, when reviewing the project from a societal perspective, it was also found that the project had brought both financial and social benefits to the mothers, the peer supporters and the community. The project aims to employ local people and thus an income was generated into the community through the peer supporters' salaries. Individual gains for the peer supporters included the enhancement of their personal development with large increases in self-esteem, many of the peer supporters having never worked previously. An important value-added benefit to the community is the social support that the peer supporters offer other than for breastfeeding. This is because the peer supporters are involved in other culturally sensitive health-related issues which include teenage pregnancy, home safety, smoking cessation, signposting, baby massage, nutrition and healthy lifestyles.

The BIBS project was found to be 'paying for itself' through the calculable health savings, but it was the value-added benefits that gave the peer support project special value (Battersby et al., 2004).

Conclusion

There were five strategic objectives for the two projects. The first was to encourage local women to initiate and sustain natural feeding methods, through the provision of high-quality and consistent information-giving and peer support. The support workers were instrumental in influencing 20 mothers to initiate breastfeeding. This clearly indicates that they were fulfilling their role in the promotion of breastfeeding. This was also demonstrated by the increase in the breastfeeding initiation rate, which had risen from 22 per cent to 49.05 per cent. This was an excellent achievement, but the number of mothers still breastfeeding at six months was even more spectacular, with an increase from 2.5 per cent to 11 per cent.

The second objective was to develop support networks that would provide social and leisure activities for breastfeeding mothers. Although these did not materialize, as envisaged initially, the peer support workers, volunteers and the mothers sought funding and inaugurated four new support groups. Consequently, during the period of this evaluation, the number of support groups for breastfeeding mothers increased from two to six. A positive aspect was that social support was also provided for other areas than just breastfeeding.

To develop a network of role models who will in the long term influence and enable cultural change so that breastfeeding is accepted as normal and 'first choice' was the next objective. Twenty-three women in the area undertook the La Léche League breastfeeding peer support training programme. All these women breastfed their own children and they were the first role models to emerge as a result of the breastfeeding projects. The breastfeeding mothers and BIBS workers increased their self-esteem and confidence and took on challenges that will further promote breastfeeding within the community.

The task of converting public opinion back to the notion of breast-feeding as normal and 'first choice' was enormous and daunting. The BIBS project 'Spreading the Word' initiated the 'turning of the tide' within the project area but recognized that it was only the start of the campaign and there was still much to do. The planned Breastfeeding Awareness Days, the fourth objective, demonstrated how knowledge could be increased, and the visits to nurseries and schools were very rewarding.

The final objective to introduce a multi-professional breastfeeding training programme for each health centre within the project area was not achieved. Due to a lack of commitment, the training sessions within the health centres and GP's surgeries were discontinued but places were still offered on the Awareness Days and the La Léche League peer support programmes.

The evaluation of both projects recommended that the work of the peer support workers and volunteers should continue, as the improvement of the breastfeeding initiation and continuation rates is vital in improving the health status for both the mothers and the babies. An improved health status will positively affect not only the individuals but the whole community.

References

Bailey, C. and Pain, R. (2001) Geographies of infant feeding and access to primary health-care. *Health and Social Care in the Community*, 9(5): 309–17.

Ball, T.M. and Wright, A.L. (1999) Health care costs of formula feeding in the first year of life. *Pediatrics*, 103: 870–6.

Battersby, S. (2001) Simply the Breast: An evaluation of a Breastfeeding Peer Support Programme. http://www.sheffield.ac.uk/surestart/publns.html.

Battersby, S. (2002) Breastfeeding is Best Supporters Project: An evaluation of the merged Breastfeeding Peer Support. http://www.sheffield.ac.uk/surestart/publns.html.

Battersby, S., Aziz, M., Bennett, K. and Sabin, K. (2004) The cost effectiveness of breastfeeding peer support. *British Journal of Midwifery*, April, 12(4): 201–5.

Bergman, V., Larson, S., Lomberg, H., Moller, A. and Staffan, M. (1993) A survey of Swedish mothers' views on breastfeeding and experiences of social and professional support. *Scandinavian Journal of Caring Sciences*, 7(1): 47–52.

Carson, R. and Thompson, R. (2000) Launch of Local Infant Feeding Audit, in *RCM Barriers to Breastfeeding: Time for a New Approach*. Conference report, 15 May, RCM, Cardiff.

Department of Health (1995) *Breastfeeding: Good Practice Guidance to the NHS*. London: Department of Health.

Dietz, W.H. (2001) Breastfeeding may help prevent childhood overweight. *Journal of the American Medical Association*, 285(19): 2506–7.

Dykes, F. and Griffith, H. (1998) Societal influences upon initiation and continuation of breastfeeding. *British Journal of Midwifery*, 6(2): 76–80.

Fox, L. (1999) *Foxhill and Parson Cross Sure Start Application Document*. Unpublished.

Heinig, M. J. and Dewey, K.G. (1996) Health advantages of breastfeeding for infants: a critical review. *Nutrition Research Review*, 9: 89–110.

Heinig, M. J. and Dewey, K.G. (1997) Health effects of breastfeeding for mothers: A critical review. *Nutrition Research Reviews*, 10: 35–6.

Horwood, L. J. and Fergusson, D. M. (1998) Breastfeeding and later cognitive and academic outcomes. *Pediatrics*, 101(1): e9, URL: http://www.pediatrics.aapublicationsorg/cgi/content/full/101/1/e9.

Humphreys, A. S., Thompson, N. J. and Miner, K. R. (1998) Intention to breastfeed in low-income pregnant women: the role of social support and previous experience. *Birth*, 25(3): 169–74.

Inch, S. and Fisher, C. (1999) *Breastfeeding: Into the Twenty-first Century*. Nursing Times Clinical Monograph Series, London, Emap Healthcare Ltd.

La Léche League (2001) *Breastfeeding Peer Counsellor Programme*. La Léche League, Great Britain.

Minchin, M. (1998) *Breastfeeding Matters*. Melbourne, Australia: Alma Publications.

Morrow, A. L., Guerrero, M. L., Shults, J., et al. (1999) Efficacy of home-based peer counselling to promote exclusive breastfeeding: a randomized controlled trial. *The Lancet,* 353(9160): 1226–30.

Mulhall, A. (2001) *The Infant Feeding Initiative: An Evaluation of Breastfeeding Practice Projects 1999–2000.* London: Department of Health.

NHS CRD (2000) *Effective Health Care: Promoting the Initiation of Breastfeeding.* 6(2).

Pabst, H. F. and Spady, D. W. (1990) Effect of breastfeeding on antibody response to conjugate vaccine. *Lancet,* 336: 269–70.

Thompson, B. (1998) Breakthrough in breastfeeding. *The Practising Midwife,* 1(5): 35–7.

UNICEF UK Baby Friendly Initiative (1999) *Towards National, Regional and Local Strategies for Breastfeeding.* London: UNICEF.

Whelan, A. and Lupton, P. (1998) Promoting successful breastfeeding among women with low income. *Midwifery,* 14: 94–100.

Wright, J. (1996) Breastfeeding and deprivation – the Nottingham peer counsellors programme. *MIDIRS Midwifery Diges,* 6(2): 212–15.

8 The impact of Sure Start on health visiting
Ann Rowe

Introduction

This chapter reports findings of an independently commissioned evaluative study that explored the impact of the arrival of the Sure Start programme on health visitors working in the Sure Start Foxhill and Parson Cross area. The research revealed how local issues impacted on the implementation of a national strategy and highlighted the need to consider pre-existing structural arrangements and service obligations when expecting a group of professionals to accommodate and work with a new initiative.

Sure Start and statutory services

Since Sure Start's inception, considerable attention has been focused on the development and evaluation of innovative services. Rather less attention, however, appears to have been paid to the requirement for Sure Start programmes to 'co-ordinate, streamline and add value to existing services' (National Sure Start website, 2003). While statutory agencies were exhorted to 'adapt their mainstream work' (Eisenstadt, 2002: 4) to accommodate learning gained from Sure Start, the extent to which Sure Start programmes have been able to collaborate with and influence pre-existing services has yet to be established. This study evaluates the impact of one particular Sure Start programme on the pre-existing statutory service of health visiting.

Health visitors in Foxhill and Parson Cross

Health visitors (HVs) offer a universal service to families with preschool children and are concerned with child development and parenting in addition to wider public health concerns (DoH, 1999a, 1999b, 2001). The health visitors working with this programme were employed by a Primary Care Trust (PCT) and were 'General Practitioner (GP) attached', each responsible for families registered with a specific GP. As Sure Start offered services within a geographical boundary, this arrangement meant health visitors worked both within the Sure Start area and outside it.

Study design

The research was designed to interpret experiences and perceptions of those involved in the delivery of Sure Start and the health visiting service. The following questions were addressed:

1   What has been the contribution of health visitors to the Sure Start Foxhill and Parson Cross programme?
2   What has been the impact of Sure Start on health visitors in the area?
3   What views do health visitors have concerning the value and effectiveness of the Sure Start programme?

Additional themes emerged in the study and are also reported.

Method

A number of sources and two methods of collecting data were used to provide breadth and depth. Multiple methods were used to ensure an in-depth understanding of the subject matter and enhance credibility (Bowling, 1997). Information was generated through interviews and focus groups, which were largely unstructured, following a guide with main areas of interest to allow the exploration of complex issues and a full understanding of the informant's point of view (May, 1993; Silverman, 1993). All health visitors working with families in the area were invited to participate, along with Sure Start workers who had contact with health visitors. A total of 10 health visitors and 11 Sure Start staff, together with the managers of the Sure Start programme were interviewed.

Voluntary participation and the right to withdraw from the study and/or retract consent at any stage were explained and data was securely managed at all times. Individual comments were not identified. However, due to the small numbers involved, it was not possible to assure anonymity. All those interviewed were given the opportunity to amend or withdraw comments made prior to publication of findings.

A cross-sectional analysis of the data was undertaken using content analysis, and data were categorized by themes from the research questions and those arising from the data itself (Mason, 1996).

This case study relates to a particular place at a particular time. Attempts to locate similar research were unsuccessful, possibly indicating that this is the first study in this field, although many of the issues raised here are likely to be replicated elsewhere.

Key issues from the study

Working together

Collaborative working between health visitors and Sure Start staff had been difficult to establish. Many of those interviewed acknowledged that structural arrangements, with HVs sited in many different premises and only partially working within the Sure Start area, made it difficult for HVs to be recognized as part of the Sure Start team.

With the arrival of new Sure Start posts, a period of negotiation was thought necessary to clarify roles and collaborative arrangements, and this had not always been given sufficient attention. As a consequence, a number of participants felt their contribution to the health and well-being of families in the area was insufficiently understood and appreciated. This had caused difficulties for some in the development of interpersonal relationships felt to be crucial for effective joint work:

> ... if you've got that personal relationship, sometimes it's easier to pick up a phone to somebody you know and get on with, ... they know what you want or they'll tell you they can't provide it (HV 9)

Health visitors generally felt that, as the long-standing service providers, their contribution was largely taken for granted. New workers in Sure Start were coming to the area fresh with ideas and enthusiasm to do the work health visitors had long wished for the resources to undertake themselves:

> They've [Sure Start] got the money and we haven't and we do feel like the poor relation quite often and it would be nice to see some money coming this way to develop our services because we can't do what they do and a lot of it is to do with finances, not ability or commitment, it's money and space. (HV 3, 4)

In addition, there was for some a feeling that Sure Start was taking credit for the work of health visitors:

> Well it's us and them, it means they start and develop all their whatever they're going to do, but we've done the groundwork and then the other thing is ... all the work we are doing, where is that shown, because every figure is Sure Start... (HV 7, 8)

For the Sure Start workers the issue was mostly around gaining acceptance into an already established set of practices. Some workers felt that their resistance to undertaking only the more mundane delegated tasks had caused difficulty:

> they [HVs] want us to mop up the things that really they feel aren't that important for them to do ... and some of the things that we're more capable of doing, they want to keep hold of (Sure Start team 2)

As a result of meetings with the Sure Start programme manager, HVs felt generally well informed about the programme with an opportunity to influence its direction. However, sharing information regarding work with families was more problematic and views on how well this was managed varied. Finding the balance between passing on information, whilst respecting the need for confidentiality, challenged all concerned:

> I don't think we've fully come to terms with the exchange of information, I think we tend to exchange information freely with HVs when perhaps we shouldn't. (Sure Start team 3)

> They [HVs] actually might be afraid of saying things which maybe they see as confidential ... they don't realize that to help the child we need a bit more information ... (Sure Start team 4)

Communication regarding work with families was important to health visitors because they described their role as one of 'case coordinator' for families:

> One of the roles as HV is also coordinating, you're doing the whole family assessment, their family health needs (HV 7, 8)

Within this role health visitors would assess families' needs, request interventions from Sure Start colleagues, and expect to receive feedback on progress. This view did not readily coincide with the understanding of Sure Start staff:

> we take on the issues that professionals want us to think about, but with all families, no matter who they are, we go out and ask them what they want, so hopefully some of it is what HVs are suggesting, but a lot of it might be other stuff, might be completely different to that. (Sure Start team 3)

This difference in perception and consequent mismatch of expectations appears to have contributed to difficulties of communication and in relationships.

Conflicting priorities

A major emerging theme was that of conflicting priorities, particularly of health visitors struggling to appreciate and accommodate the demands, requests and needs of families, managers, Sure Start workers, policy directives and local 'rules' for practice. Tension was caused for HVs by the need to provide services for families inside and outside the Sure Start area, and by the need to cope with the frustrations of those clients unable to access Sure Start services.

Tension was also felt in relation to the differing agendas of general practice and Sure Start. At the time of writing, all health visitors were 'attached' to GP practices and were part of a primary health-care team. As part of this team, HVs were expected to contribute to locally generated priority areas, which did not always coincide with those of Sure Start. Most health visitors felt there were some advantages to GP attachment but also that there would be advantages to working solely with families within the Sure Start geographical area. Although this issue had been debated, no decision had been taken to change the GP attachment arrangements and as a consequence HVs felt they were working with two divergent systems.

Another area of tension for health visitors was that between being an employee of the Primary Care Trust (PCT), with all the attendant priorities and obligations, and being seen as contributing to the success of Sure Start:

> the Sure Start team and the PCT team don't always go in the same direction (HV 9)

As a consequence of these differing priorities and organizational constructs, health visitors felt very real tension and decisions over priorities for action were often very difficult:

> We've got our core work and we're GP attached ... we've got our foot in a number of camps and we're not totally geographical, we're not Sure Start and so dedicating yourself to any one end is very difficult (HV 3, 4)

The differing agendas described by the health visitors indicated a need for them to work flexibly, particularly as they endeavoured to respond to new initiatives within Sure Start. However, a number felt that the routines and 'rules' governing their practice restricted their ability to be flexible in this way.

A further compounding factor in the quest for clarity was that of the variety of views and practices amongst health visitors themselves. They were well aware of this diversity:

There's got to be some changes in our working practice within the PCT, but then you come back to getting us all to agree, and there is division as to how we work currently. (HV 3, 4)

Some interviewees felt they would like to follow Sure Start's lead and work differently:

I think I'd like to see it [health visiting] more as a Sure Start model, it's a more community-based, health promotion model. (HV 9)

Others were less certain, either because of questions around the longevity of Sure Start, or because of concern about the constraints of the Sure Start 0–5 years focus, or because they felt they needed more flexibility to respond to local needs and agendas. The diversity of views and working practices of HVs and their need to accommodate a wide range of demands on their time resulted in divided opinion about the best way to interact with Sure Start. This had led to difficulties for Sure Start staff, who were uncertain what they could expect from their HV colleagues:

We see different HVs for different surgeries and it's so different how they work. (Sure Start team 1)

I don't feel as if they had a strategy, between them, I feel they're all separate. (Sure Start team 2)

This multiplicity of opinion also resulted in difficulties of decision-making. In a culture that anticipated that HVs would make decisions by discussion and consensus, such a wide variety of positions alongside many HVs' personal uncertainty regarding the best ways to proceed, appeared to have resulted in an impasse for many critical decisions. The Sure Start programme manager was able to reflect on a number of situations in which divergent views had resulted in deadlock and consequent inaction. For example, when health visitors debated the issue of becoming a dedicated health visiting team for Sure Start, the result was:

Half and half, I didn't even have a 60:40, it was straight down the middle and no strong voice. (SSM)

This block to decision-taking was inevitably a source of frustration for the Sure Start programme manager. As she was not the HVs' employer, she was unable to act in a managerial role.

The HV manager was also aware of the difficulties this ambiguity over expectations caused her Sure Start colleagues, and she herself was attempting to gain clarity over expectations within a newly established primary care organization. National decisions by Sure Start about priorities and targets that expected health workers' input but which did not offer additional resources also caused considerable difficulties within a cash-limited NHS.

The picture emerging from this tangled web of organizational structures, priorities, needs and agendas is one of confusion and ambiguity. Practitioners appeared overwhelmed in their attempts to make sense of this and efforts to make decisions jointly had defeated them. As a result, many were continuing to attempt to deliver across the spectrum of expectations.

Health visitors' contribution to Sure Start

Despite these difficulties, health visitors were felt to have significantly contributed to the development and progress of the Sure Start programme:

> They're quite happy to come in here and tell me when something's not right and ... when something's good and I've listened to them very carefully over the years about the posts that they've wanted developing. (SSM)

They were seen as a vital resource in efforts to ensure that local families were aware of the programme:

> they wouldn't reach the families if we weren't there giving information out, and they do acknowledge that and respect that (HV 1)

The fact that HVs were already known workers in the community was seen as giving Sure Start an advantage as they worked to establish their own credibility:

> The fact that we were already out there with the families and the community and we were a trusting faith if you like, I think that was a very positive influence. (HV 9)

Joint family work, although infrequent, was positively viewed by all.

The impact of Sure Start on health visitors

Most HVs found Sure Start presented them with both opportunities and difficulties. HVs felt that Sure Start had placed an additional burden on them in the form of increased paperwork. However, new opportunities for training and additional resources in the form of a jointly funded HV assistant post were highly valued. However, it was felt that HVs had not always made the most of the new opportunities presented by Sure Start:

> I think L [Sure Start programme manager] has given opportunities and it's really been up to us to either run with it and get money from her and get support from them. (HV 2)

> So they've all done their La Léche breastfeeding training but none of them, to date, have used their training to train local women in peer support. (SSM)

Opinions were divided on whether the arrival of Sure Start had prompted a change in the role of HVs, and examples of changes given were those of emphasis rather than approach or direction:

> I don't think its [HV role] particularly changed, obviously there are additional visits that we need to do but no it's not generated other than paperwork ... and the time spent just explaining what Sure Start is. (HV 1)

Health visitors' views of Sure Start services

Whilst some HVs were uncertain about the specific nature of the services being offered by Sure Start, most were extremely positive about the programme, feeling it was making a valuable contribution to the health and well-being of local families:

> ... they are offering lots of services and advice that we can just touch on but don't have the time to go into in any depth. (HV 1)

> Yes there are a lot more services ... when you look at issues like parenting and safety equipment and it's been better that what we had before. (HV 10, 11)

Overview of the issues

When new initiatives are developed that involve significant input from statutory services but do not bring direct additional resources for those services, one of two responses seem likely to emerge. Either existing services will have to diminish or be undertaken by others as attention is diverted to accommodate demands of a new initiative, or staff will continue to act largely as before, interacting only minimally with the incoming programme and disappointing those who hoped for their active involvement. In this case, individual health visitors displayed a mixture of these responses. These reactions appeared unremarkable to those in the study familiar with the health visiting profession, who readily accepted that there would be a wide variety of views relating to professional priorities and practices and a number of demands on their time. However, the effect of this divergence within Sure Start Foxhill and Parson Cross was to make decision-making on working arrangements between Sure Start and HVs difficult. It also meant that whilst some HVs were actively involved in supporting Sure Start, many were not. Those who anticipated joint work extending beyond sharing information and joint visits with families to joint planning and delivery of new services have largely been disappointed.

Sure Start nationally sees health visitors as an integral part of the package of services offered to families under the Sure Start banner and therefore expects their work to be counted as a part of the Sure Start output. Locally, the situation is more complex as individual health visitors work both in and outside Sure Start boundaries and are employed by an organization that does not necessarily accept targets set by Sure Start nationally. In addition, the divergence of views on priorities and working practices, the number of influences and local expectations of health visitors and recent policy initiatives identifying new roles for health visitors, have led to uncertainty over their future. Any Sure Start programme manager working within this complex situation would face difficulties in asserting that national Sure Start objectives should be a priority for these health-care staff. Equally, they would be hard pressed to gain clarity about the level of input to Sure Start that could be expected from health visitors. This was evidently the case in Foxhill and Parson Cross.

Working relationships

Inter-agency work is increasingly expected of publicly funded care services (Balloch and Taylor, 2001; Glendinning, 2003), particularly in relation to children (DfES, 2003). However, this study replicated findings elsewhere in exposing professional rivalries, organizational level difficulties and differing priorities as barriers to progress (Mattessich et al., 2001; Van Eyk and Baum, 2002; Glendinning, 2003; Harris, 2003).

Although the health visitor contribution to Sure Start was largely welcomed by Sure Start staff, and health visitors in turn mostly had positive views of Sure Start, finding ways to work together that made the most of all the skills available to families appeared very challenging.

A number of both Sure Start and health visitor staff felt that the contributions they were making to the well-being of local families were insufficiently valued. Health visitors felt that Sure Start was taking their contribution for granted, co-opting their work into Sure Start outputs without sufficiently acknowledging their source. Some Sure Start workers, on the other hand, felt that health visitors did not always acknowledge their abilities and were unlikely to encourage them to extend their skills. Sensitivities were displayed over role boundaries and skills, and individuals who felt hurt by the responses of others expressed some strong views and gave evidence of some distancing from others.

Many saw good interpersonal relationships and trust as vital to effective working practices, yet this was lacking in some areas. Although some had established effective working relationships, a number of poor experiences and lack of physical proximity combined with emotional distance between some health visitors and Sure Start colleagues seems, at times, to have resulted in somewhat stereotyped views of other groups.

Influence and example

Sure Start is expected to influence local delivery of statutory services (Eisenstadt, 2002). However, only rarely is Sure Start the employer of these staff. In this instance, the health visitors were not seconded to Sure Start and therefore the Sure Start programme manager had no direct influence over their services. Although she had managed to evoke goodwill, she had no formal mechanism through which to exert influence over decision-making. As a result, she had only been able to encourage debate, which in relation to some important issues had led to divided views and a consequent lack of action. The alternative views apparent amongst HVs were hardly surprising given the backdrop of policy change and multiple agendas outlined above.

Organizational changes in the NHS meant that formal agreements with HV employers were slow to emerge, although the two managers in this case evidently attempted to support each other despite these difficulties. External demands for health outcomes from the national Sure Start organization, implying the involvement of health-care workers, had the potential to antagonize local PCT managers already dealing with limited resources, vacancies and a multi-layered policy agenda.

Service delivery initiated by Sure Start had not had the level of HV involvement they had hoped for. Although HVs had taken up opportunities for training, this had not led to a noticeable change in the nature of their service delivery. HVs themselves felt that there had been opportunities and encouragement from the example of Sure Start to change, but they generally had not been able to make the most of these. Given the confusion over priorities and the competing agendas of families, other professionals and organizations, this seemed hardly surprising.

Conclusion

This study showed that the arrival of Sure Start had less impact on local health visitors than some originally had envisaged. The expectation of policy makers appeared to be that Sure Start, like other new initiatives, would in some way 'coordinate' the activities of local statutory workers, influencing them to change their focus and ways of practice (Eisenstadt, 2002). As has been seen in this study, a complex set of issues such as structural ambiguities, conflicting priorities, resource shortfalls, local history and a range of professional opinions all impacted on the success of this venture.

In this study, the Sure Start manager was a health visitor with an intimate knowledge of local services and with personal influence, which helped her to secure a continuing dialogue with her health visitor colleagues. However, these colleagues were unprepared to commit many resources to developing new Sure Start services, largely because they were at the receiving end of extensive demands on their time within which they, for the most part, gave developing services with Sure Start a low priority. The range of professional opinions exhibited by the HVs in this study and the apparent lack of a mechanism for agreeing profession-wide issues also contributed to a lack of focus on the Sure Start agenda.

Despite these difficulties, this study highlighted many positive features of joint working between Sure Start and health visitors. Health visitors were clear about the benefits of the Sure Start programme and felt it was having a positive effect on the health and well-being of local families. Sure Start staff were also positive about the contribution of health visitors and wanted to see them more integrated into the Sure Start team. Nevertheless, the study also revealed a number of tensions and difficulties in relation to health visitor involvement. This highlights the complex nature of interprofessional relationships and reinforces the message that such relationships need regular attention to ensure that they succeed in working profitably for the benefit of service users (Mattessich et al., 2001).

It seems likely that many of the issues reported here will be found elsewhere, and as Sure Start moves to become a 'mainstream' service the need to understand the issues, challenges and tensions for statutory service providers arising from this national programme is reinforced. Sure Start programme managers will surely need clear strategies to ensure collaboration with, and influence over, these services. Only then will the families receiving Sure Start programme services alongside those of the statutory agencies be able to experience the high-quality, coordinated care that they are entitled to receive.

Note

Linda Fox, programme manager, provides an update on Sure Start Foxhill and Parson Cross work with health visitors:

Since this report was published, there have been a number of significant changes in health visiting services. Local health visitors have moved into Sure Start premises and now work alongside Sure Start. Working together in this way has enabled relationships to be strengthened and all concerned to gain a better understanding of how Sure Start fits into mainstream children and family services. The North Primary Care Trust which hosts the health visiting service has undertaken a major reorganization so that health visiting teams work within an identified geographical boundary that is coterminous with the new Children's Centre area. The new health visiting team will manage a corporate case load; referrals between health visiting and Sure Start go to teams rather than individuals which enables a prompt response by the appropriate worker. A data-sharing protocol has been agreed between the Primary Care Trust and local programme.

Health visitors work with Sure Start at the local level and have developed many initiatives such as joint visits, sleep clinics, play and say sessions, nutritional work and exercise classes. The health visitor place on the Partnership Board enables the health visiting service to shape and influence the development of the programme.

References

Balloch, S. and Taylor, M. (2001) *Partnership Working: Policy and Practice*. Bristol: The Policy Press.

Bowling, A. (1997) *Research Methods in Health*. Buckingham: Open University Press.

Department for Education and Skills (2003) *Every Child Matters*. London: DfES.

Department of Health (1999a) *Saving Lives: Our Healthier Nation*. London: The Stationery Office.

Department of Health (1999b) *Making a Difference*. London: The Stationery Office.

Department of Health (2001) *Health Visitor Practice Development Pack*. London: Department of Health.

Eisenstadt, N. (2002) Sure Start: key principles and ethos. *Child: Care, Health and Development*, 28(1): 3–4.

Glendinning, C. (2003) Breaking down barriers: integrating health and care services for older people in England. *Health Policy*, 65: 139–51.

Harris, S. (2003) Interagency practice and professional collaboration: the case of drug education and prevention. *Journal of Education Policy*, 18(3): 303–14.

Mason, J. (1996) *Qualitative Researching*. London: Sage.

Mattessich, P.W., Murray-Close, M. and Monsey, B.R. (2001) *Collaboration: What Makes It Work*, 2nd edn. Saint Paul, Amherst: H. Wilder Foundation.

May, T. (1993) *Social Research: Issues, Methods and Process*. Buckingham: Open University Press.

National Sure Start website (2003) *Key Principles*: www.surestart.gov.uk

Silverman, D. (1993) *Interpreting Qualitative Data: Methods for Analysing Talk, Text and Interaction*. London: Sage.

Van Eyk, H. and Baum, F. (2002) Learning about interagency collaboration: trialling collaborative projects between hospitals and community health services. *Health and Social Care in the Community*, 10(4): 262–9.

9 Child Safety Scheme
Robin Carlisle

Introduction

This chapter describes an evaluation of the first year of the Sure Start Child Safety Scheme. Reasons are given why child safety schemes should be an important component of Sure Start programmes. The Fox Hill and Parson Cross Child Safety Scheme is set within the context of national and local data on the prevalence of child injuries and the evidence for effective interventions. A variety of process measures were used to evaluate the scheme which offered indicative results and led to changes in the delivery of the scheme. Findings were then used as a basis for provisional recommendations for the evaluation of other child safety schemes.

Home injuries and Sure Start

One of the overall aims of Sure Start is to improve health outcomes for children. Some interventions such as reducing smoking in pregnancy and measures to increase birth weight may well show health benefits relatively quickly. However, the life-course model of determinants of health predicts that the full health impact of improving early opportunities will only be apparent when children reach middle age and later life. Social disadvantage has a cumulative effect on health which has been compared to the effect on a car 'of putting more miles on the clock' (Chalmers and Capewell, 2001). If children grow up in less advantaged areas they tend to develop the same types of health problems as the overall population (such as heart disease and cancer), but they get them much earlier. Although most of the health benefits from Sure Start may take time to be realized, the scale of the potential health dividend should not be understated. For instance, currently boys from Fox Hill and Parson Cross can expect to live for 72 years, girls for 78 years. This is seven years less than life expectancy in other, more advantaged parts of Sheffield, some of which are only two to three miles away. In this context childhood injuries are particularly important. They are one area where health improvements can potentially be realized relatively quickly; childhood injuries are the commonest cause of death in children over age 1 and have a steeper social gradient than other causes of childhood mortality (Acheson, 1998).

Aims and description of the Sure Start Foxhill and Parson Cross Child Safety Scheme

The child safety element of the Sure Start programme started in May 2000. The aims were to support and involve local parents to improve the safety of their children.

> The scheme's original objectives were:
> * to develop a home safety equipment delivery scheme;
> * to develop an in-car seat restraint project including advice to parents;
> * to create employment opportunities for local parents;
> * to contribute to work that improves the safety of the area (such as encouraging housing providers to improve the safety of their properties).

The scheme employed a full-time project worker who previously worked for an agency with considerable experience of supplying home safety equipment to families (known as Cot-Age). Initially, the main emphasis was on providing three types of safety equipment: safety gates, fire guards and smoke alarms. Equipment was supplied and fitted free of charge, although families could make a contribution if they wished.

As the project developed, there was increasing emphasis on providing general home safety advice in addition to simply fitting equipment. All families in the area were offered a home safety assessment and the project worker also contributed to groups such as parenting classes. A portable appliance tester was used to test the safety of electric appliances and the worker also helped families with other tasks such as building external fences. There were strong links with local Cot-Age organization and the community fire service.

The evaluation of the Child Safety Scheme

The local Health Authority Public Health Department was invited to undertake a brief evaluation as part of partnership working. The evaluation took place just over a year after the scheme started. The whole review consisted of a literature review; analysis of routinely available information on childhood injuries; a description of process measures; and group interviews with parents, health visitors and Sure Start workers.

The objectives of the evaluation were to:

- summarize routinely available national and local information on childhood injuries;
- comment on whether the scheme's approach was consistent with published evidence and previous local experience;
- record progress towards achieving the scheme's original objectives;
- suggest ways in which the scheme could be improved.

Information on childhood injuries and their prevention

Policy context

Preventing avoidable injuries is an important national priority. The 1999 White Paper 'Saving Lives' set a target of reducing deaths from accidents by one-fifth by 2010 (Department of Health, 1999) and a report to the Chief Medical Officer in 2002 prioritized injuries in children (Department of Health, 2002; Towner, 2002). These priorities were also reflected in the local Sheffield Health Improvement Plan.

National data on childhood injuries and their prevention

Injuries are responsible for 16 per cent of all deaths in children aged 1–4 years (around 100 deaths in England each year). Most injuries at this age are in the home, but injuries outside the home (especially road traffic injuries) become important as children become older.

Accidental injury is also the most common reason for young children to be admitted to hospital. The best source of information on types of injury is the Home and Leisure Accident Surveillance System (DTI, 1999). This uses a sample of 18 UK hospital Accident and Emergency (A&E) departments across the country. Each year there is a 1 in 14 chance that a child under 4 will attend an A&E department with an injury. In descending order, the commonest injuries are: colliding with, or being struck by, objects in the home; burns; foreign bodies in the eye, nose or ear; and cuts. Injuries are more common in boys than girls. Injuries are much more common in less prosperous areas. This does not appear to be because of large differences in safety behaviour or in attitudes by parents (Hapgood et al., 2000; MacKay et al., 2002), rather it is the consequence of the greater number of risks in the environment in less prosperous areas and because there are fewer resources available to provide safe environments for children.

Evidence on the effectiveness of child injury prevention schemes

Although there is compelling evidence about the significance of childhood injuries, there is less consensus on the best means of preventing them. There have now been several reviews of this important topic (Kemp, 1997; Kendrick et al., 2000; Dowswell and Towner, 2002). Injuries in the home are made up of a variety of injuries with different causes. Most interventions have used several simultaneous approaches, so separating out which components of programmes are effective is difficult. Most studies have not been large enough to show statistically significant reductions in actual injuries and have reported improvements in proxies such as rating scales of safety behaviour or the use of equipment.

There is general agreement that education on its own is of limited value. Targeting 'at risk' groups for specific education programmes risks 'victim blaming' and there is no evidence that 'at risk' groups have less knowledge or are less concerned about accidents. The main problem is lack of resources to make homes safer (Dowswell and Towner, 2002).

There is some evidence (mainly from other countries) that home visits can bring about safer behaviour when they are part of packages that also offer concrete help (MacKay et al., 2002). A randomized trial in primary care in Nottingham showed that home visits combined with a low-cost safety equipment scheme increased safety behaviour (Clamp and Kendrick, 1998). However, a cluster randomized trial from the same team was unable to show a reduction in actual injuries (Kendrick et al., 1999).

A successful community-wide programme has been evaluated as part of the Healthy Cities movement in Sweden. This was reviewed by Dowswell and Towner (2002), who point out that successful community action campaigns require the sustained use of surveillance systems, cooperation between agencies and time for networks and a range of interventions to be developed.

A systematic review of the effectiveness of smoke alarms showed a similar picture to that for other safety equipment (DiGuiseppi and Higgins, 2000). Functioning smoke alarms prevent deaths from fire. Free provision of smoke alarms in Oklahoma was successful in reducing mortality (Mallonee et al., 1996), but this was not replicated by a free provision scheme in London (DiGuiseppi et al., 2002), and there is evidence that if alarms are simply provided without fitting and education a substantial proportion are not used (Rowland et al., 2002).

Building on previous local experience

Previous experience in another socially deprived area of Sheffield gave findings that were consistent with the published evidence (Jefford, 1997). Here parents reported concern about the possibility of injuries at home in young children and felt that providing safety equipment was the best way to reduce risk. Despite the relatively high levels of concern and knowledge about risks, ownership of safety equipment was low, with 60 per cent of families having no access to any safety equipment. Parents tended to use maternity grants for immediate priorities, such as baby equipment, rather than for safety equipment for toddlers. A pilot equipment loan scheme demonstrated high uptake and use of equipment but could not be continued because funding was withdrawn (Jefford, 1997).

Conclusions from the literature on childhood injuries and their prevention

Mortality and morbidity data justify prioritizing child injury prevention schemes. The Fox Hill and Parson Cross approach of providing free home safety equipment and smoke alarms, combined with fitting and advice, is consistent with the current limited evidence base for effectiveness.

Using routinely available information to enhance child safety schemes

Local information on child injury can potentially be used in three ways by child safety schemes:

- to inform the planning of the injury prevention schemes by comparing the areas with the scheme with other local areas and national data;
- to provide information directly to parents to put risks into perspective and to influence local action – for example, traffic calming schemes;
- to evaluate the impact of schemes.

The scheme covered 900 families living in an area across the boundary between two electoral wards with a total population of 16,000. Routinely available information aggregated at ward level was therefore of limited use. However, it was possible to use a full list of post codes for the Sure Start area, which supplied the level of detail needed.

There is no routine collection of data that provide a complete picture of all the injuries that occur in children. Injuries that do not require medical help go unrecorded and information from different primary care teams tends not to be combined into population-level information. Although it would have been possible to have obtained some background information from individual general practices with well-developed information systems, this option was not taken up because of the difficulties of aggregating information from a variety of manual and electronic recording systems.

In Sheffield all hospital A&E services for children are provided at a single site and electronic data were felt to be complete since 1997. There were two main problems in using A&E data:

- families living closer to the department were more likely to attend;
- separating injuries from other reasons for attendance was not always clear cut.

Comparison of information from the Sure Start area with city-wide and national data

Deaths

Data on deaths from childhood injuries on a Local Authority basis were obtained from the Office of National Statistics. Out of the total population of Sheffield of 530,000 people, there were 5 deaths from injuries in children under 5 between 1997 and 1999. This was slightly higher than the national average. Although national data show that deaths from injuries are much more common in less advantaged areas, deaths are too uncommon to be used for evaluating individual Sure Start programmes.

House fires

Information was available for South Yorkshire as a whole (population 1,320,000). There were just over 1,000 reported home fires in 1999/2000, with 10 deaths and 166 casualties in all ages. South Yorkshire has fewer fires and casualties than the national average. Again, although fires are much more common in deprived areas, their relative rarity makes them of little use for evaluating individual Sure Start schemes.

Hospital admission data

Table 9.1 shows a similar issue with small numbers when hospital admissions for accidents were collated for the Sure Start area.

Table 9.1 Annual number of hospital admissions following accidents in the Foxhill and Parson Cross Sure Start area (children under 3)

Age group	Number of hospital admissions				
	1996/97	1997/98	1998/99	1999/00	2000/01
0–1 years	3	3	2	3	3
1–2 years	6	3	1	2	4
2–3 years	4	5	4	5	2
Total under 3 years	13	11	7	10	9

Source: Sheffield Health Authority Information and Research Department

Information on accidental injuries

About half of all attendances for injuries in children under 4 were coded as accidents. This was felt to slightly underestimate the number of accidents as some non-specific codes were probably also due to accidents. However, the rank order of all the electoral wards in the city was similar if non-specific codes were included. The two electoral wards that included the Sure Start area had A&E attendance rates around the average for the city. This may reflect the fact that although the Sure Start area was in a socially deprived area, it was situated several miles from the A&E department. When attendance rates for the city overall were mapped using a geographical information package, there was a strong negative association with distance.

The A&E data also give some idea of the nature of injuries. Table 9.2 gives the number of injuries in children from the two electoral wards which each contained part of the Sure Start population and also for the Sure Start population. This showed 14 attendances for accidental poisonings and 9 for burns and scolds. There was only one attendance following an electric shock in the whole of Sheffield, but this was from the Sure Start area.

Provisional analysis showed that overall attendance rates at A&E did drop in the Sure Start area by more than the average for Sheffield in 2000/01 (9.2 per cent compared to 5.4 per cent; see Table 9.3). However, the scheme had not been running long enough to know whether this was a real effect or due to chance.

Table 9.2 First attendances by type of injuries by ward and for the Sure Start population for children under 4, 2000/01

	First attendance				
Area	All attendances	Accidents[1]	Burns and scalds	Electric shock	Poisoning
Owlerton ward	396	158	14		14
Southey Green ward	405	171	8	1	13
Sure Start Foxhill and Parson Cross	388	168	9	1	14
All Sheffield	10,477	4454	253	1	278

Source: Sheffield Health Authority Information and Research Department
[1]National A&E diagnosis codes 1–12, 14–16
(this will underestimate the true number of injuries)

Table 9.3 Rate of first attendance/1000 children at A&E 1999/2000 and 2000/2001

	Rate of first attendance		
	1999/00	2000/01	Percentage reduction
Sheffield	462	437	5.4%
Sure Start Foxhill and Parson Cross	434	394	9.2%

Source: Sheffield Health Authority Information and Research Department
The table shows first attendance for all reasons and so includes attendances that are not injuries.

Information as feedback

The evaluation was intended to be the start of the process of feeding back information to the local community on injury rates. This was timely because following efficiency savings local health visitors no longer receive routine information on A&E attendance for their clients, so providing information at Sure Start level was a useful alternative.

Conclusions on the use of quantitative information

There are practical problems in using quantitative information on injuries to evaluate Sure Start schemes. Deaths and hospital admissions are too infrequent to use them to evaluate individual schemes. Future developments that would make injury data more useful in evaluating the outcomes of injury prevention schemes include:

- the development of more sophisticated search strategies to identify attendance at A&E for more serious injuries (which are likely to be confounded less strongly by distance from the department);
- the use of primary care information systems to obtain a fuller picture of all injuries occurring;
- collaboration with other Sure Start injury prevention programmes to increase the statistical power of quantitative data.

In the short term, the most important use of quantitative child injury data is the provision of information to local communities and health professionals to empower them to address child safety issues.

Process information

The referral process and data handling

When the scheme started referrals were usually made by health visitors or Sure Start workers. The health worker only referred if they felt that a specific type of equipment was required. This was indicated on a form that also included some basic demographic data about the family. This information was used to provide information about the scheme uptake and coverage in its first year.

The evaluation reported on:

- the numbers of assessments made;
- the type of equipment fitted;
- the demography of families and children where equipment had been fitted.

Activity data

In the first year equipment was supplied and fitted to 203 of the 900 families in the Sure Start area. This included the first two months when there was less activity while the scheme was establishing itself. The scheme had not yet reached 'steady state', when the needs of all existing families would have been met and the requirement of the scheme would be to meet the needs of families with new babies and those moving into the area.

Equity of coverage

Using a geographical information system to map the uptake of equipment within the Sure Start area did not reveal any gaps in coverage within the scheme. Specifically, families living further from the family centre and families registered with more distant general practitioners were accessing the scheme.

The number of fittings made to particular target groups such as black and minority ethnic groups, teenage parents and parents with physical disabilities was quantified. However, it was difficult to monitor equity explicitly due to a lack of linkage with information about families who did not access the scheme.

Conclusions from the process description

Two changes were made following the evaluation.

- Data collection was rationalized. Data to monitor equity were no longer collected specifically by the home injury scheme; instead information on assessments made and equipment supplied was entered into the main Sure Start database. This meant that denominators and overall coverage could be more easily defined.
- Access to the scheme was rationalized. All families were routinely offered a home safety assessment and at this visit the project worker discussed with the families which equipment might be appropriate.

Views of parents

A group of four parents (all mothers) were interviewed using a semi-structured questionnaire during an open day. The mothers all had frequent contact with Sure Start and so could not comment about families who had less contact with the service. No attempt was made to interview parents who had declined to use the child safety scheme.

The mothers had found out about the scheme by four different routes: through a health visitor, through a friend, through a Sure Start outreach worker and by meeting the project worker directly at a parenting group.

In general, the mothers were very complimentary about the equipment, the fitting and the advice given. The only complaint was a refusal to fit an upstairs safety gate (because the Sure Start worker felt this would be too dangerous). 'The fitting was brilliant especially getting the kids to help.' They also valued the advice; one mother had been shown how to fully open her windows to escape in case of fire.

The mothers felt they had no unmet safety needs. They were aware of the dangers of being over-protective and felt that although small injuries would always happen they regarded their children as very unlikely now to have serious injuries.

There were different views about what they would have done if the Sure Start scheme had not been in existence. One mother said she would have found the money to buy equipment; another would have used planks or old doors rather than a purpose-built safety gate. None of the mothers said they were concerned about having to contribute financially to the additional extras – they appreciated the fact that the equipment was available at a considerable discount.

At the time of the interview, the mothers were not aware of any community involvement in planning or delivering this part of the Sure Start project but were aware of ways of getting involved with the overall Sure Start programme (one mother interviewed was a member of the partnership board). They were aware of community activity on accident prevention by the local community forum on local traffic black spots and joy riders.

Views of local health visitors and Sure Start workers

A group interview was held with four health visitors and two Sure Start outreach workers. The health visitors had all worked in the area prior to the commencement of the Sure Start scheme and came from practices that had substantial numbers of patients within the Sure Start area.

In general, the feedback was positive. The home safety scheme was seen as an important component of the overall Sure Start programme. The most important improvement was easier access to equipment. The health visitors felt that both need and demand for the three types of safety equipment were being met for families from their practices in the Sure Start area. They could not answer for patients not registered with their own practices and wondered whether patients registered with practices who had fewer patients in the Sure Start area were as informed about available services.

The health workers were happy with the type and quality of the equipment provided. They were also happy about advice given by the project worker and felt it complemented their role. It was credible because 'it came from someone who was doing something practical'. There was positive feedback about the advice given during individual assessment visits and also the usefulness of the project worker as a resource to parenting groups. Links between the project worker and the community fire officer had changed the specific advice given by the workers, for example suggesting to families they should have family fire alarm plans.

The health visitors suggested areas where the scheme should be extended, for example by financial support for cots and prams, support for safe play areas, provision of communal tools for garden upkeep and better needle and syringe disposal.

There was felt to be considerable scope for improved local surveillance of child injuries and dissemination of information. Many parents experienced worries about similar concerns, such as the fear of children falling out of bed. A newsletter was suggested as a means of communicating such information.

Criticisms of the scheme included: waits to get equipment fitted (mainly occurring during build-up to 'steady state'); problems with introductory communication for health professionals about what was available free and what not; and the problem for health visitors dealing with families who could not at that stage access the scheme because they lived outside the Sure Start area.

Recommendations

National data on the prevalence and morbidity from childhood injuries justifies including injury prevention schemes in Sure Start projects. The Foxhill and Parson Cross Child Safety Scheme has shown that it is possible to deliver an injury prevention scheme that is consistent with the evidence on what is known to be effective, builds on previous local experience and is integrated into the overall Sure Start programme.

Properly funding and planning ongoing evaluation of injury prevention schemes is particularly important because the evidence base for what is effective in practice still requires some development, and the provision of relevant local information to communities and health professionals is likely to be an integral part of successful injury prevention programmes.

References

Acheson, D. (1998) Independent inquiry into Inequalities in Health Report. London: The Stationery Office: www.archive.official-documents.co.uk/document/doh/ih/ih.htm (accessed May 2003).

Chalmers, J. and Capewell, S. (2001) Deprivation, disease, and death in Scotland: graphical display of survival of a cohort. *British Medical Journal*, 323: 967–8.

Clamp, M. and Kendrick, D. (1998) A randomised controlled trial of general practitioner safety advice for families with children under five. *British Medical Journal*, 316: 1567–79.

Department of Health (1999) *Saving Lives – Our Healthier Nation*: www.archive.official-documents.co.uk/document/cm43/4386/ 4386.htm (accessed May 2003).

Department of Health (2002) *Preventing Accidental Injury – Priorities for Action. Report to the CMO from the Accidental Injury Task Force*: www.doh.gov.uk/accidents/accinjuryreport.htm (accessed May 2003).

Department of Trade and Industry (DTI) (1999) *Working for a Safer World: 23rd Report of the Home and Leisure Accident Surveillance System*. London: The Stationery Office.

DiGuiseppi, C. and Higgins, J. (2000) Systematic review of controlled trials of interventions to promote smoke alarms. *Archive of Disease in Childhood*, 82: 341–8.

DiGuiseppi, C., Roberts, I., Wade, A. et al. (2002) Incidence of fires and related injuries after giving out free smoke alarms: cluster randomised controlled trial. *British Medical Journal*, 7371: 995–7.

Dowswell, T. and Towner, E. (2002) Social deprivation and the prevention of unintentional injury in childhood: a systematic review. *Health Education Research*, 17(2): 221–37.

Hapgood, R. et al. (2000) How well do socio-demographic characteristics explain variations in childhood safety practices? *Journal of Public Health Medicine*, 22(3): 307–11.

Jefford, S. (1997) Childhood risk and poverty. A study of parents' concerns over children's accidents in the home. Cot-Age and Sheffield Health.

Kemp, A. (1997) Childhood accidents: epidemiology, trends and prevention. *Emergency Medicine Journal*, 14: 316–20.

Kendrick, D., Elkan, R., Hewitt, M. et al. (2000) Does home visiting improve parenting and the quality of the home environment? A systematic review and meta-analysis. *Archives of Disease in Childhood*, 82: 443–51.

Kendrick, D., Marsh, P., Fielding, K. and Miller, P. (1999) Preventing injuries in children: cluster randomised controlled trial in primary care. *British Medical Journal*, 318: 980–3.

MacKay, M., Reid, D., Mohler, D. and Klassen, T. (2002) Systematic review of the relationship between childhood injury and social-economic status. *Health Canada*: www.hc-sc.gc.ca/hppb/childhood-youth/cyfh/ safe_and_supportive/resources/Injury.pdf (accessed May 2003).

Mallonee, S., Istre, G.R., Rosenberg, M. et al. (1996) Surveillance and prevention of residential-fire injuries. *New England Journal of Medicine*, 335: 27–31.

Rowland, D., DiGuiseppi, C., Roberts, I. et al. (2002) Prevalence of working smoke alarms in local authority inner city housing: randomised controlled trial. *British Medical Journal*, 325(7371): 998–1001.

Towner, E. (2002) *The Prevention of Childhood Accidental Injury*, background paper prepared for Accidental Injury Task Force, University of Newcastle: www.doh.gov.uk/accidents/accinjuryreport.htm (accessed May 2003).

Part Four
Improving children's ability to learn

10 Quality of play and learning opportunities
Simon Martinez

Introduction

The Sure Start challenge is to promote change in children and their families so that a whole range of competencies improves. These competencies are social skills (including self-esteem and social competence), readiness to learn when a child starts school leading to the development of cognitive skills and achievement, and an improvement in health. Success in these competencies, and their relationship with each other, has long-term social benefits.

Consultations with parents in the area before the programme began showed that quality play and learning experiences for their children was something that they supported and wanted to see improved. Services in the locality (health visitors, general practitioners, nurseries, Social Services, and the Child and Adolescent Mental Health Service) also agreed they were much needed. Therefore the programme was very ready to take on the third Sure Start objective quoted in Chapter 1:

Objective 3: Improving children's ability to learn
In particular, by encouraging high-quality environments and childcare that promote early learning, provide stimulating and enjoyable play, improve language skills and ensure early identification and support of children with special needs.

and the specific national Sure Start target associated with this objective:

All children to have access to good-quality play and learning opportunities, helping progress towards early learning goals when they get to school.

Children's homes are the settings where they have their earliest and most important play and learning opportunities, but as they get older, say from 18 months onwards, out-of-home community settings such as crèches, parent and toddler groups and playgroups also become important. Later, by the time they are aged 3, many children have access to nursery settings; these may be private or linked to a school or Sure Start programme.

What were the play and learning opportunities for the Sure Start area? There was a variety of provision that can be described from home to community, and from play to learning on intersecting continua. The homes of some of the families were in poor condition and lacked well-maintained private gardens to provide safe and stimulating outside play spaces. The parks in the area had generally suffered from sporadic, short-lived improvements and fallen into disrepair. There was a variety of other care and learning provision in the area, including two childminders, two private nurseries, two preschool playgroups, and four nursery classes in local primary schools. It was apparent that there were many opportunities for physical play (running, jumping, climbing and balancing), but limited opportunities for language development (rhyming, copying, role play), extension of play in a structured way that builds skills and self-esteem and social competence, and creative play that builds fine motor skills and cognitive capacity of exploration and experimentation.

Prior to Sure Start's establishment, some parents were engaged in parent and toddler and parent and baby groups, gaining from the support of their peers and from the advice and encouragement of health visitors. This social support and networking led to improved parenting, building parents' self-esteem and social competency. However, there were gaps in the accessibility of these activities. Toddler groups and baby groups meeting in some community facilities were housed in warm, welcoming and safe buildings whose management were supportive of the needs of parents and their young children. Others were the opposite, causing many parents to avoid such meetings. Parents were vocal in pointing out the limitations of the community settings. In most of the toddler or baby group settings, there were quality and capacity issues. In a minority of settings, there were concerns about safety and organizational issues.

What the programme concentrated on and why

A priority for the programme was to create entirely new opportunities for play and learning through an integrated centre that would be a hub for all services for children and families in the area, including some of the programme's own satellite activities. This required planning for additional childcare and nursery education places, developing special needs provision, supporting local parents to continue as active partners in their child's play and learning, and supporting some of them to become volunteers or workers within the broad early years provision. However, it was also recognized that community play and learning settings would continue to be important for children, especially in the 18 months to 3 years age range, and that the programme should try to increase quality in those settings by providing support for groups.

Our model of support, led by the community teacher (see Chapter 11), had a clear commitment to meeting children's developmental needs as they grow, and its foundations were set in the partnership with parents. The community teacher provided training for all staff, volunteers and parents in order to achieve better understanding of programme activities, aims and objectives. Supporting a wide range of community activities, the Community Childcare Play and Learning (CCPL) team worked with parents in all the toddler and baby groups developing play so that it was broad, structured, and extended to each child. Team members completed risk assessments so that the activities were safer and less stressful for all concerned. The workers demonstrated play with children that parents could model in their own play with their children. The team attempted to raise the quality of community settings through three main interventions.

The first intervention was encouraging groups to access a 'community chest' fund to provide small grants of up to £1,700 to buy toys and equipment to improve the resources of a wide range of groups. The 'community chest' was run by the programme partnership board where local parents had a significant voice in deciding which applications were successful. Several of the groups covered by this report received grants from this fund.

The second intervention was support for each of the groups from the Sure Start playworkers or community teacher. This support varied from group to group, with some having a regular worker for over a year to develop a particular area of play, regular visits to develop a particular activity like music making, sharing stories, or occasional visits to offer advice on routines or introducing new activities.

The third intervention was to provide a wide range of training opportunities and workshops to develop both Sure Start workers' and volunteers' skills. The workshops on curriculum issues covered all areas of the Foundation Stage of Learning with particular reference to speech and language, social, personal and emotional development, and early literacy and mark making. This training has been delivered in mixed groups of workers and volunteers to ensure lots of networking can take place. This training was largely delivered by the programme's community teacher. Other training offered to all volunteers was to strengthen their organizational skills, particularly around health and safety issues, and included food hygiene and first aid. This training was delivered by a variety of providers.

There were 12 community groups supported by the CCPL team over the years 2000 to 2002. The play and learning settings provided by these groups varied from once a week toddler group sessions and crèches, to three sessions a week playgroup, to Monday to Friday nursery. There were considerable changes in all of the groups so that supporting them was sometimes akin to climbing up sand. For every move forwards or upwards there was the risk of sliding backwards or down.

Initial research and evaluation

In the first year of the programme we carried out a study (Martinez, Hannon, van Dijk and Fitter, 2001) in which we looked at all of the out-of-home provision in the area, concentrating on what was available for children from about 18 months to their third birthday. We investigated the extent of the existing provision, its use by families in the Sure Start area, and how Sure Start provision compared to what parents wanted. We also looked at the quality of the existing play and learning settings in the community, and it is that part of the study that I want to describe in this chapter.

How could we judge or measure quality? For community settings catering for children aged 18 months to 3 years, there was no readily available method. We decided to develop our own method. We wanted a method that did not require more than one half day to evaluate each setting, did not interfere with or duplicate other agencies' roles and responsibilities, would be understood by workers and policymakers outside the programme, could be applied by an independent evaluator, and would not be threatening to workers in the settings.

We considered various possibilities, including frameworks developed by national and local agencies, Sheffield Young Children's Service Kitemarking scheme, and approaches described by Blenkin and Whitehead (1996), Griffen, 1994, OFSTED, 1998, Rouse and Griffin (1992), and Robson (1996). All these had their merits, but in the end we opted for a well-established method, the ECERS-R (Early Childhood Environment Rating Scale – Revised edition) by Harms, Clifford and Cryer (1998).

The ECERS-R is intended for use in preschool, kindergarten and childcare settings serving children from $2^1/_2$ to 5 years of age. It is a 43-item rating scale covering 7 main aspects of quality in early childhood provision: 'space and furnishing', 'personal care routines', 'language-reasoning', 'activities', 'interaction', 'programme structure', 'parents and staff'. Each 'quality item' is rated on a 7-point scale ranging from '1', inadequate, to '3', minimal, to '7', excellent, according to precise definitions.

There were alternative instruments such as that produced by the Frank Porter Graham Child Development Centre at the University of North Carolina that were intended for use in different kinds of settings or with different age groups. We examined the ITERS (Infant/Toddler Environment Rating Scale) by Harms, Cryer and Clifford (1990) and the FDCRS (Family Day Care Rating Scale) by Harms and Clifford (1989), but we decided that they were less suited to our Sure Start settings than ECERS-R. In the UK,

ECERS has been extended with additional items by the Effective Provision of Pre-School Education (EPPE) research project (Sylva et al., 1998), but we decided that, for our purposes, the additional EPPE items focused too much on learning goals for older children.

We piloted the ECERS-R in three settings. We became uneasy about applying the terms 'inadequate' or 'minimal' to community settings where staff and parents were often working hard and doing well in difficult circumstances, but we did recognize that a 1–7 scale could help everyone focus on ways of developing the quality of play and learning opportunities in those settings. We found some items were not appropriate for our community settings where sessions were of short duration and often in shared accommodation. Certain items, whilst undoubtedly important in full-day care provided by professional staff working in purpose-built accommodation, were far beyond the reach of our community groups. For example, it seemed inappropriate to rate provision for the 'use of TV, video and/or computers' when groups had no access to such facilities and it was beyond their power to improve on the quality of what was provided. We also judged that an item referring to children with disabilities duplicated other items that covered this important aspect of quality. In all, we dropped 8 of the ECERS-R items (item number 11, Nap/rest; 12, Toileting/diapering; 27, Use of TV, video and/or computers; 37, Provisions for children with disabilities; 39, Provisions for personal needs of staff; 40, Provisions for professional needs of staff; 42, Supervision and evaluation of staff; 43, Opportunities for professional growth). The remaining 35 items did seem relevant and potentially useful. Piloting showed that two raters agreed with each other and the resulting profiles distinguished between settings in ways that made sense to the workers and others who knew the settings whilst also revealing aspects that had not been so obvious.

We employed an independent team of assessors to visit settings and apply the modified ECERS-R. The profiles were summarized and fed back to the staff in each setting.

Did support from the programme increase quality?

After the CCPL team had worked with settings for a year, we wanted to know if there had been any impact on the quality of play and learning. We therefore carried out a further study (Martinez and Fitter, 2002) in which seven settings were rated a second time by the same team of independent assessors, again using our modified version ECERS-R. (There were five other settings in the community but as they were not operating in both years comparisons were not possible.)

Figure 10.1 Changes over one year in seven community settings in quality of play and learning opportunities, in terms of ECERS-R scores

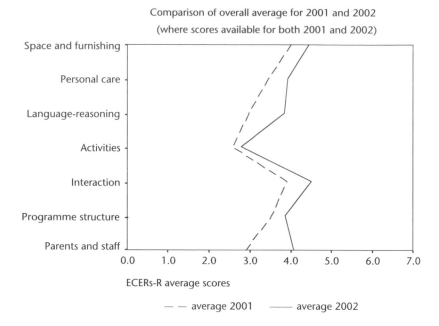

Comparison of overall average for 2001 and 2002
(where scores available for both 2001 and 2002)

ECERs-R average scores

— — average 2001   ——— average 2002

Figure 10.1 shows the aggregated profiles for the seven settings before and after input from Sure Start. One has to be cautious in interpreting aggregated data of this kind, and recognize that there may have been other changes in the community in this period apart from the arrival of Sure Start, but it does seem reasonably clear from comparing the two profiles that there had been an improvement in quality on almost all of the ECERS-R subscales. Details of the 'before-and-after' comparisons for individual settings are reported by Martinez and Fitter (2002). The improvement is reasonably clear on five subscales: language and reasoning; parents and staff; personal care routines; interaction; and space and furnishings. These reflect the input into settings of grants for equipment, support from programme staff, and training.

In two of the subscales there was no evidence of a shift, even though those areas (activities; programme structure) had been a focus of support and commitment of resources. This probably reflects the nature of some of the groups in that they met only once a week for a two-hour session and they had a number of different objectives (family support, social support for parents) which meant that the quality of children's experiences could not always be the top priority. However, in these two areas there had at least been a 'holding of the line' and the children's experiences had not deteriorated.

Overall, we concluded that there had been a positive impact on a range of different community settings.

Dilemmas of community-focused work

Within-area and out-of-area families

One characteristic of Sure Start that most parents and staff are unhappy about is the within-area/out-of-area distinction being made as to whether children and families can access services or groups. All of the work being reported is funded for children living in the Sure Start area, but that does not mean that children from out-of-area addresses have not accessed what is available. They have – and many are just as needy as those living in the area. Current proposals regarding children's centres may bring down artificial barriers.

Balancing children's needs and parents' needs

Some of the activity reported on has a dual function in trying to meet the needs of children and parents at the same time. This is as it should be because the aims of Sure Start will only be achieved by working with children *and* parents. It has been suggested above that there has not been as much improvement in the learning or curriculum areas of the provision as was wished and that a tentative explanation is that this may be a result of the needs of parents taking a priority. But for this approach, however, 'hard to reach' families would not be engaged at all with their children in Sure Start activity.

Including fathers and male carers

Fathers and male carers are clearly important in young children's lives, their development, and their happiness. Men are evidently taking more responsibility for their children. Programme staff remark on seeing men taking their children to Well Baby Clinics, to the GP and hospital when the child is unwell, around the shops and on trips, and to nursery and school. In the groups that our programme supported, women found the environment appropriate but men were absent. It is also a possibility that the absence of men makes settings more acceptable to women. There is a double benefit to children of having both parents involved in their play and learning, whether or not they are living together. Our aim in working with children *and* both their parents cannot be achieved unless we develop ways of working that are inclusive to men.

Resolving tensions between workers and volunteers

The workers that needed most support in helping parents in groups were those who had been recruited from the local community and, perhaps, were experiencing the tension of having taken on a professional role. They were more likely to take personally the negative comments received by all workers supporting groups when it comes to doing the least popular jobs, like the last tidying up. The comments are of the type of 'why should we (volunteer) do this when you (worker) are being paid for it?'. Staff who are confident in their role can cope with this. This is a staff development issue that requires sensitive support through training, supervision, and appraisal.

The danger of institutionalizing voluntary activities

Groups running play and learning settings in the community have a number of different purposes including the chance to see peers and workers playing with children. This is a chance for parents to observe what others are doing, and then gives them the space to model their behaviour on 'positive parenting'and role practice so that they develop from novice to expert. Workers and volunteers who were receiving training from the programme community teacher were anxious to put this into practice in settings and experienced tensions between what they were aspiring to achieve and what they were able to achieve. There appears to have been a danger in developing structured learning programmes based on activities that parents saw as being more appropriate for nursery. The parents then seem to have felt disempowered and withdrew from the activities, leaving the workers with the children doing 'nice' creative activities. The target group of children were pre-nursery and, as the aim was to work with children *and* their parents, this was resolved by developing activities and a programme structure that was more informal and less institutionalized.

Pointers for the future

The opportunity to work with such a range of community provision to promote play and learning is a success for the Sure Start programme. I hope I have been able to demonstrate successes in this work. What pointers for the future are there?

The range of needs of children, both by age and developmental stage, and the many opportunities to work in partnership with parents, requires a diverse model of service delivery. The 'one size fits all' model definitely does not apply. The needs of parents who are returning to work or training and who require quality, affordable, and accessible childcare are very different from the needs of depressed and isolated parents. The opportunities to work with parents whose children are in full day care are different from the opportunities to work with parents who are not working or studying.

The Foxhill and Parson Cross Sure Start programme started in an area that had community-based play and learning opportunities but no integrated centre that could offer the full range of early years services and support the community providers. Whilst it was supporting the community-based activity, the programme was developing its integrated provision, and it is possible, at times, that some of the support for the community became less of a priority. This represents a natural progression for the programme and it supports those parents who have moved on and who are needing different services such as full day care or nursery education places for their child. The programme will need to address the continuing development of services both for new parents, who need the community-based services, and for those parents who have moved on or whose children are older and can benefit from new, integrated services.

References

Blenkin, G. and Whitehead, M. (1996) *Creating a Context for Development*, in G. Blenkin and A.V. Kelly (eds) *Early Childhood Education*. London: Paul Chapman.

Griffin, B. (1994) Educare for the under threes, in L. Abbott and R. Rodger (eds) *Quality Education In the Early Years*. Milton Keynes: Open University Press.

Harms, T. and Clifford, R.M. (1989) *Family Day Care Rating Scale*. New York: Teachers College Press.

Harms, T., Clifford, R.M. and Cryer, D. (1998) *Early Childhood Environment Rating Scale (Revised Edition)*. New York: Teachers College Press.

Harms, T., Cryer, D. and Clifford, R.M. (1990) *Infant/Toddler Environment Rating Scale*. New York: Teachers College Press.

Martinez, S. and Fitter, M. (2002) *Can Sure Start Make an Impact on Community-Based Play and Learning Opportunities?* A Research and Evaluation Report for the Sure Start Foxhill and Parson Cross local programme. Available at www.sheffield.ac.uk/surestart

Martinez, S., Hannon, P., van Dijk, M. and Fitter, M. (2001) *Community Childcare, Play and Learning Opportunities in Sure Start: A First Year Report*. A Research and Evaluation Report for the Sure Start Foxhill and Parson Cross local programme. Available at www.sheffield.ac.uk/surestart

OFSTED (1998) *Guidance on the Inspection of Nursery Education Provision in the Private, Voluntary and Independent Sectors*. London: HMSO.

Robson, S. (1996) The physical environment, in S. Robson and S. Smedley (eds) *Education in Early Childhood*. London: David Fulton.

Rouse, D. and Griffin, S. (1992) Quality for the under threes, in G. Pugh (ed.) *Contemporary Issues in the Early Years*. London: Paul Chapman.

Sylva, K., Siraj-Blatchford, I. Taggart, B. and Colman, P. (1998) *The Early Childhood Environment Rating Scale – Extension (ECERS-E)*. Unpublished instrument developed by the EPPE (Effective Provision of Pre-School Education) Project at the Institute of Education, University of London.

11 Community teaching in a Sure Start context
Jackie Marsh and Jan Forde

Introduction

In this chapter, the role of the community teacher within Sure Start Foxhill and Parson Cross is reviewed. While there is very little previous research that has examined the role of community teachers, there is indicative evidence that the input given by advisory teachers to early years settings is valuable. For example, the Effective Early Learning Project (Pascal, Bertram and Ramsden, 1994) found that the role of an advisory teacher can be an effective means of providing professional development support for early years staff. Christine Stevens (in press) evaluated the work of advisory teachers, entitled Early Years Development Officers (EYDOs), in one county in England. She suggested that, from the data she collected from 138 early year settings, the EYDO's work had been invaluable in relation to three key areas: planning, record-keeping and assessment, and the writing of policies and procedures. However, neither of these studies were undertaken within Sure Start programmes and, given the complexity of a qualified teacher's role within a community-based programme, it was felt that a review of such a role would be useful in informing future developments. Therefore, this chapter addresses the following questions, using the experiences of the first community teacher appointed within Sure Start Foxhill and Parson Cross, Jan Forde, as an example:

- What were the key aspects of the qualified teacher's role within this local Sure Start programme in the first years of its operation?
- What were the key achievements and opportunities for the community teacher?
- What were the key challenges for the community teacher?
- How could the educational strand of this Sure Start programme be strengthened in the future, and what can be learned from this analysis that would be useful to similar programmes?

In 1997, Sheffield Young Children's Service (SYCS) had introduced the role of community teachers and established a community teacher post in Foxhill. When Sure Start Foxhill and Parson Cross was launched in 1999, this community teacher post became jointly funded by SYCS and Sure Start. This was one of the first Sure Start programmes in the country to fund education work in this way and it is, therefore, timely to review this work in order to identify the strengths and challenges faced by the community teacher.

The data in this chapter arise from a series of three in-depth interviews with Jan Forde, undertaken soon after she had left the role to take up a post in a school. The chapter is structured around the four questions outlined above, questions which guided the interviews and provided opportunities for Jan to reflect on a wide range of issues. To begin with, we outline what the key roles and responsibilities of the community teacher were, given the pioneering nature of this work within the national context, at that stage without extensive external guidance and precedents.

The role of the community teacher

The role developed by Jan was very diverse and the key characteristic was that it encompassed a much broader set of practices than is usually the case with an advisory teacher role. This was because of the community element, which was central to the work within Sure Start. In such circumstances, it is not feasible to implement a unidisciplinary model of education, but educative processes should be situated within a wider set of community practices, as will be made clear later in this chapter. Overall, the role of the community teacher appeared to have three main aspects: training, consultation and modelling. It is important to note that training was not conducted in a didactic manner, but was participatory and started from the participants' understanding and experiences. The consultation role was similarly sensitive to the needs of the community and was based on the self-identified needs of various groups and individuals. The modelling element of the role needed to be undertaken with care in order to develop the knowledge *and* the self-esteem of early years workers, and was necessary to the effective development of good practice. Table 11.1 provides an overview of the main roles and responsibilities under these headings.

Table 11.1 Roles and tasks of the community teacher

Role	Key activities	Description
Training	• Courses for parents	The community teacher organized and co-delivered, with Sure Start workers and staff from settings, a range of courses for parents, such as 'Finding out about the foundation stage of learning', Story Sacks[1] and family literacy/ numeracy programmes.
	• Ongoing support for providers	The community teacher provided training for settings on a wide range of issues, including planning and assessment and curriculum development across all areas of learning.
	• Training for providers	Initial training was followed up by regular support, consisting of additional staff development sessions and regular visits. Settings were also supported in making judgements about children who potentially had special educational needs.
Consultation	• Liaison role	The community teacher had a key liaison role, providing a link between settings in the area. She also ensured that settings developed effective links with other services, such as the Library Service, local FE college and the LEA support service for children with special educational needs. The community teacher also liased with workers on a range of other Sure Start programmes, when an educational input was needed.
	• Development of resources	The community teacher supported settings in their planning for inspections. Support was also given in devising follow-up action plans.
	• Supporting transition	Settings and groups were given advice by the community teacher on the purchase of educational items. The community teacher was also asked to choose and purchase resources for a new Sure Start nursery. *cont.*

Role	Key activities	Description
	• Quality assurance	The community teacher facilitated meetings across settings in the Sure Start area, at which issues relating to transition could be discussed.
Modelling	• Work with parents	The community teacher modelled work with parents through the provision of specific courses and one-to-one work.
	• Pedagogical modelling	The community teacher provided a model for workers in settings by teaching alongside them.

This list is by no means exhaustive; nevertheless, it presents the main activities carried out and suggests something of the flexibility which is needed in a post of this kind. During the interviews, a number of key themes emerged which underpinned much of the work of the community teacher outlined in Table 11.1. These were: the pioneering and developmental nature of the role in the first years; the need for sensitivity to the Sure Start context; and the multidisciplinary nature of the work.

Community teacher as pioneer

There was an immense demand for training and support across the Sure Start area. It was as if, once offered, such provision created its own demand as settings became increasingly aware of their needs. The approach was also more systematic than had previously been the case. Jan recalled that, 'Everything seemed a bit like an amoeba ... that somehow grew and spread and grew and spread and this sparked off that ...'. Therefore, in those early years, one of the main aspects of the role of the community teacher was establishing its remit. Jan suggested that:

> what happened in terms of the [Sure Start] Family Centre was that probably one of the things that I helped to do was lay down the foundations for the actual role of outreach teachers – outreach education – because up until that time the Family Centre did not have its own dedicated educationalist. Over the three years and one term I supported the project, I felt as though foundation stones were being laid down ...

An important aspect of the establishment of the role of community teacher within Sure Start was to allay concerns early years workers had about the role of a teacher:

> I remember one of the first times I went into one nursery ... one of the workers turned to me and said, 'I think I'm frightened of teachers' and I said, 'Oh you've no need to be frightened of me, you know more about your nursery than I do, just tell me what to do.' That made me realize that people were coming with a lot of baggage about their own education, you know their own attitude to education and this went on to be borne out by other members of staff and also parents. Many people didn't have good memories of their own school experiences and so to have a teacher in the midst of all this was actually quite difficult for some people. So in the beginning it was about putting human faith very much, I think, on the role of the teacher.

The fact that many people within a Sure Start community may have had very negative experiences with schools and teachers needs to be considered when setting up an advisory teacher's role; time needs to be allowed to develop positive working relationships and the creation of trust.

Need for sensitivity to the context

Another underlying theme of the role appeared to be the need for the community teacher to be sensitive to the needs of the Sure Start community. This meant engaging in activities which might not be so necessary in other areas. For example, an important aspect of Jan's role had been the pastoral work with parents. She had undertaken a number of activities which had provided specific types of support to individual parents and families because she felt that this helped to build up relationships within the community:

> It went on to be developed in various ways actually, what I would call a sort of caring role, the caring side of the job. Sometimes parents would say, ... 'Oh I don't know which school to send my child to when he leaves nursery' and on several occasions I actually took parents in my car with their child to look at different schools. I had numerous conversations about sleepless nights and faddy eaters. But this is the side of community teaching which would never get written up and never get reported ...

One of the important aspects of the role was its developmental nature. Because parents were often struggling with a range of social, economic and personal difficulties, the community teacher had to be sensitive to these needs and not insist that education had priority. In addition, the community teacher felt that it was important to acknowledge that her work should be seen as long term, in that practitioners and parents would be supported in developing their confidence and skills in an incremental way over a long period of time. It was also important that the community teacher was sensitive to the work of other Sure Start workers in bringing parents to the Family Centre in the first place and ensure that parents shouldn't be frightened off by an overly formalized curriculum and an over-emphasis on educational objectives. Jan commented on her involvement with one group that:

> ... these were the family support worker groups, they weren't my groups at all it was just that one of the family workers wanted teacher input into the baby group and so that is how I became involved with that, but it had to be very low key ... Some weeks I would go and I wouldn't do anything apart from sit around and we'd talk. It seemed to be what they needed at that time and we would just talk and it didn't seem appropriate to start banging instruments and singing ... some of these parents are referred parents as well so it is important not to frighten anybody away because that could undo the work that other people have done to get these people into the centre in the first place.

These aspects of the role, and the careful, sensitive approach required to fulfil them, were necessary for the specific context within which the community teacher operated.

Multidisciplinary nature of the role

One of the main aspects of the role of community teacher in Sure Start was to work alongside other Sure Start workers, rather than operating autonomously:

> I see it as working alongside, really. With the Story Sack[1] groups, tutors from the Open College Network eventually supported the groups along with our story sacks support worker to gain a qualification in Story Sack making ... On other occasions, I worked alongside a teacher or learning mentor in school to support a parents' Story Sack making group. I would also advise other development workers on setting up and running Story Sack groups. This work eventually widened out to include advising workers in new Sure Start areas. We were all supporting each other, working alongside each other and learning from each other.

This notion of mutual support and dependency was important. The community teacher needed the knowledge and contacts of the other Sure Start workers in order to operate successfully. It was difficult for the community teacher to identify projects she had set up autonomously because:

I might have set a group up, but it would have been with the knowledge and information that the team leaders had provided about the parents and their needs. It is very difficult initially for a community teacher to get cold call customers. You can't do that because you haven't got the links established in the same way. Once I had been around the Sure Start nurseries for a long time, I could approach parents with ideas because I knew people but in the beginning you can't do that, you very much rely on the workers and settings to actually get people to join groups or act as volunteers ... and I always found the most successful work I did was where I always worked alongside an existing member of staff, for instance family literacy workshops.

It was important to recognize that, in a multidisciplinary team, people needed to learn from each other:

I had a lot to learn from the people I was working with there. I'm not a social worker, or a speech therapist and I haven't worked with drug abusers, within the domestic violence or breastfeeding advice services. I haven't got any of those skills. The speech therapists who I eventually ended up working closely with on a pilot project to develop speech and language in the area provided me with so much new information. I didn't have those skills so, obviously, as much as I could talk about education, they could actually teach me things and similarly, the parents had knowledge and understanding of their own children and the area where they live that I couldn't possibly have, so everybody, in a way, we all had things to share with each other.

Within this multidisciplinary work, a qualified teacher had a specific contribution to make:

I think one of the main things is that as a teacher my training, my knowledge base is based on child development and learning through play and it is a case of making sure that those two things go together so that any planning is child age/stage appropriate and that the workers ... as they develop they constantly remind themselves and bring them back to the child development side of things.

This confidence in articulating the nature of the role of the teacher in a multidisciplinary team is noteworthy, given that this has been a problematic area in other 'joined-up' provision. For example, in a review of the work of Early Excellence Centres, Anning (2001) notes that:

> Teams of workers from different professional practices are appointed with the brief to work in 'joined up' ways. However, little attention has been given to two significant aspects of operationalizing integrated services. The first is the challenge for workers of creating new professional identities in the emergent communities of practice (who I am). The second is for workers to articulate and share their personal and professional knowledge in order to create new versions of knowledge (what I know) for new ways of working.
>
> (Anning, 2001: 9)

In this instance, Jan felt able to articulate both 'Who I am' and 'What I know', important for effective multidisciplinary work. Given this rich range of roles and activities, it was inevitable that there were a range of key achievements for the community teacher. In the next section, some of these are reviewed.

The value of the involvement of a community teacher in an early years intervention project

One of the main achievements and key roles of the community teacher was the effective liaison work which meant that very diverse, and often isolated, settings were provided with opportunities to make links and share good practice. Jan often offered training across settings, and also set up a networking group which focused on transition. She reflected that this:

> ... enabled one conversation to be held once a term with about 12 settings instead of having to have 12 separate conversations ... it also meant that the settings, this was another achievement, the different settings in the area who had never really had anything to do with each other were actually talking. The private, the voluntary, the Local Education Authority settings were actually coming together and talking and realizing that they were ... singing from the same hymn sheet ... it was great to have people actually coming together like that.

The community teacher, therefore, had a vital role to play in the dissemination of good practice across settings in the Sure Start area and the facilitation of meetings to discuss areas of shared concern.

A second area of success and important aspect of the role was the work with parents. Jan felt that her work had enabled a number of parents to develop confidence and self esteem. This included parental attendance at Foundation Stage training sessions, in addition to the Story Sack project:

> the unqualified parent workers who not only agreed to come on training for the first time but found themselves getting involved and enjoying it and the looks on their faces when they got the certificates, a first certificate often for a lot of them, that for me personally was the most important thing and the fact that they attended and kept coming back.

In addition, the focus on quality assurance and supporting settings through OFSTED inspections meant that an important success and aspect of the community teacher role had been impacting positively on quality and standards across the settings. This is, of course, a key driver in the current governmental policy of ensuring that all early years settings have some level of qualified teacher support.

There were some challenges to the role of community teacher, however, all of which need to be considered when developing a similar model in other projects. The main challenge to Jan's work had been the varied and complex demands of the job and, related to this, the limitations of time. Jan commented that:

> I think the hardest part about this job, which comes into the weaknesses if you like, is that you are trying to gather lots and lots of fine strands together and keep ever so many balls up in the air all at the same time and also ... the practical issues of how you travel from A to B and how many settings and how many groups of staff you can actually physically get round in a week. But within that, how many relationships are properly formed and ... properly thought through and satisfied. I think that is the hard bit ...

The nature of the role meant that the community teacher was frequently asked to respond to immediate needs:

> I mean all the time I was based there, there was always somebody constantly coming in and saying, 'Can you just tell me this?' or 'Can you just tell me that?' or, 'Do you think you can just do this or just do that?' Those sorts of informal things ... that was going on all the time.

The lack of time for the demands of the role and these on-the-spot requests for support were a source of constant pressure that had to be managed. In addition, there were times when education was not given as high a priority as it could have been by other Sure Start workers, and Jan felt that, '... their focus has been on care and health and it is a health visitor driven project. I think they have found it hard ... to see things with equal value'. This issue, of course, is not specific to this programme. In a review of multidisciplinary work in Early Excellence Centres, Anning (2002) notes that:

> These practitioners are trained in different ways, have different priorities and espouse different beliefs/values.
>
> (Anning, 2002: 2)

It is inevitable, therefore, that issues of this nature should surface in Sure Start programmes. The success of this particular Sure Start project was in providing opportunities for workers to voice these areas of concern and to develop effective communication. This meant that an aspect of the role that was identified as challenging, the multidisciplinary aspect, was also for Jan a clear strength:

> I think a strength was working with the Sure Start workers – an amazingly talented group of people with all sorts of educational backgrounds themselves. I mean amazing workers, amazing workers.

A further difficulty experienced by the ccommunity teacher had been finding the balance between allowing groups to develop autonomously and identifying appropriate ways to intervene to provide guidance. This had particularly been the case in relation to the purchase of resources:

> One of the difficult areas that I found being involved with Sure Start is this balance between workers and parents having the freedom and being given the responsibility to buy resources, to spend money and buy resources for their work, and originally the programme manager wanted my support with the groups, where possible, to guide the buying and where possible I did, but I found this was a difficult animal to control. Often, it seemed as if things were bought that were not always age/stage appropriate and then I'd suddenly find I missed that opportunity ... it is this balance between ... not taking away from people, especially parents, their own progress and their own development. It is a sensitive area.

This delicate balancing act was necessary in order to ensure that parents and Sure Start workers had autonomy in relation to the purchase of educational resources and meant that the professional expertise of the community teacher sometimes had to take a back seat to other concerns, such as maintaining effective relationships with groups.

Further considerations

From the review of the work of the community teacher in Sure Start Foxhill and Parson Cross, a number of areas deserve further attention if the educational strand of this Sure Start programme were to be strengthened further. These issues are not specific to this context, of course; they could be applied usefully to other Sure Start programmes. First, the community teacher should be involved with long-term planning of their work with Sure Start managers and help to ensure that the balance of work between health, care and education within Sure Start is overtly recognized at a strategic level. In a situation such as the one outlined in this chapter, where a post is jointly 'shared' by a Sure Start programme and an education authority, a clear working mandate could be established between Sure Start and its community teacher involving, for example, a system of regular appraisal introduced in order to ensure that the community teacher's agenda related to Sure Start's targets. Having said that, a key strength of the role as envisaged in Sure Start Foxhill and Parson Cross was that flexibility was central and the community teacher was able to respond to immediate demands. A careful balancing act is needed to maintain flexibility within a clearly strategic role. In addition, the roles and responsibilities of the community teacher within individual Sure Start programmes could be made explicit to all settings and other Sure Start workers in order to ensure effective use of the teacher's professional expertise.

When Jan worked as community teacher in Sure Start Foxhill and Parson Cross, there was not a room available for her to store resources. If possible within space restrictions, programmes could provide a base in family centres for the community teacher, which might then offer space for drop-in sessions for parents and Sure Start workers. An important part of the role is providing advice and support on the purchase and use of educational resources such as toys, books, games and videos. A base such as this would enable displays to be set up for this purpose. In addition, the community teacher could seek opportunities to disseminate information about her or his work in order to ensure that it is sufficiently recognized within Sure Start programmes. This could include offering submissions for a newsletter, or putting on displays about the work within Sure Start settings. This kind of promotional work is important in raising awareness and building rapport within a community setting.

Conclusion

The work of the community teacher within Sure Start Foxhill and Parson Cross has been, and continues to be, highly successful and of central importance in raising quality across settings. In addition, the work has permeated other projects within Sure Start and this multidisciplinary work is very exciting and offers a range of opportunities for innovative work. The fact that there was no blueprint for the role of community teacher when the role was originally created did not limit its potential. Indeed, this freedom to develop a model which met the needs of the communities and the Sure Start aims and vision was an important factor in the development of the current role. As Sure Start provision continues to change in response to community needs and government initiatives, the flexibility embedded within the role of community teacher will enable that work to also develop and change accordingly, thus ensuring its long-term relevance and impact.

It is clear from this brief review that the role of community teacher is one of central importance within Sure Start. Although a Sure Start programme in its totality can be seen to be educational in nature in its work with parents and members of the community, there is a clear role for someone with qualified teacher status because of that person's training and in-depth expertise in the field of children's learning. The need for such expertise in relation to the support of voluntary and non-maintained settings has been recognized by the DfES and is now a requirement for all local authorities. The role of the community teacher as developed by Sheffield LEA is an excellent model within the national context. In particular, the way in which this role has been integrated into the work of Sure Start Foxhill and Parson Cross has been highly innovative and creative and could, we feel, offer valuable insights for others.

References

Anning, A. (2001) Knowing who I am and what I know: developing new versions of professional knowledge in integrated service settings. Paper presented to the British Educational Research Association Annual Conference, University of Leeds, 13–15 September.

Anning, A. (2002) Investigating the impact of working in integrated service delivery settings on early years practitioners' professional knowledge and practice: strategies for dealing with controversial issues. Paper presented at the Annual Conference of the British Educational Research Association, University of Exeter, England, 12–14 September.

Griffiths, N. (2001) Once upon a time. *Literacy Today*, 26(9).

Pascal, C., Bertram, T. and Ramsden, F. (1994) *The Effective Early Learning Research Project: The Quality Evaluation and Development Process.* Worcester: Worcester College of Higher Education.

Stevens, C. (in press) Perceptions of the value of Early Years Development Officers' support for voluntary pre-school playgroups, in K.M. Hirst and C. Nutbrown (eds) *Perspectives on Early Childhood Education: Contemporary Research.* Stoke-on-Trent: Trentham Books.

Note

[1] Story Sacks are a resource, developed by Neil Griffiths (2001), used to promote early reading. They consist of a sack which contains a picture storybook, along with related games and artefacts. These are intended to be used by parents with their children in the home. Many parents' groups have been involved in making these throughout the UK since their inception. For a report on the development of Story Sacks within Sure Start Foxhill and Parson Cross, see: http://www.shef.ac.uk/surestart/ssfrnt.html

12 Screening and language development
Caroline Pickstone

Introduction

Language development for young children was a main area of focus for all Sure Start programmes from the earliest thinking and was included in the PSA targets[1] set to monitor the impact of the government expenditure. Although the PSA targets evolved over time, the language targets retained their emphasis on 'normal' language and on the pattern of language attainments for the whole community as indicators of change. In 1999, one target was to have 'at least 90 per cent of children with normal speech and language development at 18 months and three years'. There seemed to be two requirements for Sure Start programmes included in this PSA target, one stated explicitly, to find out about the language attainments for the community as a whole, and a somewhat less obvious requirement, to identify children who could benefit from interventions to improve their language skills.

Although the targets have evolved to reflect changes in thinking, this first target encouraged programmes to examine the attainments for children at 18 months and 3 years. In a later development, the Sure Start Language Measure (SSLM) (SSU, 2001) was developed by a team at City University in London in the hope that it could provide a baseline measure at 24 months against which programmes could measure change. The SSLM was developed as a survey measure rather than a screening measure and was not available when Sure Start Foxhill and Parson Cross began. The programme needed to find a way of understanding language attainments in the local community.

Whilst the PSA targets provided a common focus for programmes and brought language into the foreground for discussion, there were problems in understanding and addressing them. The use of the term 'normal language' seemed to assume that language skills were easy to measure in the preschool child and that there was widespread agreement on which children fell outside the 'normal' limits. These assumptions were only partially true. Many of the problems inherent in screening children for language delay were highlighted in a systematic review (Law et al., 1998), including a lack of agreement on what constituted 'normal' language development and therefore disagreement on which children were 'cases' of delayed language. The review also highlighted concerns about predictive validity because language delay at two years of age did not necessarily lead to language problems in the long term. The proposed age points were also problematic because testing children younger than 3 years of age can be difficult, partly because tests may not have been developed using populations with similar demographic profiles, meaning that interpretation of results is difficult. Despite the challenges inherent in the task, Sure Start presented new opportunities to understand the local picture in terms of language attainments.

The local programme

The nature of work carried out in Sure Start depended to a great extent on the perceived local needs and the staffing infrastructure which was put in place to carry out the work. The local programme employed a team of support workers to visit families with children under 4 years of age in their homes to offer support with parenting. These staff had previously undertaken training in child development (nursery nursing) and had experience with young children. Could they take on the additional role of screening and surveying language skills in the local population? Asking support workers to take on a screening role was innovative because screening had typically been part of the professional role (Aylward, 1997). Screening had been regarded as 'diagnostic', requiring the practitioner to understand case history information, to test and interpret the child's presentation, and integrate all the findings in reaching a decision. However, the task for the local programme was somewhat different. The purpose was to identify children whose skills suggested that they were language delayed or 'late talkers' (Kelly, 1998), so that they could access assessment by a speech and language therapist. The major advantage of employing the support workers in this role was that they offered *universal* home visiting to minimize stigma and therefore hoped to contact the majority of local families with eligible children. Reaching a high proportion of the local population would provide the most accurate overview of language attainments and might increase the use of early assessment and intervention by the local population.

Prior to Sure Start, there was evidence that use of speech and language therapy (SLT) services by children in the local area was low. A routine local audit revealed that only 10 per cent of the expected number (based on a 10 per cent estimate of prevalence) were referred for SLT by health visitors or other referral agents. This was a somewhat unexpected finding and contrasted with the high level of language delay amongst local children at nursery entry (Locke et al., 2002). Having agreed that involvement of the support workers in a screening role would have advantages for involving families, we looked at the nature of the task.

There were several ways in which the task could be brought within the skills and training of these staff. First, the screening could focus on particular age points. Although the reason for choosing those age points was driven by the PSA targets, we recognized very early on that testing children at 18 months was likely to be difficult because of the limited availability of testing instruments (Law et al., 1998) and the acknowledged variance between children (Fenson et al., 2000). A review of instruments available for screening language in preschool children was carried out to find instruments suitable for use by support workers which were standardized on a population of children similar to the local population in terms of demography (Pickstone et al., 2002). Although 36 instruments were examined, few fulfilled the requirements. Finally, the First Words Test (FWT) (Gillham et al., 1997) was selected as a suitable instrument for use by support workers because it had been standardized on a UK population including disadvantaged families, had an appealing format, and was quick to use. The normative data for this instrument included 20–36 months and this influenced the choice of age points for the screening visits. The ages chosen for language checks were the periods 20–24 months and 31–35 months, but only the 20-24 month data will be described here.

The chosen instrument had one additional benefit in the context of a Sure Start programme in that it included parent report of language skills. Sure Start placed considerable emphasis on active involvement of parents in every aspect of programme activities. Research suggested that parent report of language skills tends to be reliable when parents are asked about current skills, when they use a structured format for the report, and when the child has fewer than 300–400 words, in the earliest stages of language development (Bates et al., 1991). This parental involvement enhanced the screening method, meaning that the child was not necessarily required to cooperate with a stranger for direct testing. This combination of methods of parent report and direct testing is not unique but was of particular value in this application.

Methods

Training

Once the decision had been made to use the First Words Test using a model of home visiting, it was possible to identify the training and supervision needs for the support workers. Although they were trained nursery nurses with experience of children of 3 years and above, they were less familiar with working in home settings and including parents. They were given additional training in language development in young children with emphasis on 18–36 months, including risk factors and training in the use of the selected instrument (a total of two days' training). Following the training, the agreement between the workers and the therapist was checked to determine whether workers made reliable recordings of the child's output. Overall, the interjudge agreement comparing the record of each word or utterance spoken by the child was good to substantial (Kappa, 0.7–1.0), confirming that workers could record child language output accurately as the basis for scoring and decisions about the child's skills. Workers received regular monthly supervision from within the programme and their day-to-day support was provided by local health visitors.

Participants

Each month, support workers received a list of those children eligible for screening (called a Talking Check), generated by the programme database and they contacted families directly. Initially, the database did not include phone numbers and so most often this contact was by letter. Having made an arrangement, the support worker visited the home and carried out the check. First, parents were asked to complete the Parent Checklist indicating words they knew that their child could say. In cases when the parent could not read, the worker went through the form with them. Parents then looked at the First Words Test picture book with the child asking 'What's this?' and the worker recorded the child's output. Parents were asked whether they would be prepared to take part in the research and a sample of those who agreed were randomly selected for follow-up by the researcher (a qualified speech and language therapist, SLT). The follow-up home visit was arranged as soon as possible after the support worker visit to minimize loss to follow-up and the researcher carried out in-depth testing to establish the child's profile on more comprehensive testing using standardized measures. The instruments used at this stage of the study included the Vineland Adaptive Behaviour Scale (VABS) (Sparrow et al., 1984) and the MacArthur Communicative Development Inventory (MCDI) (Fenson et al., 1993), both of which are parent report instruments. The development of the study sample is shown in Figure 12.1.

Research questions

The research explored the validity of this application of screening. The First Words Test was developed for use by professionals and in order to establish whether it was valid for the application by support workers, several questions were posed.

Figure 12.1 Development of the study sample at 20–24 months of age

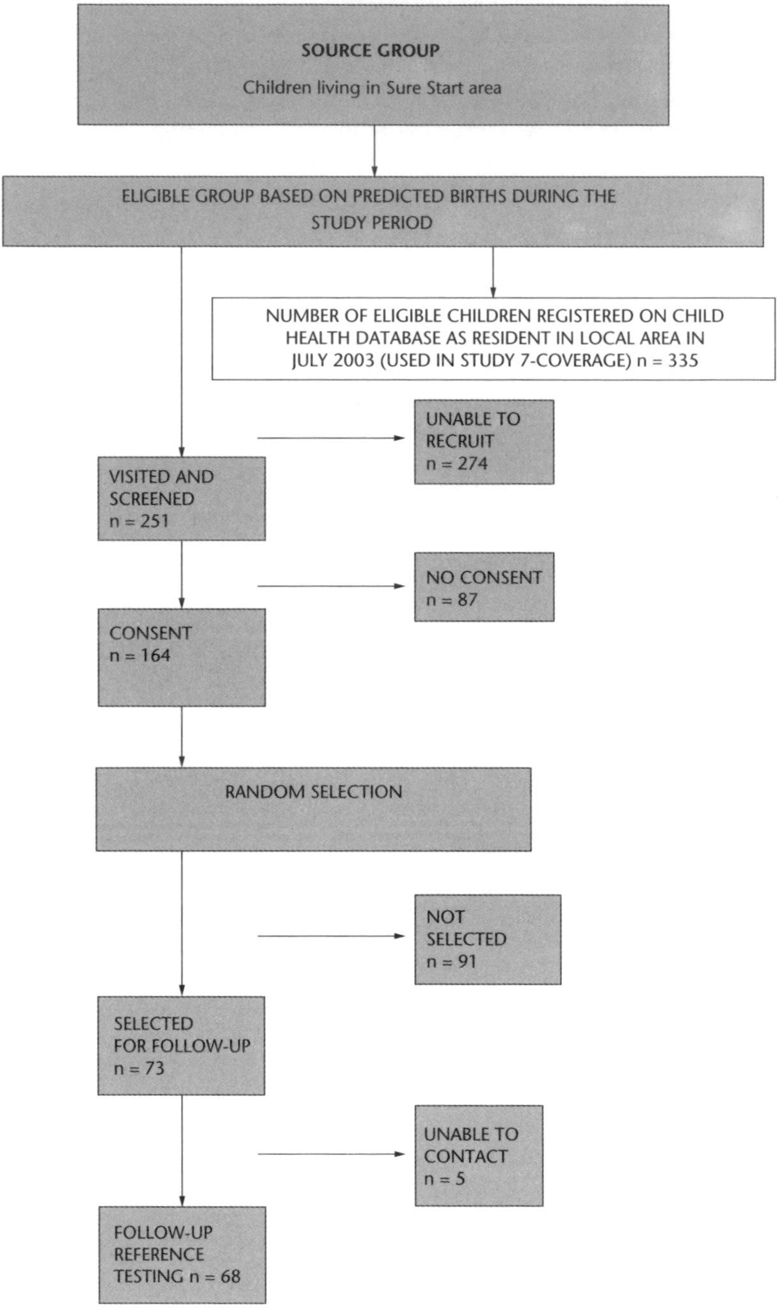

- What was the level of participation in the screening?
- Did the results of screening agree with the results on in-depth testing by a specialist?
- What was the pattern of language skills in the community at 20–24 months of age?
- Did the results of screening at 20–24 months predict later outcomes?

Results

What was the level of participation in the screening?

It can be seen from Figure 12.1 that of 525 children eligible to take part in the screening, it was not possible for the support workers to visit 274. In some cases, this was because families left the area. In other cases, repeated attempts to visit were unsuccessful. One of the first findings of this study, therefore, was that although the testing programme reached a large number of families, it was a long way short of reaching the intended number. Another source of information about participation was the Child Health database, holding records of all children who had taken part in the Child Health Surveillance programme typically offered by health visitors (HVs) in the UK. Given that workers did not engage many local families for the current study, was there any evidence that support workers engaged a different group of families, perhaps those who had no previous contact with health visitors? If such evidence could be found, it would strengthen the belief that the support worker visits had offered new opportunities for screening to families who were not reached by existing methods. If no such evidence could be found, it would strengthen the argument for visits being complementary to those offered by health visitors. In fact, an analysis of the Child Health database revealed that all the children reached by the support workers had a record of contact with the HV during the first year of life. Whilst this is not a high level of engagement with health visitors, it confirmed that workers reached a group who had at least one previous contact with a health visitor, suggesting that the visits were in fact complementary to those offered by the health visitors.

Did the results of screening agree with the results of in-depth testing by a specialist?

In order to know whether the screening tests gave a good indication of a child's performance, the results of screening were compared with in-depth testing using a number of measures by the researcher (CP). The range of language skills seen in children can be represented as being on a continuum.

This means that there is not a clear dividing line which separates children who are developing as expected from those about whom there is a concern. This requires decisions to be taken about the cut-off point to determine which children give cause for concern. For this study, the level of the 10th centile was used on the in-depth testing as the level denoting children who were delayed. The first question examined whether the results of the screening and in-depth testing agreed. The purpose of screening is to identify those children whose skills place them at the low end of the range of skills expected at that age (typically taken as performing below the 10th centile), so that they can access early intervention. Spearman rank order correlations were carried out to establish the level of agreement between the screening and the in-depth testing. The level of agreement deemed acceptable depends to some extent on the application. Where the agreement is for 'diagnostic' purposes, a level of 0.8 or above is needed (Breakwell et al., 1995). The results of the rank order correlations are shown in Table 12.1. The results of the First Words Test were highly correlated. The MCDI in-depth parent record of the child's expressive vocabulary correlated with the VABS parent report of communication skills and with the Parent Checklist by workers.

Was the level of agreement sufficient for the screening to identify children with delayed language?

Given the results of the correlations, was the agreement sufficient to distinguish those children whose skills were at or below the 10th percentile for in-depth assessment? By calculating sensitivity and specificity, it is possible to ask whether the agreement was adequate for the purpose of screening. Calculations for sensitivity (how well the test detected those children who were delayed) and specificity (how well the test detected those children whose skills were within the expected range for their age) were both 0.8 or above. This indicates that 80 per cent of children whose language is delayed would be detected by the screening tests. However, this level was achieved only when the Parent Checklist and First Words Test were both used together identifying those whose scores were below the 10th percentile on either test. When the Parent Checklist was used as a stand-alone test, the results were 0.75 (sensitivity) and 0.93 (specificity), meaning that only 75 per cent of the delayed children would have been detected. Additional analyses confirmed that the combination of tests and the use of the 10th centile as the cut-off to identify children whose skills were delayed was the most accurate way of using the instruments in this application.

Table 12.1 Correlations between support worker screening and in-depth testing including substituted median values for missing values (raw scores)

	FWT support worker	Parent Checklist SLT	FWT by SLT	VABS-C SLT	MCDI SLT
Parent Checklist support worker	0.78**	**0.87**	0.63**	0.73**	**0.85**
FWT support worker		**0.81**	**0.83**	0.64**	0.771**
Parent Checklist SLT			0.74**	0.77**	**0.88**
FWT by SLT				0.64**	0.74**
VABS-C SLT					0.75**

Abbreviations: FWT First Words Test; SLT Speech and Language Therapist; VABS Vineland Adaptive Behaviour Scale; MCDI MacArthur Communicative Development Scale
** denotes significant at the alpha level of 0.001

Did the results of screening at 20–24 months predict later outcomes?

The next question related to whether the results of screening testing in the second year of life predicted the child's skills at 4 years of age. Children in the local area were tested at entry to nursery (51–53 months of age) to show the patterns of change in terms of school readiness. The battery of tests used included the British Picture Vocabulary Scales (Dunn et al., 1997), which is a test of vocabulary comprehension. Known as 'predictive' validity, the relationship between scores at one age and another is important for screening because it confirms that the children identified at one age are those who continue to have problems with language at some later age point. The sensitivity of the screening (the statistic conventionally used to look at predictive validity) was calculated by examining the proportion of children below 10th centile at 20–24 months who scored at or below the 10th centile at 4 years. The results were disappointing (sensitivity, 0.25), meaning that there was a low level of agreement. This suggests that low expressive language scores at 20–24 months did not predict low performance on the BPVS II. However, although it was not possible to demonstrate predictive validity in this study, three factors may have influenced this: the high variance amongst children at 20–24 months; the suitability of the BPVS II for distinguishing those children with delayed language skills; and the high loss to follow-up in the sample. Of those eligible to be followed up, only 32 children were reached and 28 were lost to follow-up mainly because they had moved out of the area.

Surveying language skills and reach

A further question that arose from the findings related to whether the data from the screening tests could be applied to 'survey' language attainments in the local community. As noted above, the PSA targets had emphasized the need to establish language levels for local children as one way of measuring change as a result of Sure Start. Locally, we attempted to use the data from the screening tests to do this. There was a need to compare the result for local children with norms provided in the test manuals for the screening tools. The process of choosing a test for use in this research had emphasized standardized instruments which had been developed with populations that included disadvantaged children. The test selected was one such instrument. The norms for the Parent Checklist and for the First Words Test were compared with the norms given in the manual. When the scores were compared, local children obtained lower scores than expected and the differences were significant ($t = -7.152$, df = 72, $p = 0.0001$). When the scores were compared using the measure of effect size (showing the differences in terms of standard deviation units), local children obtained scores which were on average one standard deviation below the norms given in the manual on both the Parent Checklist and the First Words Test.

Discussion

What do these results reveal about an application of screening for delayed language in Sure Start? Mass screening for language delay was not indicated, but targeting towards those at increased risk seemed to hold promise of increasing the referrals for assessment and for improving attainments at school entry by offering early interventions (Law et al., 1998). In the case of Sure Start, targeting was based on geographical areas of disadvantage, but families living in such areas are very varied and not all the children will be at higher risk for delayed language. Although there were no obvious differences between the sample of children who took part in the screening and those who did not, the comparisons were somewhat limited being based on birth weight (target group, birth weight, 3279.18gm, eligible group 3268.09gm, support worker group 3284.27gm, $p = ns$) and probably could not reflect some of the subtle distinctions that were operating. Some of the reasons for low participation are well recognized, including high mobility of the local population. Although the screening proved to be valid when current screening scores were compared with in-depth testing, the predictive value of scores in the second year of life for outcomes at 4 was more limited. There may be several reasons for this. The BPVS may be too limited to identify children with concerns at nursery entry, focusing as it does on comprehension of vocabulary. Second, almost half the children in the screened sample were lost to follow-up having moved out of the area and of these 28 children, 6 were cases of delayed language at 20–24 months. This very high mobility makes it costly and difficult to trace children for follow-up testing, but the results are essential for a full and fair evaluation of whether this method of identifying children is a valid way to detect language delay. There is a risk that studies fail to demonstrate predictive validity because of loss to follow-up rather than because screening is not predictive. Part of the difficulty with predictive validity of screening results at 20–24 months is the wide variance amongst children developing language at this age. Some children who appear to be showing language delay at this young age will go on to show a vocabulary spurt during the third year, a pattern which seems to be encouraging for their outlook in terms of spontaneous progress. Others, however, will not show this spurt and this may be a marker for a much increased risk of persistent problems. Language checks that take place late in the third year of life may show higher predictive validity but would also be more difficult to carry out because of the much more complex nature of language development in children over 30 months. This increased complexity could mitigate against support worker involvement and, additionally, there is evidence that it remains difficult to achieve coverage at this age (Laing et al., 2002).

Even if the screening tests could be shown to be both reliable and to have predictive validity, there would inevitably be some families who choose not to take part. Children who have either missed out on the screening programme or who have not been detected by the tests will need to be able to access interventions on starting nursery or later. The emphasis on early interventions should not prevent careful consideration of other intervention possibilities and research into their potential and effectiveness.

Acknowledgement

This work has been supported by a Department of Health National Primary Care Researcher Development Fellowship to the author (granted July 2000). Thanks are due to all the families who took part, the support workers, the staff in the programme, and Professor Peter Hannon and Professor Pam Enderby at the University of Sheffield who provided advice and insights throughout.

References

Aylward, G. P. (1997) Conceptual issues in developmental screening and assessment. *Developmental and Behavioural Pediatrics*, 18: 340–9.

Bates, E., Bretherton, I. and Snyder, L. (1991) *From First Words to Grammar: Individual Differences and Dissociable Mechanisms*. Cambridge: Cambridge University Press.

Breakwell, G. M., Hammond, S. and Fife-Schaw, C. (eds) (1995) *Research Methods in Psychology*. London: Sage.

Dunn, L. M., Whetton, C. and Burley, J. (1997) British Picture Vocabulary Scale (BPVS-II), 2nd edn. Windsor, Berks: NFER-Nelson.

Fenson, L., Bates, E., Dale, P., Goodman, J., Reznick, J. S. and Thal, D. (2000) Measuring variability in early child language: don't shoot the messenger. *Child Development*, 71: 323–8.

Fenson, L., Dale, P. S., Reznick, S. J., Thal, D., Bates, E., Hartnung, J. P., Pethick, S. and Reilly, J. S. (1993) *MacArthur Communicative Development Inventory*. San Diego: Singular Publishers.

Gillham, B., Boyle, J. and Smith, N. (1997) *First Words and First Sentences Test Manual*. London: Hodder and Stoughton Educational.

Kelly, D. (1998) A clinical synthesis of the 'Late Talker' literature: implications for service delivery. *Language, Speech and Hearing Services in Schools*, 29: 76–84.

Laing, G., Law, J., Levin, A. and Logan, S. (2002) Evaluation of a structured test and a parent-led method of screening for speech and language problems: prospective population based study. *British Medical Journal*, 325: 1152–9.

Law, J., Boyle, J., Harris, F., Harkness, A. and Nye, C. (1998) Screening for speech and language delay: a systematic review of the literature. *Health Technology Assessment*, 2.

Locke, A., Ginsborg, J. and Peers, I. (2002) Development and disadvantage: implications for the early years. *International Journal of Language and Communication Disorders*, 37: 3–16.

Pickstone, C., Hannon, P. and Fox, L. (2002) Surveying and screening preschool language development in community-focused intervention programmes: a review of instruments. *Child: Care, Health and Development*, 28: 251–64.

Sparrow, S. S., Balla, D. A. and Cicchetti, D. V. (1984) *Vineland Adaptive Behaviour Scales (Interview Edition)*. Circle Pines, MI, USA: American Guidance Service.

SSU (2000) Annexe B, PSA targets for 2001–02 or earlier. London: Sure Start Unit.

SSU (2001) Sure Start Language Measure (SSLM) Information Pack. London: Sure Start Unit.

Note

1   In order to appraise value for money from Sure Start, the PSA targets were related to broad areas including 'Improving the ability to learn' SSU (2000) Annexe B, PSA targets for 2001–02 or earlier. London, Sure Start Unit. Prominent among this group of targets were those relating to language development.

13 Media, popular culture and young children
Jackie Marsh

Introduction

The lives of young children are changing rapidly in the new media age but we have, as yet, little data on the extent of these changes in UK communities. This chapter outlines a project that sought to explore the techno-literacy practices of children in the Sure Start Foxhill and Parson Cross area. This information was felt to be important for a number of reasons. First, we need to determine children's patterns of use of new media in order to understand more about their development in these crucial early years. Second, we need to explore the implications of their media use for the early years curriculum if schooling is to provide relevant and meaningful learning opportunities for children. Finally, there is much media hype about a new generation of 'couch potatoes' who face a number of perceived dangers from the leisure activities in which they engage, including increased violent behaviour (Wazir, 2001), obesity (*Guardian*, 17 September 2002), and even enlarged thumbs from playing console games (Dunning, 2002). In the face of such media hysteria, many parents and teachers may be concerned about young children's media use and there is a need to explore these practices in order to identify how they are contributing to children's education and well-being. In this chapter, findings from a small-scale study are shared and the implications of these data discussed.

Although there have been a number of studies which have provided information about the out-of-school techno-literacy practices of older children (Sanger et al., 1997; Livingstone and Bovill, 1999), there have been fewer studies which have indicated how younger children engage with a range of technologies such as television, film, computer games and mobile phones.

In Marsh and Thompson's (2001) study in the UK, 18 families in a white, working-class community in the north of England were asked to keep literacy diaries for a period of four weeks. These literacy diaries documented the number and titles of texts which 3- and 4-year-old children read over that four-week period, including televisual texts. Key findings were that, as is the case with older children (Livingstone and Bovill, 1999), televisual texts were a primary source of narrative satisfaction, with children watching television and films far more often than engaging in any other type of literacy activity. However, embedded within children's literacy practices in the home were a range of popular cultural texts such as computer (mainly console) games, comics, books based on television char acters and environmental print linked to media texts (stickers, labels, video labels, computer game boxes, and so on). This central role of television in preschool children's literacy experiences in the home has also been noted by Orellana (1994), Rodriguez (1999); Xu (1999) and Kenner (2000). These studies have analysed the place of television and media texts in bilingual children's home literacy practices and all have emphasized how children are active meaning-makers in relation to this material.

Despite the lack of extensive research in the field, the studies above provide indicative evidence that media texts and new technologies are embedded within many young children's lives. In this study, the focus was on children who were aged between $2\frac{1}{2}$ years and 3 years 11 months, and the primary aims of the study were to
identify the emergent techno-literacy practices engaged in by the children and to examine the attitudes of parents towards these practices.

Research design

The aim of this project was not to achieve a fully comprehensive picture of techno-literacy across all families in the Sure Start community, but rather to open up a new area of study by gathering the views of those families able and willing to share data with the researcher. Indeed, I would suggest that it was not possible to collect data that were representative of this community, as the concept of a homogenous community on this scale is open to question (Barton and Hamilton, 1998; Moje, 2000).

It was decided that it would be desirable to have at least 20 families in the study. Many families in the community studied would, of course, have more pressing priorities than participating in a research study. Therefore, the strategy adopted was to invite a large number of families to participate in the hope that this would generate a sufficient number of volunteers able and willing to share data. The names and addresses of 260 families, with children aged $2\frac{1}{2}$ to 3 years 11 months at the time of the study, were randomly selected from a list in the Sure Start database of families, and a questionnaire sent out to them. The questionnaire had been piloted with a group of five parents who attended sessions at the local Sure Start Family Centre. Forty-four questionnaires were returned and the average age of children in the families who returned the questionnaires was 2 years, 8 months. The questionnaires also invited respondents to volunteer to be interviewed in the home about their children's media use. Twenty-six families responded to this invitation and so the parents of 13 boys and 13 girls were interviewed. This balance in gender was not planned. In summary, the sampling strategy succeeded in reaching a sufficient number of informants (26) willing to be interviewed about techno-literacy practices in the homes of young children and almost twice that number willing to supply information in questionnaire responses.

Questionnaire and interview questions focused on children's literacy practices in the home in relation to a wide range of media such as books and comics, environmental print, television and film, computer games, mobile phones and music. Parents were asked about patterns of children's use of each of these media and then parents' attitudes towards this use were explored. Parents were also questioned about their own interaction with children as they used these media and their feelings about the use of such material in nurseries and schools were probed. Field notes were completed during home visits, notes which focused on the use of space in the living room with regard to children's artefacts and technological items and the actions and responses of children during the visit. Selections from across this range of data have been chosen in order to provide indicative examples of these children's multi-modal meaning-making practices in relation to technology. There are three aspects of children's multi-media worlds which are focused upon in this paper: television (which includes film), computer games and mobile phones.

Television

The findings from the survey indicate that television is the primary source of textual pleasure for the young children in this study. All of the families reported that children watched television regularly. Livingstone and Bovill (1999) surveyed 1303 children aged 6 to 17 years to determine their uses of new media and found that they watched, on average, two and a half hours of television per day. In Figure 13.1, it can be seen that 45 per cent of the children in the present study watched more hours of television per day than that. This may be a result of the more limited options available to younger children for engaging in other leisure activities.

There has been a range of work that has indicated that older children are not passive viewers, but active meaning-makers with regard to television (Buckingham, 1993; Robinson, 1997). In this study, parents were asked what their children did as they watched television. Only one parent responded that their child sat quietly and did not engage in other activities. Data from the other 43 families all suggested that children sat quietly at times, but they also took part in a whole range of other actions:

Figure 13.1 Hours of television viewing per day

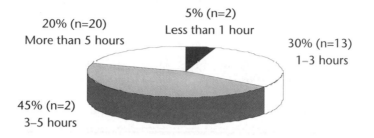

5% (n=2)
Less than 1 hour

20% (n=20)
More than 5 hours

30% (n=13)
1–3 hours

45% (n=2)
3–5 hours

Figure 13.2 What children do when they watch television

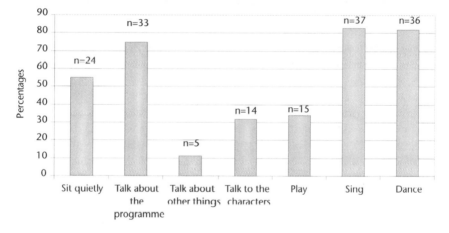

When watching television, therefore, these young children are both audience and co-performers. The data from the interviews and field notes indicated that many children acted out aspects of the programme along with the characters and imitated screen behaviour. Far from being 'couch potatoes' they were, indeed, an extremely 'lively audience' (Palmer, 1986).

The central importance of play in young children's literacy development has been extensively explored (see Roskos and Christie, 2001, for a review of this work). Through play, children make sense of the narratives they encounter in a range of modes and relate these narratives to their lived experiences (Vygotsky, 1978; Barrs, 1988). In this study, parents were supportive of their children's play and in particular encouraged playful responses to television narratives, describing how they themselves took active parts in this role play under the children's direction. For example, one parent said 'He'll role play it afterwards. You know, he'll be so and so and you've got to be such and such.' Parents frequently stated that children involved them in such play and that they were happy to take on roles in these narratives:

> Yeah, he's always Bob the Builder anyway. He's always adapting into one role or the other. But he puts me in the role as well. If he's Tigger, I'm Winnie and Pooh and things like that, you know. We always have to play out the different things, yeah.

John's mother described, as did other parents, how her child needed to have the narrative unfold in a predetermined way:

> Rug Rats – he likes to act that out after he's watched it and we have to, we all get a character. He's usually Chucky, aren't you John? He likes to play Chucky and then we all get a little bit to do and he'll just pretend to do something that's happened in that programme. And we have to respond like they do. And if you get the story wrong, you've had it!

The need to constantly revisit and/or re-present the story as experienced is also a feature of the readings of other kinds of texts, such as picture books, and is an important contribution to young children's literacy development (Campbell, 1999; Martinez, Roser and Dooley, 2003). The fact that the narratives played out in the study were based on televisual narratives may have increased parents' confidence to take part in them; in an earlier study of children's media literacy practices and parental involvement in these, parents reported that they felt more secure with popular narratives than those contained in the unfamiliar, canonical picture-book texts found in nurseries (see Marsh and Thompson, 2001). This level of familiarity with a text is important in developing parents' sense of confidence and may enhance the quality of the interaction between child and parent around a text.

The use of space in the living rooms of the 26 families visited also indicated that the television was a primary text within the home. In many of the homes visited, the area around the television appeared to be demarcated as a space for celebrating and extending children's relationship with the screen. Often, children's dressing-up clothes, toys or books which were associated with television characters were situated there, ready to be taken up by children when necessary. For example, Keiran, aged 3 years and 7 months, loved to wear his grandmother's high-heeled shoes as he watched *101 Dalmations*. The shoes were always kept next to the television. His mother stated:

> He re-enacts it. That's why we've got my mum's shoes over there. [To child] Cruella Deville, aren't you? You are Cruella Deville, aren't you? [To interviewer] And he re-enacts everything that he watches in 101 and 102 all the time … and then we'll re-enact it but we'll re-enact it for about two weeks. Honestly, if he's really

found it funny or something he can talk and talk and talk and talk. And he talks about the same thing over and over again.

As suggested earlier, the links between language, literacy and play are well established and parents in this study generally provided implicit support for this through their unquestioning acceptance of, provision for, and involvement in these responses to televisual narratives.

In addition to the recognition by parents of the importance of play as a response to television narratives, families also suggested that television had contributed to the development of a range of skills by their children, including linguistic, mathematical and social skills (see Marsh, 2002). For example, the mother of 3-year-old Dale felt that television had been instrumental in the development of his knowledge of the alphabet:

JM: Do you worry about the amount of TV he watches?
Mother: No, because he learnt all his alphabet off the telly. You know, from watching Wheel of Fortune, he just picked up the letters and it came to the point when he knew every letter, and he knows the adult alphabet, not child's ... and he knows all his colours, shapes and the lot.
JM: How old was he when he started watching the Wheel of Fortune?
Mother: Oh, about 2 and by the time he went to nursery at 3, Dale went to nursery at 3 and he knew all his alphabet.

Whether or not Dale had developed knowledge of grapheme/ phoneme correspondence through television viewing was not verified by this study, as the aims of the study did not include attention to this aspect. However, there is a range of research which suggests that such learning can indeed occur (see Singer and Singer, 2001). What is of interest here is that the data in this study provided evidence that this group of parents valued highly the role of television in their children's lives and saw it as facilitating imaginative, social and cognitive development.

Computer games

Of the 44 families surveyed, 32 stated that they owned either a computer or a console games machine, or both. Of the 26 children whose parents were interviewed, 14 played PlayStation games and half of these were girls. In this under-4 age group, therefore, there was little evidence that boys were more likely to play console games, although there is evidence that boys do dominate use in older age groups (Livingstone and Bovill, 1999). However, gendered patterns were noticeable. Many of the 14 families who stated that their children played console games described how men in the family had inducted young children into the genre:

> Well, he's always – his dad always had a PlayStation so he's also like had it from being a baby. His Dad would have him in his lap and Dan liked to sit and play, thinking he were playing it.

> Daddy'll sit behind her and she just pushes arrows to go forwards or sideways as he presses the button.

> Yeah, my husband plays with her on it. She obviously didn't know what she were doing. He were just – she just started playing with him.

In this study, it was fathers, brothers and uncles who modelled game playing for young children; only one mother reported playing the PlayStation games with her daughter. In some interviews, the mothers indicated that they knew little about playing the consoles:

> He uses the buttons. We've not got a joystick. And he does think he's playing with it – controlling the cars, you know. Daddy helps him because I don't know how to do it.

The lack of interest in playing the games expressed by mothers obviously did not deter a number of the girls from playing on PlayStation. However, the way in which gender was constructed in relation to the use of these texts was important in terms of the messages given and the potential for reinforcing essentialized gaming identities. The children were joining highly gendered communities of practice (Lave and Wenger, 1988; Paechter, 2003) in relation to PlayStation games, in contrast to the way in which traditional print literacy practices are primarily associated with female members of families (Millard, 1997).

There is emerging work which suggests that console games encourage the development of a wide range of spatial and problem-solving skills and are often based on sound learning principles (Gee, 2003). As argued elsewhere (Marsh and Millard, 2000), these games are embedded within the intertextual media universe (Kinder, 1991) of young children's lives and so they are texts that integrate with the wider popular culture interests of children. Engagement with such games may motivate children to read across categories. In an earlier study of children's media literacy practices, for example, 3- and 4-year-old children were engaged in reading computer games covers and magazines (Marsh and Thompson, 2001). Therefore, it would seem important to take a closer look at the opportunities offered by playing such games for children's learning. This is not to suggest, however, that all such games are good and that endless game-playing is appropriate for young children; rather, we should look carefully at the advantages and disadvantages of this medium and attempt to build on the positive elements in the early years curriculum. For example, creating socio-dramatic role play areas or small-world play scenarios related to some of the more popular games can be highly motivational for some children who may not otherwise be drawn to such activities (Bromley, 2002).

Mobile phones

Gillen (2002) states that 'when reference is made to ICT in curriculum documents ... it is relatively rare to see the telephone included' (Gillen, 2002: 28). This is also generally the case in relation to analyses of young children's techno-literacy practices. Yet the ubiquitous place of text-messaging in contemporary social lives must inflect itself at some level on the literacy practices of very young children. Certainly, traditional 'Loveheart' sweets which contained short messages or acronyms on them and played a popular role in many childhood games now contain text-message acronyms and messages, an indication of the way in which the text-message genre pervades the iconography of contemporary childhoods. Toys have always played a vital role in inducting children into the sociocultural practices and values of a society (Sutton-Smith, 1986; Agamben, 1993; Barthes, 1993) and many children own artefacts such as toy computers, laptops, DVD players and mobile phones, from an early age. Of the 44 children in this survey, 36 owned toy mobile phones, from an average age of 12 months. Although none of the children used text-messaging, many were aware of it and knew when a message had arrived for their parents. The mother of Kay, aged 2 years, 9 months, stated that:

> If the phone beeps, 'Mom, you've got a message!', like that – that's all they ever say, yeah. They know what the beep's for. They're more bothered about tones and rings. You know, the ring tones what you can get on it?

Some children watched as their parents read and responded to text-messages and were thus becoming acculturated into the world of electronic print mediated through mobile phones. It is inevitable that the family context is a key site for the induction into text-messaging practices because, as Alexander et al. suggest (2001):

> family life is embedded in recurring activities and mediated by particular discourse practices, and ... young children come to orient

themselves within particular systems of meaning by participating in these everyday social practices.

(Alexander et al., 2001: 379)

In addition to mobile phone practices within the home, toys, sweets, adverts and television programmes all reflect this technological landscape of text messages, ring-tones and emoticons, and thus the communicative practices related to mobile phones are firmly embedded within the lives of contemporary children.

Conclusion

Throughout the paper, it can be seen that these young children's engagement with a range of contemporary texts and artefacts contributes to our understanding of 'emergent techno-literacy'. These contemporary communicative practices were recognized and encouraged by parents, but, when children begin to attend nursery, only very selective areas of their home literacy experiences are normally focused upon – largely story-book reading and writing on paper (Marsh, 2003). Thus, the literate identities of these young children as they begin formal schooling will, no doubt, have to accommodate to this selective focus and this may lead to the marginalization of their competence in the use of electronic media. Instead, these practices should be valued and the place they play in the development of children as competent users and producers of media texts and artefacts acknowledged in curriculum frameworks for the early years. If this does not happen, then the gap between home and school for children in this Sure Start community, as in many others, may continue to be wider than it needs to be.

References

Agamben, G. (1993) *Infancy and History: The Destruction of Experience*, trans. Liz Heron. London: Verso.

Alexander, K.J., Miller, P.J. and Hengst, J.A. (2001) Young children's emotional attachments to stories. *Social Development*, 10(3): 374–98.

Barrs, M. (1988) 'Maps of play' in M. Meek and C. Mills (eds) *Language and Literacy in the Primary School*. London: Falmer Press.

Barthes, R. (1993) *Mythologies*, trans. Anette Lavers. London: Vintage.

Barton, D. and Hamilton, M. (1998) *Local Literacies: Reading and Writing in One Community*. London: Routledge.

Bromley, H. (2002) I've got that man at home: roles, realities and representations in children's play. Paper presented at ESRC Seminar on Children's Literacy and Popular Culture, accessed 25 June 2004 at: http://www.shef.ac.uk/literacy/ESRC/seminar2.html

Buckingham, D. (1993) *Changing Literacies: Media Education and Modern Culture*. London: Tufnell.

Campbell, R. (1999) *Literacy from Home to School: Reading with Alice*. Stoke-on-Trent: Trentham Books.

Dunning, M. (2002) 'Thumbs', *Guardian*, 25 March 2002.

Gee, J.P. (2003) *What Video Games Have to Teach Us About Learning and Literacy*. New York: Palgrave Macmillan.

Gillen, J. (2002) Moves in the territory of literacy? The telephone discourse of three- and four-year-olds. *Journal of Early Childhood Literacy*, 2(1): 21–43.

Guardian (2002) Childhood obesity at 'epidemic' levels, 17 September.

Kenner, C. (2000) *Home Pages: Literacy Links for Bilingual Children*. Staffordshire: Trentham Books.

Kinder, M. (1991) *Playing with Power in Movies: Television and Video Games from Muppet Babies to Teenage Mutant Ninja Turtles*. Berkeley: University of California Press.

Lave, J. and Wenger, E. (1991) *Situated Learning: Legitimate Peripheral Participation*. Cambridge: Cambridge University Press.

Livingstone, S. and Bovill, M. (1999) *Young People, New Media*. London: London School of Economics.

Marsh, J. (2002) *Children and Media Project: A Research and Evaluation Report for Sure Start Foxhill and Parson Cross*, accessed October 2002 at: http://www.sheffield.ac.uk/surestart/reports/Foxhill/pdf/ch_media.pdf

Marsh, J. (2003) One-way traffic? Connections between literacy practices at home and in the nursery. *British Educational Research Journal*, 29(3): 369–82.

Marsh, J. (2004) The techno-literacy practices of young children. *Journal of Early Childhood Research*, 2(1): 51–66.

Marsh, J. and Millard, E. (2000) *Literacy and Popular Culture: Using Children's Culture in the Classroom*. London: Paul Chapman.

Marsh, J. and Thompson, P. (2001) Parental involvement in literacy development: using media texts. *Journal of Research in Reading*, 24(3): 266–78.

Martinez, M., Roser, N. and Dooley, C. (2003) Young children's literary meaning making, in N. Hall, J. Larson and J. Marsh (eds) *Handbook of Early Childhood Literacy*. London, New Dehli, Thousand Oaks, CA: Sage.

Millard, E. (1997) *Differently Literate: Boys, Girls and the Schooling of Literacy*. London: Falmer.

Moje, E. (2000) Critical issues: circles of kinship, friendship, position and power: examining the community in community-based literacy research. *Journal of Literacy Research*, 32: 77–112.

Orellana, M.F. (1994) Appropriating the voice of the superheroes: three preschoolers' bilingual language uses in play. *Early Childhood Research Quarterly*, 9: 171–93.

Paechter, C. F. (2003) Masculinities and femininities as communities of practice. *Women's Studies International Forum*, 26(1): 69–77.

Palmer, P. (1986) *The Lively Audience: A Study of Children Around the TV Set.* Sydney, London: Allen & Unwin.

Robinson, M. (1997) *Children Reading Print and Television*. London: Falmer Press.

Rodriguez, M.V. (1999) Home literacy experiences of three young Dominican children in New York City. *Educators for Urban Minorities*, 1(1): 19–31.

Roskos, K. and Christie, J. (2001) Examining the play-literacy interface: A critical review and future directions. *Journal of Early Childhood Literacy*, 1(1): 59–89.

Sanger, J. with Willson, J., Davies, B. and Whitaker, R. (1997) *Young Children, Videos and Computer Games*. London: Falmer Press.

Singer, D.G. and Singer, J.L. (2001) *Handbook of Children and the Media*. New York: Sage.

Sutton-Smith, B. (1986) *Toys as Culture*. New York: Gardner Press.

Vygotsky, L. (1978) *Mind in Society: The Development of Higher Psychological Processes*. Cambridge, Mass.: Harvard University Press.

Wazir, B. (2001) Violence makes games 'unsuitable for children', *The Observer*, 16 December.

Xu, S.H. (1999) Young Chinese ESL children's home literacy experiences. *Reading Horizons*, 40(1): 47–64.

Acknowledgement

This chapter is based on a paper which appeared in the *Journal of Early Childhood Research* (Marsh, 2004).

14 A dialogic reading intervention programme for parents and preschoolers
Anne Morgan

Introduction

This chapter describes a short intensive programme designed to enhance children's vocabulary and descriptive language skills by introducing parents to specific techniques for reading with their young children. The programme was tried in the Sure Start area to investigate its suitability and effectiveness within Sure Start. The dialogic reading programme was originally developed in the United States (Whitehurst et al., 1988). Its aim was to enhance children's vocabulary and descriptive language skills by encouraging parents to use specific techniques when reading with their children. It was devised using a combination of techniques taken from existing studies and theories. There were three general principles:

- *Evocative techniques.* These are techniques that encourage the child to take an active role; for example 'what' questions are encouraged because they require a verbal response from the child, whereas 'where' or 'yes/no' questions are discouraged because they require a limited or non-verbal response.
- *Feedback.* This should be informative and where possible include corrective modelling, with the adult encouraging the child to recognize the correct form and to say it. If possible, expansions of the child's response should also be incorporated.
- *Progressive change.* This refers to adjusting questions to the child's developing abilities; the adult helps the child to achieve just a little more than they ordinarily would through questioning and encouragement.

Dialogic reading had achieved encouraging results in the US, with the most significant developments occurring in children's vocabulary skills. Taking Sure Start principles into account (building on evidence of effectiveness, involving parents and carers and being culturally appropriate and sensitive to particular needs), there were some concerns regarding parents' receptiveness to a prescriptive programme such as this. The programme was therefore trialled with a relatively small number of families, and, before considering extending the programme, its appropriateness could then be assessed by seeking participants' views.

Aims and content of the dialogic reading programme

The main aim of this programme was to enhance children's vocabulary skills. A secondary aim was the development of children's early book skills, which would enhance their ability to thrive once they started school. These aims were to be achieved by introducing parents to specific techniques for reading with their children.

Target group

The target group was parents and children within the age range of $2\frac{1}{2}$ to 3 years old.

Methods

The programme was implemented using an experimental design, with an experimental programme group and a control group. This was considered to be the most appropriate method, since it enables causality to be established. If the programme group were significantly ahead of the control group on language skills after the intervention, the only plausible explanation would be that the programme itself had affected these skills. Interviews with parents were also used to find out more about the effects of the programme. The experimental design meant that there was a technical component to the way the programme was conducted and the way it is reported here. It will be described in sufficient detail for those interested in the work to find sufficient information to replicate it elsewhere.

Model of delivery

This was a short, intensive programme which lasted for six weeks. Forty parents were interviewed before the programme and children were assessed on language and literacy skills. The children and their parents were then randomly assigned to programme or control groups. Those assigned to the programme group were invited to attend a session introducing the dialogic reading techniques at their local Sure Start Family Centre. Three weeks later, they were invited to a second session to explain ways of extending the techniques. The sessions were very informal, with light refreshments and a crèche provided. There were also weekly home visits when books were exchanged and families' experiences and concerns discussed. At the end of the programme, children's language and literacy skills were assessed and parents interviewed about their experiences. The parents and children originally assigned to the control group were offered the dialogic reading programme several months later.

Resources

A videotape introducing the dialogic reading techniques was obtained from the United States (Huebner, 2001). Eighteen different book titles were used so each family could borrow three books each week for the duration of the programme. Four sets of each title were available, which meant that the programme required a total of 72 books. Since dialogic reading encourages discussion of pictures, books were selected primarily for picture quality and their potential for interaction. Language and literacy assessment materials were required, to evaluate the programme.

Staffing

The programme was designed and implemented by a single researcher (the author). A colleague who did not know which group families had been assigned to also conducted a number of the post-programme assessments.

Contribution to the Sure Start programme

This programme principally contributes to the Sure Start objective of 'improving children's ability to learn'. Specifically, the programme was designed to address Sure Start's concern with ensuring that the majority of children have normal speech and language development in their first four years, since the dialogic reading programme targeted language skills. As such positive results had been achieved in the United States, the programme appeared to have much to offer. In addition, young children's early literacy skills could be enhanced through participation in a dialogic reading programme.

Research questions for the dialogic reading programme

There were three key research questions for this programme:

1 What is the nature of the home literacy practices of the families before the intervention?

This question was included because it was considered helpful to determine the extent to which families used 'dialogic'-type techniques before participating in the programme. Information about families' home literacy practices could also help in judging the amount of support parents were likely to need when implementing the new techniques.

2 Can parents be taught to use dialogic reading techniques?

The most rigorous way of determining the extent to which parents were using the techniques would involve observations of parents and children reading together. A less precise, but still valid method would be through interview and informal discussion. After careful consideration, it was decided not to observe dialogic interactions, mainly because this would be intimidating and parents might have felt that they were being judged. Instead, the extent to which parents adopted the techniques was gauged through informal weekly visits to each family, reading diary entries and through interviews.

3 What is the value of a dialogic reading programme?

The value of the programme was measured in three ways: the parents' views of the programme, parents' perceptions of the benefits of the programme and a statistical analysis of children's assessment scores.

Method of conducting the dialogic reading programme

Subjects and sampling

Forty parents and children participated in the study. All participants lived within the programme area. Names of 101 children aged $2\frac{1}{2}$ to 3 years living in the area were obtained from a database held by Sure Start. Families in difficult situations and children identified with behavioural or learning difficulties were excluded from the study after discussions with health visitors. Although it was anticipated that the programme might benefit such children, children with typical development were the focus of this trial. The sample was then allocated at random from the 78 remaining families. Forty postal invitations to participate in the study were sent out and these postal invitations were followed up with a home visit. In cases where parents declined to participate or could not be contacted after three visits, a replacement was randomly chosen.

Pre-test assessment

The study used a matched pair experimental design. This means pairs of children were matched as closely as possible in terms of age, gender and language assessment scores. One of the pair joined the programme group and the other joined the control group. For the language assessment, the Preschool Language Scale-3 (PLS-3; Psychological Corporation Ltd. 1997) was chosen, because it measures a broad range of language skills and includes both expressive and receptive language. In addition, the 'books' strand of the Sheffield Early Literacy Development Profile (SELDP; Nutbrown, 1997) was used to evaluate children's book knowledge. The books strand assesses knowledge about the features of books, asking children to identify, for example, the front of the book, pages, pictures and words. It also asks children to recount the main events in the story after looking at the pictures.

There were no significant differences between the two groups before the programme took place on either assessment, although the control group were slightly ahead on mean scores for all the assessments.

Post-test assessment

Immediately after the programme, children were assessed on tests of receptive vocabulary (British Picture Vocabulary Scale, BPVS, Dunn et al., 1997) and expressive vocabulary (Expressive One Word Picture Vocabulary Test, EOWPVT, Gardner, 2000). A second test of expressive vocabulary, 'My Word', a non-standardized vocabulary assessment of the author's devising, was also used. It consisted of black and white photographs from the books used in this study that were judged to call for novel vocabulary. The books strand of the SELDP (Nutbrown, 1997) was also used.

Previous studies had assessed children's descriptive language skills. However, in this programme, assessments had to be carried out in one session. As a result, the number of assessments had to be limited, since children may tire or become stressed if sessions are too long. Therefore, the decision was made not to test for descriptive language skills.

There were two types of analysis of these assessments. In the first 'between subjects' analysis, results for children in the programme and the control groups were compared on all assessments. In the second 'within *subjects'* analysis, children's scores on the pre-programme SELDP (books) were compared with those from the post-programme SELDP (books).

The dialogic reading programme in action

Two sessions introducing the techniques to parents were provided three weeks apart. At each session, the importance of daily reading was emphasized and the dialogic techniques were introduced using a videotape (Huebner, 2001). Some procedures for parents were presented (see Table 14.1) and these were followed by taped extracts of an adult reading a book with a child. The dialogic reading techniques were demonstrated using a child's picture book, with the session leader playing roles of both adult and child. Parents were then given a children's book and asked to think of appropriate questions they could ask their child.

Table 14.1 Procedures for parents

	Procedures for parents	*Goals for the child*
Session 1: Tips to build vocabulary	Ask 'what' questions	Noun labels
	Follow answers by the child with questions	Attribute and function labels
	Repeat what the child says	Turn taking
	Help the child with answers when needed	
	Praise and encourage	
	Follow the child's interest	
	Have fun	
Session 2: Tips to build sentence skills	Ask open-ended questions	Multiword expression
	Ask follow-up questions	Story and picture structure
	Expand what the child says	
	Have fun	

Source: Whitehurst, Arnold et al., (1994: 683)

At the end of the initial session, parents were given a folder containing three books to read dialogically with their children over the following week. The folder also contained some 'hints for questions', a summary of the procedures for parents and a reading diary, which they were asked to complete each time they read. Parents were asked to read dialogically every day for between five and ten minutes. They were visited each week to exchange books and to discuss any concerns or queries they had.

What are we learning?

The findings of the programme are discussed in relation to the research questions.

1 What is the nature of the home literacy practices of the families before the intervention?

Forty families (both control and programme groups) were interviewed about their home literacy practices before the programme. Literacy activities, in particular interactions around books, were occurring in the majority of families, although the nature and frequency of home literacy experiences varied. Most parents felt their children were interested in books, and virtually all parents sometimes read with their children. Parents all had aspirations for their children's later reading and writing attainment.

Parents were asked to describe features of their reading interactions. Seven said that they read the book while the child listened. Five parents made comments such as 'I don't think we do anything consciously', implying perhaps that they read the whole book from beginning to end. One described shared reading as an interaction in which the mother read the text while the child lifted the flaps and turned the pages. Twenty-seven parents described certain dialogic aspects of their reading interactions with their children. The technique most frequently mentioned was asking questions.

The majority of parents were already interacting with their children during reading to some extent. The dialogic reading programme could provide an opportunity to build on these existing practices and increase interaction. This was a solid base from which to begin the programme.

2 Can parents be taught to use dialogic reading techniques?

Attendance at programme sessions varied. Nineteen parents arranged to attend the first session, although only 13 parents actually attended. The remaining seven were introduced to the techniques at home. Only six parents attended the second session three weeks later, although 13 had arranged to attend. Twelve were introduced to the techniques at home. Two families dropped out of the programme. One gave no reason, while the other felt the programme books were not appropriate for her son.

Of the 18 parents who completed the programme, 9 said they found the techniques quite difficult to use initially. For these parents, it seemed dialogic reading was very different to the shared reading methods they had used previously. The techniques required practice. Seven parents said that the techniques were not difficult to apply, and two initially felt that they might find the techniques difficult to use, although when they began to read with their children, found this was not the case.

Fourteen parents described using specific aspects of the programme, suggesting that they were using the techniques. These 14 all mentioned they had increased their use of questioning. Six of these also mentioned an increase in discussions with their child, implying that shared reading sessions had become more interactive, with the roles of both parent and child being of equal importance. For example, one parent said:

> Rather than just reading the book to her, I let her get more involved by stopping me and saying 'Look mummy, look what he's doing!' whereas before I'd have just said 'Quiet, let me read the book!' Now she stops me and we talk about it more.

Only one parent mentioned techniques introduced in the second training session, which focused on encouraging the child to say a little more than they ordinarily would:

> I'm more aware about asking questions now, and about taking him that 'little bit further' part of it.

No parents mentioned increasing their use of praise and repeating the child's correct response, and only one described how she asked her son to repeat her extended response.

Parents were asked how frequently they had read with their child over the duration of the programme. Ten answered 'on average, several times a week'; five had read 'most days'. Only three said they had managed to read dialogically every day. Fourteen felt being in the programme had increased the frequency of their shared reading sessions. This was often because reading together had become more enjoyable with the dialogic reading techniques.

The information gathered suggested that virtually all parents were implementing the techniques to some degree. While most reported an increased use of simple questioning, few reported using open-ended questions or expanding children's responses. However, there were varying rates of participation, with few families managing to read every day.

3 What is the value of a dialogic reading programme?

Parents' views of the programme

The majority of parents made positive comments about the programme. All felt the video training method was appropriate. The only slightly negative comments, made by four parents, related to the fact that the techniques were not really different to methods they already used. None reported finding participating in the project a pressure.

Parents were asked to describe positive and negative features of the programme. Views about positive aspects varied from learning a new way of reading to benefits for the child. Only seven parents could identify a negative aspect of the programme. In every case, this related to difficulties in finding time to read, or feeling guilty about not reading every day.

Concerns that the programme may not have been appropriate appeared to have been unfounded; no parents felt that the programme was too prescriptive.

Parents' perceptions of the effects of the programme

Parents were asked whether they thought their children had been affected at all by the programme. Sixteen believed that their children had benefited in some way. All sixteen mentioned the enjoyment aspect of reading together dialogically.

Most also mentioned general benefits such as, 'I think it's fetched her on really well.' Two said that their children's confidence had increased. Eight specifically mentioned an improvement in concentration during shared reading. Most of these parents felt that, as a result, their shared reading sessions were longer, for example:

> We seem to spend a lot longer looking at books now; before she used to get bored quickly.

Eleven parents said the techniques had helped to develop their children's language. Most of these spoke of an increase in verbal participation during reading, such as:

> Emily anticipates that I'm going to ask her more questions, so she's started saying more about the pictures without being asked. She's definitely saying a lot more now.

A few parents mentioned an enhancement of vocabulary skills, for example:

> … She seems to know more words, and if she hears a word now and she doesn't know what it means, she'll ask me what it means.

When asked whether the programme had made any difference to them, most parents responded in terms of the effect it had on their reading methods. One mother said it had brought her and her child closer together.

Only one specifically described the impact the programme had had on her. This parent, who had found learning to read difficult herself commented:

> I've enjoyed reading, whereas before I hated the thought of books.

All parents said that they would continue reading using dialogic reading methods and all were in favour of the programme being offered to other families. One felt the programme should be extended to include parents of nursery children:

> ... people don't know how to read with children. They (in nursery) give you the books but they don't tell you what to do.

In summary, the majority of parents valued the programme and felt it had helped their children in a variety of ways. Some thought their children had benefited in terms of vocabulary acquisition, a number mentioned enhanced concentration, confidence or enjoyment of books. Some said the programme had increased their own awareness of what to look for when reading with their children. All felt the programme should be offered to other families.

Post-programme assessments

This section reports the technical findings of the assessments, which basically show that there were no statistically significant differences for the programme group over the control group for vocabulary or early book skills. However, the tests showed that the early book skills of the programme group were significantly enhanced by the intervention.

Table 14.2 shows the means and standard deviations for the children in the two groups. The means for the programme group were slightly above those for the control group on every assessment. Although the scores for the programme group were lower than those of the control group on the pre-programme language and literacy assessments, they were now higher than those of the control group.

For the between groups analysis, a t-test was carried out. No statistically significant differences between the programme and control groups existed for any of the four post-programme assessments. For the standardized EOWPVT: $t(32) = -.876$, $p = .388$, for 'My Word': $t(30) = 1.572$, $p = .126$, for the BPVS: $t(26) = .384$, $p = .704$ and for the SELDP (books): $t(26) = 1.056$, $p = .301$.

Table 14.2 Children's post-programme assessment scores

	EOWPVT	'My Word'	BPVS	SELDP
Control group				
Mean	87.71	4.75	25.86	3.64
SD	9.51	3.73	11.79	2.17
N	17	16	14	14
Programme group				
Mean	90.88	8.00	27.36	4.57
SD	11.54	7.38	8.66	2.47
N	17	16	14	14

*Note regarding numbers: Not all children completed all post-programme assessments, usually due to lack of cooperation or tiring. If this was the case, that child and the child they had been matched with in the other group were excluded from the analysis for that particular test. This was felt to be the most rigorous method of analysis. Thus, there were different numbers of children in the analysis for different tests.

Table 14.3 illustrates the means and standard deviations for SELDP (books) scores before and after the programme. The control group performed slightly better at post-test, whereas the mean for the programme group increased markedly, from 2.93 before the intervention to 4.57 at post-test. A paired samples t-test was carried out for each group on the pre- and post-programme SELDP (books). This was significant for the programme group, t (13) = –3.453, p = .004; mean difference –.96 ± 1.95 (95 per cent CI), and not significant for the control group, t (13) = .747, p = .468; mean difference –.279 ± –.64 (95 per cent CI). These results suggest that the programme group's early book knowledge increased as a direct result of the dialogic reading intervention programme. Effect size for the SELDP (books) was 0.40. According to Cohen's (1977) convention, this is approaching a medium effect size. Thus, although there were no statistically significant differences between the programme and control groups' SELDP (books) scores, there may have been some practical, or educationally significant effect.

Table 14.3 SELDP (books) pre- and post-programme scores

	SELDP (books) pre-programme	SELDP (books) post-programme
Control group		
Mean	3.50	3.64
Median	3.0	4.0
SD	3.03	2.17
N	14	14
Programme group		
Mean	2.93	4.57
Median	2.0	4.5
SD	2.37	2.47
N	14	14

Discussion: What have we found out from the dialogic reading programme?

The most notable feature of the programme was that, while there was no measurable effect on children's language skills, most parents were able to engage, and felt that their children had benefited from taking part. Programme children's early book skills were significantly enhanced. Parents and children enjoyed reading using the techniques and said that they would continue to read dialogically.

There were a number of problems involved in actually putting the programme into practice which need considering for future research. First, attendance at programme sessions tended to be relatively low (in keeping with other work reported in the area, see Chapters 12 and 13), so a large number of parents were introduced to the techniques at home, which was very time-consuming. Second, although they were asked to read daily, only three families said they had managed to do this. In such a short, intensive programme, low participation is likely to have affected the overall result. Future research could possibly consider whether it is possible to increase attendance and participation on such programmes.

Another problem related to assessment administration. It was felt that conducting assessments in homes was not ideal, as children were often distracted in the home environment. The 'community-based' nature of the programme also needs reconsideration. Many hours each week were spent visiting families at home in order to change books. While this was a valuable experience, and provided an opportunity to discuss issues with families in their own homes, it was extremely time-consuming. Sometimes, families were not at home. If the study had been based in a nursery, parents could have exchanged books there on a given day. A nursery-based programme would also have meant that children could have been assessed within the nursery environment, rather than at home. Parents may have been more likely to agree to participate in a nursery based programme, viewing it as being associated with school, and therefore worthwhile. A number of studies (Tizard and Hughes, 1984; Hannon and Nutbrown, 2001) which approached parents through nurseries and schools reported a 100 per cent take up rate. The programme reported here achieved a lower take up rate of 56 per cent, which is in keeping with other work conducted in the area, and with 'hard to reach' families. This was probably due to a number of factors, one of which was because it involved 'cold calling', but also due to the overarching difficulty of engaging the whole cross-section of families in activities Sure Start has to offer.

To summarize, this programme achieved mixed results. Although parents valued the programme and adopted the techniques to some extent, there was no evidence that the main aim of the programme, that of enhancing children's vocabulary skills, was achieved. It is possible that language skills not assessed may have been affected, since a number of parents reported an increase in interactions between the parent and their child after the programme. There was evidence that children's early book knowledge had increased. Equally important, however, were parent reports of increased enjoyment and their child's interest in reading.

References

Cohen, J. (1977) *Statistical Power Analysis for the Behavioral Sciences*, revised edition. New York: Academic Press.

Dunn, L.M., Dunn, L.M., Whetton, C. and Burley, J. (1997) *The British Picture Vocabulary Scale*, second edition. London: NFER-Nelson.

Gardner, M.F. (2000) *Expressive One-Word Picture Vocabulary Test* [Revised]. Novato, CA: Academic Therapy.

Hannon, P. and Nutbrown, C. (2001) *Emerging Findings from an Experimental Study of Early Literacy Education Involving Parents*. Paper presented at the UKRA Annual Conference, Canterbury, July.

Huebner, C.E. (2001) *Hear and Say Reading with Toddlers*. Rotary Club of Bainbridge Island, Washington.

Nutbrown, C. (1997) *Recognizing Early Literacy Development: Assessing Children's Achievements*. London: Chapman.

Psychological Corporation Ltd. (1997) *The Preschool Language Scale – 3 (UK)*. London: Psychological Corporation Ltd.

Tizard, B. and Hughes, M. (1984) *Young Children Learning: Talking and Thinking at Home and at School*. London: Fontana.

Whitehurst, G.,Arnold, D., Epstein, J., Angell,A., Smith, M. and Fischell, J. (1994) A picture book reading intervention in daycare and home for children from low-income families. *Developmental Psychology*, 30: 279–689.

Whitehurst, G. J., Falco, F., Lonigan, C.J., Fischel, J.E., Valdez-Menchaca, M.C. and Caulfield, M. (1988) Accelerating language development through picture-book reading. *Developmental Psychology*, 24: 552–8.

Part Five
Strengthening families and communities

15 Community involvement
Helen Lomas and Peter Hannon

Introduction

Sure Start aims to have community involvement in the delivery and management of services. This was a concern of the Foxhill and Parson Cross group before the Sure Start programme was approved. After it began, there was a commitment to meeting the fourth of Sure Start's objectives.

> **Objective 4: Strengthening families and communities**
> In particular by involving families in building the community's capacity to sustain the programme and thereby create pathways out of poverty.

One of the specific national targets associated with this objective also matched the programme's aims.

> All Sure Start programmes to have parent representation on the local programme board.

Families may want to *use* services in a programme but is it, in practice, realistic to *involve* them in the programme itself? Can a programme achieve genuine parent representation on its management board? In this chapter we want to reflect on these questions and on what we have learned about involving members of the community, particularly parents.

Learning about community involvement

This chapter is written by Helen Lomas, a local parent and, at the time of writing, the Community Development and Training Co-ordinator for the programme, and Peter Hannon from the University research team. It was in 2002, the second year of the programme, that we started looking seriously at community involvement. By then, the programme already had two years' experience of community involvement (three, if the months of work and consultation leading up to submitting the original application for a Sure Start programme are counted too).

We thought about how we could learn from past experience and how that could influence further work to involve the community. We decided to begin by the two of us having taped discussions about the different ways in which parents became involved in the programme and about Helen's role in working with parents. In 2004 we taped a further discussion. Tapes of discussions were transcribed and the two of us met to review the transcripts. That developed our thinking and led to the idea of Helen writing a personal account of her own involvement in the programme. We also invited two other parents (both mothers) to write their stories. The three stories appear later in this chapter. We were interested in how much parents were really engaged in decision making in the programme, so Peter observed one of the Partnership Board meetings to check what the various members did and said. We devised a simple open-ended questionnaire for parents who had served on the Board. We also looked at records of attendances at Board meetings from the start of the programme.

Learning about this aspect of Sure Start therefore meant using a mix of methods: reviewing past experience (by taping, transcribing and reflecting on a series of conversations); collecting stories from individual members of the community who had become involved in the programme; observing involvement in action, counting attendances and seeking views through a questionnaire survey.

What the programme did to promote involvement

When the original bid for a Sure Start programme was publicized in the area, it was met with reservations and a certain amount of uncertainty due to previous projects having insecure funding and running only for short periods of time. Some comments were 'Oh, how long is this one going to last for?', 'Six months and you'll all be gone again' and 'I'm not getting involved – it's not worth it'. But gradually, those barriers were broken down by holding focus groups with other local parents all the way through the process, asking them what they would like to see in their area. One of the parents agreed to help with the actual writing of the original application.

When the programme was approved, a group of local women worked alongside parents to involve them in the development of the programme and its services. All local toddler groups, playgroups, baby clinics, and other community groups were visited in the area to promote Sure Start and its aims, and information leaflets were given out to parents, who registered with us to inform them how they also could become involved in the programme itself.

The programme's aim was to initiate, involve and maintain participation and involvement of local parents in all aspects of the programme. This was to be done by providing support and informing all local parents about the Sure Start programme and its services and activities through holding meetings visiting groups, visiting other community places, centres and so on, visiting people's homes and also holding fun events.

'Check It Out' groups were monthly events, giving the chance for parents to raise any issues. They were a sounding-board – really informal, coffee, no agenda and a chance for programme staff to check out any new ideas for the programme. From this group, parents who were that little bit more interested in working alongside the programme, and maybe becoming involved in decision making, came forward or showed interest in moving on to the next stage.

'Parent Forum' meetings were developed as the next stage of involvement. Before we developed this group it was straight from the Check It Out group to the Board meetings and there was nothing in between. Subgroups were set up to become part of the structure of the newly formed Partnership Board. Their meetings were held bi-monthly and supported by a worker and a crèche. Parents who attended the forum meetings could also access any training available.

Partnership Board meetings were held monthly at first, and then every three months as the programme developed. Parents were supported to attend these by the parent involvement workers and also by providing training where necessary. Refreshments and crèches were available at all meetings.

As the programme has developed, the parent involvement work has increased and a team is now in place to cater for all parents who want to become more involved in the programme or who want to return to education, training or employment.

Volunteers are also a vital part of parental involvement. The programme has an increasing number of parents who have become involved and moved on to volunteer officially for NCH (the voluntary organization that acts as the 'accountable body' for the programme). Volunteering is very rewarding for some parents, and after being involved in meetings and groups it was the natural next step for them before employment.

In 2002, in the course of one of the discussions she had with Peter, Helen came up with the idea of a 'ladder of involvement'.

A 'ladder' is only one way to describe parents' developing involvement in the programme. It emerged during the research process but later turned out to be a useful way of getting ideas across to parents. Figure 15.1 shows how it is presented to parents. The Parent Involvement Team uses the ladder, now part of an information pack, to explain different ways of becoming involved in the programme. They explain that support is available

Figure 15.1 The involvement ladder

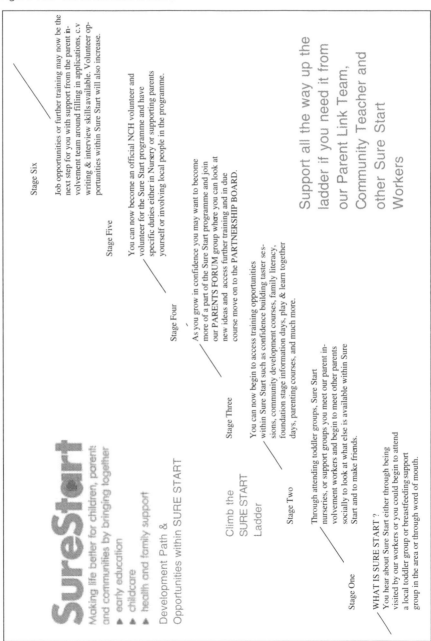

all the way up the ladder, but also emphasize that not everyone has to go to the top. It is not necessarily 'better' to be on a higher step. People can step off when they have gone as far as they want. Also, some people can skip a step or two.

Parents as decision makers

The main way in which parents are involved in making decisions about the programme has been as members of the Partnership Board, the committee responsible for the programme and to which the programme manager and other staff are answerable. The Board makes decisions about major contracts relating to programme agreements, management structure and premises developments. It has consisted of 13 members, drawn from the community and from relevant organizations working in the area. It has had five subgroups: Finance, Capital, Parent Forum, Partners, and REAC (Research and Evaluation Advisory Committee).

To evaluate parents' input into the Board, we began by reviewing their attendance over its first three years, during which time it met 19 times. Low attendance would mean that parents' involvement in decision making would be limited. We found, however, that there was an average attendance of four parents per meeting (and no trend upwards or downwards during the period).

Next, we considered the nature of parents' and the other community members' participation in Board meetings. Did they sit silently while professionals from outside the community made decisions, or were they part of the process? To investigate this, Peter attended a Board meeting as an observer. Observations of one meeting can only be a snapshot, but that is better than no picture at all. The meeting took place in 2002. There were four parents present (three with children in the Sure Start age range, one with an older child). One other member of the community (a local councillor) gave apologies. The remaining members of the Board, one of whom was absent, were professionals working in the area (in social services, the local authority young children's service, a local school, an adult education agency), a health visitor, a GP, a midwife, and a vicar. It was interesting that one of the parents was Chair of the Board. The agenda was a review of work carried out in the previous three months in the programme (covering some ten services), reports from three subgroups, and a report from the programme manager. Six programme workers presented written reports, spoke to them, and took questions. The reports were detailed but clear. Business was dealt with briskly and efficiently, due mainly to the way in which the meeting was chaired (it emerged later that the parent chair had recently attended a course on running meetings). A tally of spoken contributions showed that, on average, parents spoke as often as the professionals (although many of the parent contributions came from the chair). The professionals, however, asked more questions of the programme staff. On the whole, this was not a decision-making meeting, although the discussion of several items did conclude with action points for programme staff. Some decisions may have been made in subgroups (which include parents). The observations therefore indicated that parents were genuine participants in the programme Board and, even if there was little direct evidence of the Board making decisions in the meeting observed, the parents were certainly treated with respect by the staff presenting reports.

To gain another perspective on parents' roles in the Partnership Board, current and past parent members of the Board were asked to complete a short open-ended questionnaire. The questions asked how the parents first got involved in the programme, how they became members of the Board, what was 'good' about being on the Board, what was 'not so good', whether involvement in the programme had changed their lives in any way, and whether, and why, they would recommend other parents to get involved in the programme. Five out of eight questionnaires were returned.

Most parents had become involved by using services and being drawn into the programme to the point where they were asked to join the Board, 'a natural progression' as one parent put it. What they liked about being on the Board was 'being involved in decisions that affect my community' and 'being able to give input and pass on views as well as listening to other ideas, etc. that were raised'. One said she 'met lots of people and found out loads of things about the community'. When asked what was 'not so good' about being on the Board, the more experienced members said there was nothing, but one of the newer members expressed doubts about their ability to speak in meetings and another felt unsure about whether the board was advisory or decision making. The strongest views expressed concerned how parents felt they had benefited personally from experience of the programme up to Board level.

It gave me more confidence as a person.

I was given a chance to leave the house and take part in the groups. I'm now involved in community groups. I've the confidence to access funding, etc.

It was a very good confidence builder. I loved it at the time.

Only a few parents in the community can be involved at Board level in the programme, but what we have learned is that those who have been involved have found it worthwhile personally and feel it has enabled them to give something to their community.

Helen's story

In the summer of 2004, in preparation for this chapter, Peter suggested to Helen that she write her own story of how she became involved in Sure Start, from being a parent using services to becoming a member of staff in the programme. Here is what she wrote:

It all started in 1998, and who would believe then that I would be doing what I am doing now?

In 1998, as a local parent with young children, I attended a Mother and Toddler Group at the Family Centre that was later to become the base for Sure Start. The group was held twice a week. It was a nice and friendly and both myself and Hannah my youngest daughter gained a lot from the group.

The Family Centre then was just beginning to house a project called Women Supporting Mothers, a befriending project for women. I was bored and thought it was about time I got my brain working again so I took an interest in the training course that they were putting on around community development and befriending skills. I found myself on the next round of training and enjoyed every minute. I began to volunteer for a couple of hours a week and befriended two mothers. I really enjoyed this and it gave me a sense of satisfaction knowing I helped them to help themselves.

In 1999 along came this brand new initiative from the government, Sure Start, aiming to support families with young children and with a big agenda about involving parents. I was approached by another volunteer and by the future programme manager, who was then a health visitor, looking at developing this new programme. It felt right and I really wanted to get involved. I began volunteering for this project, informing parents, getting their views on what they want to see improved in the area, and so on. Before I knew it a year had gone by. In June 2000 a part time job came up as Parent Involvement Worker. It all felt right. It was the right time and so I thought, 'Yes, go for it'. I did and was successful in gaining the post. For two years I worked constantly, talking to parents, informing them, holding focus groups and Check It Out groups, parents meeting. I became part of the Partnership Board, making decisions about what should happen in the area with the Sure Start money. Running alongside this, I was also taking part in numerous training opportunities for myself gaining confidence by the minute and facilitating my own workshops for parents.

In 2002 my job had evolved so much I was successful in gaining the position of Parent Involvement Co-ordinator and extending my working hours. We also recruited another Parent Involvement Worker to work with me to engage parents in the programme. My skills just grew and grew and I found myself not only continuing to engage parents in meetings and groups but supervising another member of staff and gaining a City and Guilds adult learning qualification.

In 2003 I ran my first training course – on community development and health. It lasted for 14 weeks and the learners could gain six OCN credits. This was me! I loved training this course and seeing parents grow themselves, not only in understanding about health issues and how they affect them but growing in confidence and self-esteem as the course went on. All eight parents gained full accreditation and I have since trained this course again. Also in 2003 a neighbouring Sure Start came along after a lot of hard work fighting for it and I was lucky enough to be offered the chance to develop services in that area. I jumped at the chance and it was agreed I would again increase my hours and work a split role across two programmes. The timing was perfect for me as both my children were now in full time education and luckily my partner's work was flexible. Three more parent involvement workers were recruited and we worked as a team over the two areas, involving new parents, informing the community about Sure Start and consulting with parents for their ideas.

It's now 2004 and I am currently undertaking a Diploma in Management course. My position again has grown and changed. I now have a title of Community Development and Training Co-ordinator, supervising five members of staff. I continue to train, inform, consult and advise parents on Sure Start, building up their confidence where necessary.

My life in the last six years has changed so much – from volunteering to managing – all thanks to Sure Start giving me the opportunity to learn new skills, take up further education and gain employment.

Thanks, Sure Start.

Parents' stories

Two stories from other parents speak for themselves.

Cheryl's story

I was first approached by someone I knew on the way home from taking my children to school one morning and asked if I would like to attend a meeting at Sure Start.

I didn't know whether to go or not but she encouraged me by offering my youngest child and my baby a place in the crèche – which, as well as a break for me, would also be good experience for my children.

The other matter to take into consideration was the fact that it was to be held at the Family Centre on Palgrave Road. I wasn't sure about the Family Centre as I had never actually visited it – it used to be a place where 'problem families' went. As far as I was concerned, if I went there people would think I was going to have my children taken into care.

It was quite a long way for me to walk to with a young child and a baby but I wasn't on my own and I made the effort.

The meeting was quite daunting at first. My doctor was at the meeting, which felt strange. We sat outside under a gazebo as it was a nice day and this lightened up the atmosphere a little for us all. I had a great time meeting new parents in the Parson Cross area and professionals who were there. Before I knew it I was questioning people, putting my views forward and those views of people too shy to speak up too! Everyone made us really welcome and we had a lunch provided too.

Once I had been to the meeting and got to know about the services that Sure Start was going to be offering in the future I was hooked. I passed the word around at school and got more parents to attend the meetings – admitted, I encouraged them with the free crèche and lunch but everyone was the same as me once they knew what Sure Start was about they wanted to get involved too.

I attended all the meetings from that day on and then signed up to be in the check-it-out-group. Unfortunately around this time my children had moved on in age and I had to go out to work. I got a part time job but I couldn't bear the fact that I wasn't going to get any information through (basically I was scared I would miss something!). So I phoned Helen and asked her to still send the meeting dates and any information to me and I would attend when I was able if I wasn't at work.

After this I helped out when I could and kept my foot in the door to speak where possible I attended the centre one day and Helen informed me of a Sure Start administrative post which had been advertised in the Sheffield Star. The closure date for the applications was pretty soon – she took me into her office and let me use the phone to request an application pack. She also issued me with paper and pen and helped me put together a letter.

By the time of the interview I was really nervous wondering if I had done the right thing and kept thinking that I would probably not get the job and how would I feel? The interview went really well. I asked what training would be available etc and then went home to await the phone call. They phoned me and gave me the good news that they would like to offer me the post and I couldn't believe it. And the rest as they say is history!

Debbie's story

Becoming involved with Sure Start was one of the best things I have done in the last few years. As you can imagine, having 3 young children is stressful in itself but my youngest was having speech delay and this was really worrying me. I attended a Mother and Toddler group, supported by a Sure Start worker, and my son's speech improved enormously. I began to attend different groups on different days and enjoyed them all. I found out more about Sure Start and attended one of the Check It Out group meetings I thought it was great to be able to be in the know about what was happening in the area you lived in.

I started to become more confident, attended a few training courses Sure Start had put on which made me feel better about myself. I began to help run the toddler group and by now had also given birth to my fourth child and received extra help along the way from Sure Start around breastfeeding and postnatal care which I hadn't received with my other children. I began to attend further training and completed my breastfeeding peer supporter training and also have engaged in further training days, building my confidence. My most recent was the Introduction to Community Development and Health course which was the longest course I have done since leaving school but I have enjoyed every minute and gained 6 OCN credits at levels 2 and 3 which I was very proud of.

I am now a member of the partnership board and also have become an official volunteer for NCH/Sure Start. I am shortly going to undertake my NVQ 2 in Administration which without support over the last 3 years from Sure Start I know I wouldn't be in a position to do. Sure Start has not only helped me personally a lot but my family too, helping with my son's speech and also my youngest daughter's behaviour and since she began at the Sure Start nursery this has improved a great deal. Having a Sure Start programme in your area certainly gives you that bit of extra support people need.

How far have we come?

We have come a long way in five years. We have learned that *how* people are consulted is important. For example, before parents come to a meeting (whether it is a Board meeting or for consultation) it can be very helpful to have a pre-meeting so they can gain information and have a chance to talk about issues amongst themselves. Being open with parents, informing them and also supporting them helps to build confidence and a productive relationship. It is important to provide a crèche at meetings so that parents are not excluded because of childcare responsibilities. The locality and timing of meetings matter. Even apparently small things such as providing refreshments, to make people feel welcome and valued, are important. We have found that when local people realize they have influence, and when they see opportunities to volunteer or even become employed in the programme, there can be knock-on effects throughout the community. Finally, we have learned to accept that parents who are willing to be involved will become involved at different levels, and that we must not pressure them in any way. It is all these things combined together that build confidence within the community and encourage involvement.

Obviously our commitment to involving the community has not worked perfectly. There are always improvements that can be made and lessons to be learned. For example, meetings have not always been well attended and there have been times when just one or two parents have turned up at the Parent Forum, or even times when no parents came to the Check It Out group. We have learned not to feel a failure on such occasions. It is natural for it to happen sometimes, as there will always be times when parents have good reasons not to attend.

We have also failed to involve fathers as much as hoped. We have learned that we need to do something different to bring this about. Thinking that a male role model or member of staff could influence and encourage involvement, we have recently appointed a men's project worker to work with dads in the area. The early signs are that this worker is having an impact in supporting fathers, encouraging them to become involved in projects within the programme such as gardening, and also supporting them to attend meetings.

Overall, the main lesson we have learned is that parents *are* willing to be involved in a Sure Start programme, not just as users of services but as members of the community with ideas to contribute. For some, involvement means stepping up a ladder that can lead to employment or a role in

shaping the programme. We have learned that, to be successful, a programme must have people's involvement and input into the decisions that
affect them.

16 The Young Families' Advice Service
Imogen Hale

Introduction

The Young Families' Advice Service (YFAS), funded by Sure Start, is a dedicated advice service for Sure Start families, to help them tackle the causes and effects of poverty. The aim of the service has been to provide free, independent advice on a range of issues including housing, debt and benefits. The project has been delivered by a full-time advice and development worker and has been managed by the Foxhill and Parson Cross Advice Service (FPCAS).

Foxhill and Parson Cross families have distinct advice requirements, linked to their poor socioeconomic situation. Many local people are reliant on welfare benefits, and debt is a common problem. The area includes large estates of local authority inter-war housing, where families often experience unsuitable or insecure accommodation, including disrepair, overcrowding and eviction threats because of rent arrears.

FPCAS is a well-established neighbourhood advice centre, part of a city-wide network of voluntary sector organizations. It provides advice via 'drop-in' sessions at the main premises, and outreach bases that include libraries and GPs' surgeries. Unfortunately, despite the commitment to making advice available to everyone, some of the most vulnerable sections of the local community have traditionally not accessed the service. Young people, teenage parents, single parents and people with caring responsibilities have proved to be reluctant or unable to access drop-in sessions, despite frequently being most in need of the service. Sure Start presented the opportunity for FPCAS to develop a more focused service for local families, as an integral part of the overall Sure Start programme.

The role of the Young Families Advice Worker was to develop the new service in the following ways:

- promoting the service to families who had not used the existing advice provision;
- delivering advice through home visits, appropriate outreach locations and other appointments;
- establishing a referral network with other Sure Start projects, health workers and local service providers;
- providing training to local workers about advice issues for families.

Evaluating the service

Six key questions were addressed in an evaluation of service effectiveness:

1 Was the client group using the YFAS different from that using the general 'drop-in' advice service?
2 How many families used the YFAS?
3 What types of advice were provided?
4 To what extent did the YFAS result in an increased income for Sure Start families?
5 To what extent did the YFAS help people address their housing problems?
6 Was the provision of advice integrated into the overall Sure Start programme?

During the 26 months studied in this chapter, detailed records were maintained. Every client's enquiry was recorded, including advice provided, follow-up action and outcomes. Daily records were kept of all client contact for statistical purposes. Client questionnaires completed throughout January 2002 enabled comparison between people using the general 'drop-in' sessions to people using the YFAS. Case studies illustrate various aspects of the service, and how it related to the overall Sure Start programme.

Question 1: Was the client group using the Young Families' Advice Service different from that using the general 'drop-in' service?

At FPCAS the general advice service was delivered through daily 'drop-in' sessions at the main premises, and outreach locations in the local area. These sessions did not require appointments, using instead, a first-come-first-served system.

The YFAS was predominantly appointment based, and provided home visits as needed. To ensure as many families as possible knew about the service, it was actively promoted through talks to target groups, and a referral network with other agencies was established.

The survey referred to earlier provided a comparison between clients using the YFAS and general advice service.

The comparison revealed that the YFAS was attracting a different client group to the general advice service. Ninety per cent of the YFAS clients were female, compared to the fairly even male/female ratio for clients using the general advice service. The client group was also younger. Fifty-nine per cent of YFAS clients were aged 18–24 years, whereas 59 per cent of people using the general advice service were aged 25–49 years. The YFAS attracted a higher proportion of clients aged under 18 than the general advice service. Only 16 per cent of clients using the general advice service had young children. Unsurprisingly, 100 per cent of YFAS clients had young children or were pregnant. Both services saw almost the same percentage (36 per cent) of clients who regarded themselves as disabled.

Clients' routes to advice were very different for each service. The majority of YFAS clients (63 per cent) came through the established referral procedure (21 per cent of general advice service clients stated another agency had referred them, which generally meant another agency had recommended FPCAS). Most (63 per cent) general advice service clients acted on family and friends' recommendations, past experience or local knowledge, compared to only 37 per cent of YFAS clients.

These findings show that the YFAS was attracting a client group that did not use the general advice service, confirming that the drop-in system presented a significant barrier for some people who needed advice. For example, parents with young children found the unpredictable waiting times very difficult. General advice service users seemed to take an active approach to accessing advice. A high percentage of general advice service clients cited personal knowledge, and recommendations from family or friends as the main reason for using the service. Clients of the YFAS seemed more hesitant about asking for help. The active referral network proved invaluable in ensuring vulnerable and isolated people were able to access the YFAS.

The YFAS client figures from January 2002 were typical of the period covered by the evaluation. The project did seem to succeed in engaging a client group regarded as hard for programmes to reach.

Question 2: How many families used the YFAS?

During the evaluation period, 318 individual families used YFAS. Forty-two of these returned for further advice once or more. Other families went on to use the general FPCAS advice service as a result of contact with the YFAS (no figures available). Approximately 394 children under the age of 4 years benefited from their parents' contact with the YFAS.

After an initial one-month period spent developing a referral system and promoting the YFAS, demand was soon high for the new service, with a general monthly increase in families seen. At first, local health and community workers referred most families using the YFAS. As the service became established, families began to refer themselves. Towards the end of the first year of the project, the YFAS began to see families who had used the service before returning with fresh enquiries.

Families whose enquires required in-depth advice would remain clients of the YFAS for as long as necessary, often several months. On average, the YFAS dealt with 35 families per month, including new and existing clients. The majority of families received advice about more than one issue, for example a combination of housing, debt and welfare benefits, as the following case study shows.

Case study 1

Karen was referred to the YFAS by her Sure Start Family Support Worker. Her income support had been stopped when her two children were taken into local authority care. She needed urgent advice about entitlement to other benefits.

During a home visit to sort out benefits, Karen mentioned she had received a letter from her landlord, Sheffield Council, asking her to move out. This turned out to be a 'notice to quit' issued because her housing benefit ceased as soon as income support was cancelled. She had a temporary tenancy after being re-housed through the Homeless Section.

The YFAS contacted Karen's housing officer who explained that in addition to housing benefit stopping, Karen had failed to keep to a rent arrears repayment agreement. After negotiations, the rent officer proposed that the notice to quit would not be pursued if Karen reclaimed housing benefit, and caught up with the missed arrears repayments. The housing officer also confirmed that after 26 weeks of regular payments, the temporary tenancy would be replaced with a secure tenancy.

The YFAS, on Karen's behalf, approached Social Services, who agreed to award a Section 17 payment to bring the repayment agreement up to date. YFAS helped Karen re-apply for housing benefit and council tax benefit.

When Karen's children returned to live with her, YFAS helped her reclaim child benefit and income support, and obtained a new washing machine from the Family Welfare Association.

Soon afterwards, Karen got back in touch. She had started working part-time and needed advice about entitlement to Working Families Tax Credit. The YFAS helped her claim this, and advised her about entitlement to Children's Tax Credit and the housing benefit extension period.

Question 3: What types of advice were provided?

The Young Families' Advice Service provided advice on a broad range of welfare issues. Below is a proportional breakdown of types of advice provided during a 6-month sample period August 2001 to January 2002. This period was typical of the overall study period. While the examples are context-specific, incorporating technical information, the issues they encapsulate relate to other families dealing with challenging circumstances.

> *Means-tested benefits (18 per cent)*
> This category encompassed issues about income support, job seekers allowance, housing benefit and council tax benefits, including benefit arrears. The YFAS also advised clients on related issues, for example fraudulent claim allegations, co-habiting rules and ways of maximizing entitlement to means-tested benefits.
>
> *Re-housing/Housing disrepair (13 per cent)*
> Many families were struggling to cope in unsuitable accommodation, and teenage clients had problems getting tenancies until they were 18 years old. The YFAS advised families about those and other housing-related issues. Advice included negotiating with local housing offices and the homeless section, and referring cases on to solicitors, if necessary.
>
> *Tax credits (13 per cent)*
> Most enquiries in this category involved advising families about returning to work, using 'better-off' calculations based on tax credits. Advice about tax credits resulted in families coming off income support, and returning to work.
>
> *Disability benefits (10 per cent)*
> This category of advice included Incapacity Benefit, Invalid Carers' Allowance, and Disability Living Allowance (DLA) for children and adults. In cases where an application had been refused, the YFAS could apply for a reconsideration and if necessary, represent the client at a Disability Appeal Tribunal.
>
> *Maternity benefits (11 per cent)*
> This category included enquiries about statutory and contractual maternity pay, maternity allowance and maternity grants. Many clients in this category had never claimed benefits before, and were unaware of their entitlement beyond statutory maternity pay (SMP). The YFAS produced a self-help leaflet about SMP. *cont.*

Rent and council tax arrears (8 per cent)
Arrears advice aimed to prevent families being evicted by negotiating with the landlord, representing families at County Court, checking entitlement to council benefits, and general debt advice.

Debt (7 per cent)
Debt advice involved helping families develop strategies to deal with their debts, such as budgeting and prioritizing debts, and negotiating affordable payments with creditors. If debt problems could not be simply resolved by negotiation, or careful budgeting, the YFAS helped families to obtain administration and bankruptcy orders.

Social Fund (6 per cent)
The YFAS helped families obtain financial assistance from the Benefits Agency Social Fund section. The Social Fund provides interest-free loans, crisis loans and community care grants, intended to help alleviate short-term need for people in receipt of certain benefits.

Charities (6 per cent)
Work in this category involved applications the YFAS made to a range of charities on behalf of clients. These included requests for household items and nursery equipment, and grants for families experiencing severe hardship. Charity applications were usually made if the Social Fund and Social Services had been unable to help.

Employment (4 per cent)
Most employment enquiries concerned parental and maternity rights. The YFAS also advised parents who were considering returning to work about tax credits, help with childcare costs and back-to-work bonuses.

Miscellaneous (4 per cent)
This category included all other types of advice provided.

Question 4: To what extent did the YFAS result in an increased income for Sure Start families?

The positive benefit for families using the Young Families Advice Service was most easily quantified in terms of financial gains, recorded on a case-by-case basis.

Most benefits and tax credits are calculated weekly. For evaluation purposes, and to gauge the full extent of increased income, gains were translated into annual amounts. However, where the length of award was for less than 12 months, for example Working Families Tax Credit (WFTC) which lasts for 26 weeks, the figure given as annual was actually the total value of the award, rather than a pro-rata figure.

The scores were collated quarterly to track the development of the YFAS. A general monthly increase in generated income reflected the overall development of the service.

Breakdown of income raised for YFAS clients

In the study period there was a total increase in income for Sure Start families of £191,261.50. It is reasonable to expect this level of increased income to continue. The amount was broken down as follows:

- 29% – Disability Living Allowance for adults and children (£96,787.60)
- 27% – Working Families Tax Credit (£86,944.22)
- 21% – Income Support, JSA or Incapacity Benefit (£66,050.40)
- 11% – Housing and Council Tax Benefit (£35,202.96)
- 7% – maternity benefits (£22,100.00)
- 5% – Child Benefit and Children's Tax Credit (£14,752.40)

In addition to increased income through awards of weekly benefits, the YFAS also monitored one-off financial gains that resulted from advice. Benefit arrears, debt write-offs and charitable grants were included. These amounts were recorded as distinct one-off payment, and were not included in the figures above. The £145,668 total was generated as follows:

- 53% – debts written off (£77,204.04)
- 27% – benefit arrears obtained (£39,330.36)
- 13% – Social Fund grants (£18,936.84)
- 4% – miscellaneous payments (£58,26.72)
- 3% – charitable grants (£43,70.04)

Question 5: To what extent did the YFAS help people address their housing problems?

Housing and rent problems accounted for one-fifth of the YFAS enquiries, and covered several main areas. Case studies are used in this part of the evaluation to illustrate how the YFAS helped people address typical housing problems.

Security of tenure

The YFAS worked with families to prevent them losing their homes. Usually this involved cases of threatened eviction because of rent arrears. During the 26 months evaluated, the YFAS represented nine Sure Start families at County Court possession hearings. As a result, all nine families were allowed to remain in their homes. In eight cases the judge agreed to suspend possession orders and warrants. The other family's application was initially refused, but allowed at appeal.

Case study 2

Joanne and her partner had been under considerable pressure for several years. Postnatal depression following the birth of their fourth child had prevented Joanne from returning to work. A drop in income, coupled with an extra child, led to escalating debt problems. A housing benefit claim took over 12 months to be processed, and when eventually done, was for much less than the couple had expected. They found themselves liable for several thousand pounds of rent arrears. Joanne had agreed to pay the rent arrears off at a rate the family could not afford. They soon defaulted on the repayment agreement, and the Council began proceedings to evict them. By the time Joanne was referred to the YFAS by her health visitor, she felt completely unable to cope, and was suffering from worsening depression.

The YFAS helped Joanne work out what she could afford to offer the housing office, whilst providing ongoing debt advice. The advice worker then represented the family at court. The repayment proposal was accepted, and the possession order suspended.

Unfortunately, Joanne did not keep to the court order because of increasing problems at home. Sheffield Council obtained a warrant to evict the family. The YFAS helped Joanne apply for the warrant to be suspended. When the application was unsuccessful, the YFAS instructed a solicitor on Joanne's behalf, to appeal against the decision. The YFAS succeeded in persuading the Homeless Section to allow the family to remain in the house while the appeal was being considered.

A successful appeal application resulted in the warrant being suspended for two years, to allow time for the family to get back on their feet financially. As long as the family regularly paid their rent, and a small sum towards the arrears during that time, they would keep their home.

Applications for re-housing

Families had various reasons for needing to be re-housed. Some families were simply struggling in overcrowded accommodation. Others were isolated, and wanted to live closer to friends or family, often following the birth of a new baby or relationship breakdown. The YFAS also helped families whose homes were unsuited to special needs arising from disability.

Young people's housing needs

Teenage parents presented specific housing problems. They were excluded from accessing housing through the housing offices due to a policy of only allocating tenancies to people aged 18 or over. If teenage parents asked the Homeless Section for help, they were generally encouraged to accept hostel accommodation, out of the area. The YFAS advised 16- and 17-year-olds about their housing options, and supported them in achieving the best outcome. This work was regularly done in collaboration with the Sure Start family support workers (see Chapter 3).

Case study 3

Sarah was a 16-year-old single parent. Her relationship with her mother was poor, and she had lived with various relatives since the age of 13. After having her son, Sarah desperately wanted a house of her own, so she could provide a secure home for him. The local housing office refused her application for a house, telling her to come back when she was 18.

The Sure Start teenage mums' group put Sarah in touch with the YFAS. Sarah was clear that she wanted her own house, rather than a place in a mother and baby hostel. She wanted to remain in Parson Cross where she had a strong support network of relatives. A hostel placement would have been more suitable for someone without the life-skills Sarah had already developed. The YFAS arranged an appointment for Sarah with Sheffield Council's Young Person's Accommodation Unit to discuss her housing needs.

Sarah was assessed as being in priority need of housing, and mature enough to manage living independently. The accessing officer was impressed that Sarah had accessed an advice service, and was receiving support from various Sure Start projects. Sarah was offered a house in the area she wanted.

When Sarah accepted a tenancy, the YFAS provided advice about claiming housing and council tax benefits. It also helped Sarah obtain a £900.00 community care grant for household essentials, and a fridge and washing machine from a charity.

Disrepair problems

The housing stock in the Sure Start area includes many unmodernized properties. In addition to porch-toilets and insufficient heating, many Sure Start families were living in homes in very poor repair. If negotiations with the local housing offices failed to get repairs carried out, the YFAS referred clients to specialist solicitors who were able to obtain independent surveys, and seek court orders on the disrepair.

Question 6: Was the provision of advice integrated into the overall Sure Start programme?

From the outset, the Young Families' Advice Service was intended to be an integral part of the overall Sure Start programme rather than just a resource that Sure Start would use. How well that aim was achieved was evaluated by monitoring referrals made to the YFAS.

During the 26 months studied, a total of 233 referrals were received by the YFAS, with a general quarterly increase that echoed the establishment of the YFAS and Sure Start itself. By the end of the study period, an average of 16 families were being referred each month.

The majority of referrals came from local health visitors and community midwives, 34 per cent and 17 per cent respectively. Thirty-eight per cent of referrals came from other Sure Start projects. The BIBS team, Family Support team and Outreach team made 17, 13 and 8 per cent of the total referrals, respectively. The YFAS often worked alongside other Sure Start projects with individual families after a referral was received. Other Sure Start partner organizations, including Women Supporting Mothers, and the Domestic Abuse Project, made 5 per cent of all referrals. Four per cent of referrals came from other FPCAS advice workers. The remaining 2 per cent came from Social Services, youth services and the local housing office.

Overall, the YFAS was well used by other Sure Start projects and local health workers. The levels of referrals indicated that families were routinely offered access to advice as part of the Sure Start package of support.

Conclusion

The partnership between Sure Start and FPCAS marked a new direction in advice provision in the area. By recognizing the impact of poverty on children's early experiences, Sure Start made funding available to provide a service that directly tackled that issue. The reality of integrated working resulted in a service that was accessible to the families who needed it. To the best of our knowledge, a dedicated advice project was unique in the first round of national Sure Start programmes. Sure Start funding enabled FPCAS to develop flexible new ways of promoting and delivering advice to an under-represented client group. This was particularly valuable in a climate in which new projects are increasingly dictated by funders' remits, rather than community needs.

The evaluation demonstrates that the Young Families Advice Project consistently contributed to the aims of the Sure Start programme.

- Demand for the service took off quickly, and remained consistently high. Through the provision of advice, the project came into contact with, and assisted, a high proportion of Sure Start families.
- The YFAS succeeded in establishing a new, distinct client group. This was achieved by linking up with health and support workers, actively promoting the service in the community, and making access as flexible as possible. Families could have home visits, or attend advice sessions by appointment or on a drop-in basis.
- The YFAS provided a general advice service with an emphasis on income maximization, debt and housing, issues that significantly affect young children's preschool experiences.
- Certain aspects of the YFAS work can be easily quantified. Families' income increased substantially as a result of receiving advice. The project helped families resolve housing problems including disrepair, overcrowding and threatened evictions. This work directly contributed to children's well-being and security.
- This evaluation indicates that the YFAS succeeded in establishing itself as an integral component of the overall Sure Start programme. Referrals were received from all the Sure Start teams, with collaborative working where appropriate. It appeared that families using the service also perceived the YFAS as part of Sure Start. One YFAS client commented in a service evaluation questionnaire:

> 'I thought my case was managed very well. [The YFAP] was a great help throughout and seems to care a lot about my needs. I would like to thank [the YFAP] and Sure Start for helping me when I was in need.'

At this early stage in Sure Start's life, it is hard to accurately accredit definitive achievements to individual projects. Sure Start's 'partnership' approach involves collaborations resulting in (hopefully) cumulative successes. The use of case studies in this chapter serves to indicate the contribution to this process, made by the Young Families' Advice Service.

The future

There are four general recommendations for the future that arise from the issues raised in this chapter, which would help work of this nature to develop:

1 A continued commitment to retaining and developing networks with other agencies, particularly those that were not yet referring to the project.

2 The YFAS to develop and deliver training for other Sure Start workers around advice issues to encourage more appropriate referrals.

3 The YFAS to work with FPCAS to encourage the main advice centre to develop and implement more family-friendly practices.

4 Greater emphasis on social policy work around benefits and housing issues affecting families with young children.

In the work reported to date, it is clear that the Young Families' Advice Service had a positive contribution to make to the families in the Sure Start area, and it is work that could usefully be replicated elsewhere.

17 Community research
Jo Weinberger

Introduction

This chapter describes a key aspect of community involvement in research in the Sure Start area. Local community interviewers were involved in conducting a survey, in which they interviewed parents of all 4-year-olds within selected year groups, to find out about parents' experiences of bringing up young children in the area. The process of this detailed and sensitive work is documented, with details of recruiting, training and supporting the community interviewers and contacting families. It offers reflections on the process of conducting the work by the local community interviewers. Wider implications relate in a general way to evaluating work within community contexts.

A distinctive feature of conducting the survey of parents' view (see Appendix 2) was the involvement of local people, working as community interviewers. They visited and, where possible, interviewed parents of 4-year-olds living in the area, at the beginning of the programme using a structured interview. (A second, comparative survey was undertaken once Sure Start had been in the area for four years, see Chapter 2.) The aim was to find out about parents' experiences of bringing up young children in the area, to establish their views on parenting and to monitor the difference the Sure Start programme made to families.

Recruiting, training and supporting community interviewers

The intention was to recruit local people as interviewers who were not involved in the delivery of the programme. Community organizations were contacted to find individuals who might be interested. One of these, a health promotion project, had experience of conducting a health needs assessment using local people. Initially, a small group involved with this organization expressed an interest in the survey work. Because of issues of payment and other work opportunities, only two of this group were able to continue the interviewing, one for a short period and the other throughout the length of the first survey. Other potential interviewers were contacted through previously expressed interest in community-based involvement. Information about the work was made available, and opportunities to find out more about what it might entail were organized.

This recruitment process proved successful, which meant that interviews were all conducted by a team of people who lived in or near the Sure Start area. Everyone in the team had previous experience of work within the community, or of undertaking a course concerned with community issues. Team members changed over time as other commitments and community work opportunities arose. This meant flexibility was essential. Regular meetings were an integral part of maintaining and monitoring the process.

The number of interviews at any one time was shared between those available and trained to do the work. This meant that the community interviewers could work hours to suit themselves, choosing times when they thought they were most likely to find parents at home. Often it took more than one visit before they found the parent in and could conduct the interview. As we were anxious to hear the views of *all* parents of 4-year-olds, we encouraged interviewers to keep trying to arrange an interview (and paid for their time in doing this), although obviously parents could decline to be interviewed. To set up an interview, the interviewers were given names and addresses of children who were 4 within the specified time range and lived in the area. We supplied ready-printed letters to send to parents and the interviewer added their own name, the time they would call and a contact address and phone number. Letters could then be posted in stamped addressed envelopes that were supplied. Support and training was available throughout the time they were involved in the work. As well as being essential to the work, it was also part of Sure Start's commitment to capacity-building in the local area:

> ... training and supervising people in the community ... will help to increase such skills within the community and will ensure a higher degree of community involvement in the process.
> (Hawtin et al., 1994: 43)

Training was interactive and carried out in a group, so interviewers could offer one another support, share experiences, and pose questions. From the outset, the *purpose* of interviewing parents was emphasized (to find out detailed experiences of parenting, and the impact of Sure Start), and they were given opportunities to become familiar with the interview schedule through role play, group feedback and discussion. There was discussion of sensitive topics, with a midwife and a domestic abuse worker giving input around difficulties that might be triggered by questions on postnatal depression, breastfeeding and about family life. It was made clear that it was not appropriate for interviewers to debrief parents after the interview. However, relevant professionals were available if needed, and interviewers had access to phone numbers for parents, should they become distressed or wish to talk sensitive issues through further.

It was important to ensure support for the interviewers was adequate and accessible, with easy ways of contacting research staff and one another. To start, each interviewer undertook to arrange and conduct a pilot interview, a chance for the interviewers to practise using tape recorders. These pilot interviews showed the interview schedule was workable, with only minor adjustments necessary. Detailed notes about the way their interview had gone were given to each person. Further feedback and support was given in a group context. There were opportunities to meet programme and research staff so the interviewers felt an integral part of the whole enterprise. Background information about Sure Start and where the survey fitted in to the research and evaluation of the programme was given and discussed, and the interviewers had packs of information they could give to families they interviewed. Queries were answered as they arose, and group meetings provided the opportunity to share comments and experiences. Once the interviewers had completed their training and were conducting interviews, there were regular meetings to allocate and return interview schedules, and share their experiences. Forms were devised to help document the process, which included the number of visits made, the time and date of completed interviews or reasons an interview was not carried out.

The interviewers visited parents at home (although alternative arrangements were possible if requested). They took brief notes, and, with permission, tape recorded the interviews, marking the interview schedule when parents made more than a short response, so what they said could later be transcribed. This allowed everything to be recorded accurately and meant rich qualitative data was collected. The interviewers practised the preamble to the interview, where they explained this process to the parents, and gained their consent. After the interviews, a summary of the main findings of the survey was sent to all the interviewers and the families who had contributed.

Contacting families

Initially, parents were contacted via nurseries their child attended. They were given details about the survey and asked to return a pre-paid postcard if they agreed for an interviewer to contact them. This method had been used successfully in previous research (Nutborwn, 2005), but in this instance the majority of families did not respond. After consultation with workers experienced in contacting families within this particular community, a more direct approach was adopted. A letter was sent by the community interviewer directly to parents, explaining about the survey and proposing a time for the interview, with details of how to make contact to cancel or rearrange the appointment. Because the community interviewers knew the area well, and were persistent in their efforts to contact parents, they managed to achieve a very high rate of response using this method. Many parents did not keep diaries, and had busy lives looking after young children, so were often not found at home at regular or specified times. One visit yielded a response rate of 36 per cent, but because they were prepared to return to make new appointments, a second or third visit greatly enhanced the level of response (see Figure 17.1).

Figure 17.1 Visits made to obtain interviews: effect of persistence

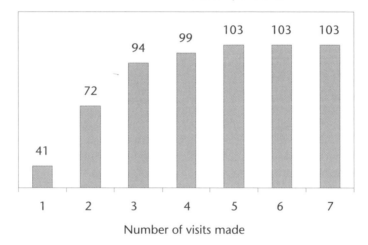

Number of visits made

▨ Number of interviews completed (N = 103)

Occasionally, additional attempts to visit were successful, but visiting more than three times was not particularly effective and not a cost-effective use of interviewers' time. It was left to individual interviewers to decide how many times to attempt an interview, striking a balance between finding a mutually convenient time and not wanting families to feel under pressure to take part. The highly sensitive issue of passive refusal was discussed at length. Often parents did not say outright that they did not want to be interviewed, but were simply not in at the times arranged. It took considerable local knowledge and judgement to decide what action to take. Options were to post a friendly note through the door arranging another time, to agree with the parent (if they were in), to call back another time, or to accept it was not possible to conduct that particular interview. The interviewers also voiced concern about not looking too official, and not enquiring about the families' whereabouts, except when neighbours themselves volunteered information.

Local interviewers' reflections

All five of the community interviewers involved in working on the survey at the time this chapter was written responded to a questionnaire about their experience of conducting the survey. In addition, four of the interviewers attended a meeting to share their experiences as a group (the fifth was unwell). One of the interviewers, who remained involved in the process from the outset, was also interviewed on her own, about her experience of the work. What follows is a summary of their views, explaining their experiences.

The interviewers were asked what attracted them to take part in the survey. For some, interest was generated by involvement in a health needs survey, others by attending a community-focused course and also by a general interest in what Sure Start could offer the area. They identified previous experiences relevant to the survey work, including taking part on a community development and health training course (two of the interviewers), training on the health needs assessment, which included designing the questionnaire, collating data, and reporting the findings (two of the interviewers), and doing voluntary community work in the area.

Experiences of the work and its impact

The community interviewers explained their initial feelings about the work. They expressed nervousness and apprehension, excitement, and being pleased to have the opportunity to become involved in more survey work.

They also explained how their feelings about doing the work changed over time. Three of them talked of gaining in confidence, for instance:

> I became more confident and relaxed – this also allowed me to interact better. Being more relaxed myself seemed to relax the person/people being interviewed and, in turn, meant they 'opened' up to me more.

One of them mentioned that at first she had felt uncomfortable using a tape recorder, but she also appreciated its usefulness. Another was surprised how many people assumed she was interfering, rather than agreeing straightaway to take part. She commented how many visits and appointments it took to actually conduct a successful interview, although, as she said:

> ... when I actually got to interview it was mostly a pleasant experience.

The interviewers described the main things they had learned from doing the work. Their replies included perseverance, patience, the differences in different types of research work, gaining better listening skills (mentioned twice), more information about Sure Start, and concern that there were many young families in the area living in poverty, many of whom were not yet taking advantage of Sure Start (mentioned twice). They revealed insights into the level of difficulty many of the families in the area faced, for example:

> It's surprising how many problems families have got. You don't realize what people have to face every day. It's quite shocking really.

> It's like I walk round street and I see people I don't know and I think 'I wonder what horrible lives you have to put up with'.

They all responded that they had sufficient support in coping with their responses to encountering these difficulties, as clearly it is important to have adequate opportunities to discuss feelings arising from the experience.

The nature of disadvantage

Four of the five interviewers mentioned things that surprised them in doing the work. Two talked about how people opened up and were keen to share their views. Also mentioned were the suspicion and resentment shown towards Social Services, how reluctant some people were to give Sure Start a chance, and the extent to which many families had so many problems in their lives, for instance:

> Social Services are there like a safety net to help these people that really need it and they won't entertain them half the time because they live in fear that they're going to interfere that much and the children are going to be maybe taken away from them ... There were about 3 that wouldn't even entertain the survey because they

thought 'Oh, from Social Services'. But once I made it clear they were willing to go ahead with it. I found that really sad.

I've been surprised at the poverty that some people live in.

The community interviewers were asked about the most rewarding aspects of doing the work. One mentioned the satisfaction of completing interviews and another had no doubt in identifying the sense of achievement in, 'getting a completed survey at the first attempt!!' This comment emphasizes how difficult it was to complete interviews without making a number of arrangements to find families at home and available to respond. As has been discussed earlier, this partly reflects the nature of family life with young children, but was also a feature of families in this community, where keeping a diary was unusual and pre-arranged appointments often forgotten. Giving people an opportunity to air their views, and creating a relationship with the people interviewed were mentioned as rewarding aspects of the work. One of the interviewers expressed the privilege it was to talk with the families, especially if it was going to affect work and planning in the future:

> Just the opportunity to be invited into someone's home, and listening to them say what they felt, thought et cetera about different issues is, I think, a privilege to be given. Listening to the parents open up in a frank and honest way to a total stranger is rewarding, especially if something comes out of what they have said.

The most difficult aspects of doing the work seemed to be actually setting the interviews up, mentioned by all the interviewers, for example:

> Arranging the interviews – setting up times and dates. This became quite frustrating at times, especially having called three to four times and still not getting a response.

> Probably going to someone's home, and them not being in, arrangements had been made and we did give our phone numbers … but some did not let us know and this was sometimes frustrating.

It is to the interviewers' credit that they were persistent in following up families to interview. This was due to their intrinsic belief in the value of the process, and their eagerness to make the sample of families interviewed as representative as possible. This also reflected the fact that the interviewers thought the Sure Start programme had the potential to improve circumstances for families in the area. On the whole, they did not have much knowledge about Sure Start before they began the work on the survey, but, having been given information and experience, felt it was worthwhile. One commented on the grass-roots nature of the organization, and hoped that their practices could become embedded in the area:

> I am surer than ever that Sure Start is needed and needs to be sustained for years to come to get 'people' to trust them. Sure Start is really starting from the ground up, and I think that more than ever.

The one interviewer who knew about Sure Start from the outset of the survey was convinced of its usefulness, but also aware of its limitation:

> Sure Start is a really good project. It's a pity it only helps families with children under 4.

This points to the frustrations inherent in programmes that have boundaries imposed by funding considerations, which cut across people's actual needs. This is now addressed in new arrangements for mainstreaming the services that Sure Start provides.

Interviewers' views of research

The interviewers expressed a more comprehensive and rounded view of research as a result of working on the survey. They were surprised at the amount of paperwork involved and that the research enterprise was not as straightforward as appeared at face value. They needed to learn strategies to deal with disappointment, taking support and holding on to a wider view, for instance learning:

> … not to take it personally if someone is abrupt and refuses to take part, at this point it's quite easy to question the reason to carry on. It's essential to take each day individually.

It gave them more incentive to respond to research themselves:

> … if I am asked to fill in a questionnaire, I feel that it is important to do so! No matter how little information has been given it does help to make a difference to the findings of a survey.

The importance of helping people to express their real views was recognized:

This research that involves young people and their children needs
to be done face to face and the emphasis should be on real opinions, not 'right answers'.

This was certainly something that was taken on board by all the interviewers in the way that they talked with the families, and aimed to establish
rapport. In listening to tapes that they made, it was clear that they were able
to adopt a conversational style, creating every opportunity for families to
express what they really felt.

Personal development through community research

There were clear personal development gains from involvement in the
work. The interviewers enjoyed the work, and meeting and working with
new people. They gained in confidence, and learned better listening skills.
In addition, they mentioned learning:

> ... to view things with a more open mind. People have hidden
> depths and initially only let you see what they want you to see.

> ... about the amount of excellent people that are working to make
> things better for people in the area, not only in Sure Start but other
> agencies.

> ... skills I can use to find further employment.

Confidence increased, and the interviewers found carrying out the
interviews rewarding, saying, for instance, the work offered:

> a reason to get out of bed ... It's helped me ... because ... I get out
> and talk to people.

> I really enjoyed meeting new people.

The interviewers liked feeling part of a team and meeting people
through the work. It was an important feature of the capacity-building
nature of the work, that the interviewers were given training and feedback
to increase their skills and confidence. As one expressed it:

> My opinions and views were encouraged all the way through, I was
> kept informed and up to date – it made me feel like a valued
> member of the team.

In terms of work, all but one (who had reached the age of retirement) were at a time of transition in terms of employment. Three of the interviewers went on to posts in some form of community work. As one of them expressed it, through involvement in the survey she realized:

> I wasn't happy with my current job and it made me look long and hard at what I was doing and the direction I wanted to go … I've since terminated my employment … and have taken a part-time job … This allows me to volunteer … as a trainee advisor and I've just started a training course – so who knows what the future will hold!

Two other interviewers mentioned that being able to refer to the survey work helped them in job applications. One of the interviewers was waiting until her children were in school full time before looking for more work.

Implications of the work

The implications of this work reach beyond the present programme. As numerous research studies (particularly in the field of health) demonstrate, involvement of local people in the research process itself adds value to research by making it more valid, and offer a lay perspective on issues that are pertinent to the particular communities in which the work is undertaken (for example, Entwistle et al., 1998; Macaulay et al., 1999).

Local people have wide-ranging experience of key issues for the community and ways to enhance the quality of life there. Part of the task is to raise the expectations of people in the area. As one of the interviewers described it:

> There's an awful lot of people and an awful lot in this area, they've been deprived for so long that they don't expect enough.

This work is cumulative. It takes a long time for new ways of working to become embedded and accepted. As one of the interviewers expressed it, she was hopeful that by the time the second set of interviews were conducted, people would have had more of a chance to interact with Sure Start and find out about what it had to offer. The first group of parents interviewed had had only limited engagement with Sure Start, but this was likely to change over time:

> When we go and these 4-year-olds are down the line, the mothers will know already about Sure Start because they've had some kind of help and support for when their 4-year-old were 1 year old. But

now you are going out and doing 4-year-olds and unless mothers are out in community, which a lot will come home from school and shut door and that's it, isn't it? They don't know about Sure Start.

One of the interviewers gave an example of how long-established ideas are hard to change:

A lot of people in area associate Sure Start with social services ... 'cos it [the building] used to be a children's home ... That stigma will stay with Sure Start because it's in that building as well. Even my next-door neighbour, she's in her sixties, I tell her about Sure Start and she still thinks it's the children's home. And my children go across there and she still thinks it's children's home. She doesn't listen to what I say.

Work needs to be given time to become established. As one of the interviewers who had had considerable experience of community ventures commented:

I've seen too many things start and disappear because they've not been there long enough for people to get roots and people know them.

The interviewers were starting to pick up that while there were still a large number of families contacted during the initial stages of the survey who had not heard of Sure Start, for many that had, it was starting to make a difference. As one of them said:

I've learned that there's a lot of good young parents out there without a lot of money and that a lot of them are good mums and dads but they're not overly well educated themselves ... the one's I've gone to that are involved in Sure Start in some way do talk differently, I don't mean more proper, I mean when you ask them a question about what's it like being a parent they'll say 'It's alright, it's good being a parent' ... Whereas the one's that aren't find it more difficult.

Work on the survey contributed fundamental information needed for evaluation of the programme. It also raised the profile of the work within the community, and contributed to the capacity-building nature of the work by giving new skills and opportunities to the people who trained and worked as community interviewers, and who made the whole venture possible.

References

Entwistle, V. et al. (1998) Lay perspectives: advantages for health research. *British Medical Journal*, 316: 463–6.

Hawtin, M., Hughes, G. and Percy-Smith, J. (1994) *Community Profiling: Auditing Social Needs*. Buckingham: Open University Press.

Macaulay, A. (1999) Participatory research maximizes community and lay involvement. *British Medical Journal*, 319: 774–8.

Nutbrown, C., Hannon, P. and Morgan, A. (2005) *Early Literacy Work with Families: Policy, Practice and Research*. London: Sage Publications.

Part Six
What have we learned?
What do we need to know?

18 Bringing it together: the role of the programme manager
Linda Fox, programme manager, talks to the editors

In the book, we present a variety of different perspectives on the Foxhill and Parson Cross programme but, as we see integration as a key theme, we wanted to offer an overview of the whole enterprise. Linda Fox, who was involved from the outset, was interviewed about her experience, from the point of view of a programme manager. Questions were sent out in advance, so Linda had time to think about the issues. We asked her to reflect on key issues that stood out for her. To help the process of reflection, we prepared a 'spider diagram' of Linda's role. This informed our discussion. The final version of the diagram is shown in Figure 18.1. What is offered here is in the form of a conversational response as Linda talked about her observations in an interview context. This was taped, and the transcription provides the basis of this chapter, with key phrases highlighted. While this is a personal point of view, the key ideas will have resonance for those engaged in similar contexts.

Jo: 'We're reflecting on the programme as a whole from your perspective of the leadership role. What have been the greatest challenges and the worst moments for you?'

New roles and expectations

Linda: 'OK, the greatest challenges I think have been *employing a whole new staff team*. Writing every job description, every person specification, getting them all graded against jobs that weren't there. There was absolutely no historical script from which to draw on. Some of the jobs were an educated best guess at the time. Some initial errors have come back to haunt me a little as the years have gone on. Bringing a whole new staff team in, in new roles with blurred boundaries has been a major challenge.

You need a lot of time with staff to enable them to *step out of historical roles*. I would particularly say that was pertinent to home

Figure 18.1 Aid for interview with Linda Fox, February 2004 Role of Programme Manager

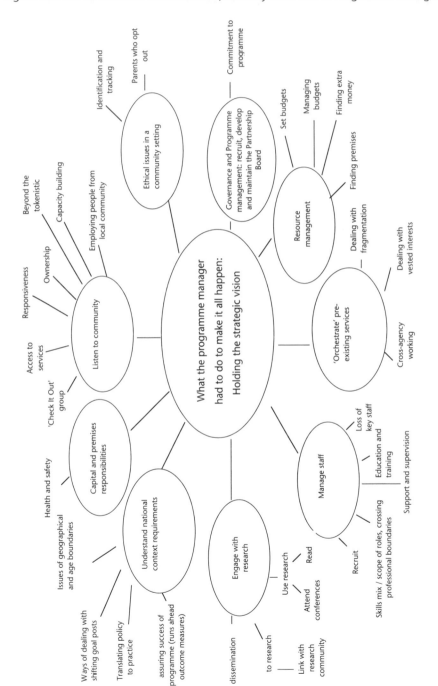

visitors and to early years staff where we wanted a different way of working in Sure Start. Home visitors as an example were trained to do one thing – maybe visit with a previously set objective, but we wanted them to visit families with a different open agenda. That has been very challenging.

... I've thought about the current challenges to me, particularly regarding the programme as a whole. One is getting the actual *programme accepted as a credible service within statutory agencies'* ... think getting some aspects of the service accepted by some individuals has been OK, but some professionals in particular in key positions have more difficulty in accepting such a new way of working.

I think the biggest challenge for me at the moment is perhaps managing change as the local programme becomes part of a much bigger Sure Start organization and *children's centre* initiative.

Perhaps some of the other challenges are relate back to the workforce. *Developing a multi-skilled and a multi-agency team.* Getting social workers, midwives, health visitors and local peer workers to understand the same language work towards a common aim and not to be vying for position. I didn't want one worker to feel that they were superior to another. We've been very keen at interview to tease this out, to get the right people in post with the right attitude, I think we've done that pretty well with 90 per cent of my workforce. But the 10 per cent where we haven't got it quite right, is an issue that comes back to haunt me every day of my working life and causes a lot of difficulties within the team.'

Jo: 'About the need to be really diplomatic, to be able to engage with all those very different people in different ways and make them feel on side...?'

Linda: 'I think you need a lot of **tact** and a lot of **diplomacy**. I also think it's about **timing**. I've learnt not to react so quickly when somebody tells me something negative about a worker, it's important to get the facts first when dealing with staff issues ... I think it's been quite a surprise to me how little self-esteem and confidence some of the workforce have got. I think the other big surprise and challenge I have faced is the fact that many workers have brought a lot of personal problems to work. Dealing with this, separating it out, takes time, takes being part of a workforce, takes maturity and it does take an awful lot of diplomacy.'

Jo: 'It's interesting because you're talking about an organization where roles are being forged and that's in contrast to agencies where people go in and they know what their task is. That gives them that shield.

So what you're saying sounds as though it would be quite widely replicated. It's not these particular people, is it, it's the roles...'

Linda: 'I know it's replicated. I know it's the same with the other Sure Starts in the city. We talk about this issue when we meet; it is a challenge and a dilemma we try to work it through together ... All the Sure Starts have tried to create, a very supportive management team, but we're not everybody's friend, I think I've learned to be much clearer about what's expected of workers as time has gone on. We have had to impose boundaries in some roles, because the edges can be blurred, but you would ... expect people to know their own boundaries in certain positions and that hasn't always been the case. So it's caused some problems with some staff. We haven't had any major disasters. I wouldn't for instance be expecting, and this is just an example, I wouldn't be expecting a peer support worker with half a day's training in child protection to manage a child protection case. But sometimes they think they have to.'

Jo: 'Yes, yes. It's a very good example because there will be quite a few of those sorts of issues that come up. Presumably one of your roles is to be very attentive?'

Linda: 'Absolutely. And discuss issues with staff and bring them back to the role without making them feel that they've done it wrong. But also to be clear that there are other people who have got skills and experience in certain areas that can do it better. I think that has taken quite a lot of management time.'

Jo: 'As you're talking I'm thinking of this as a sort of overview of what this job entails. So the things you're saying also apply across other Sure Starts, other circumstances.'

Linda: 'I think a word that we probably need to include is expectations. I think there has been an awful lot of *expectation of unqualified staff*. I think as well as this applies to qualified staff who working in different roles ... I guess an example there would be that of the Sure Start midwife and health visitor, a statutory midwife or a statutory health visitor might be expected to do some of their statutory work. In actual fact we've brought them out of that to do a completely different role. That has caused some tensions. And it has also caused ... a number of *key staff* to feel *isolated from their own professional peers*. It's easier now but it has taken four years. It's another factor that we've had to deal with together by supporting each other. I've personally had to pick a few of the key staff up off the floor on a number of occasions. It's a very difficult thing to be suddenly isolated by your peers. I guess the easiest thing for them would have been for them to go back. It's a credit to them that they didn't and that they stayed for the course. So that's good isn't it?'

Jo: 'And what you're describing is a process isn't it? Some of these things when you started you wouldn't have known which way it would go.'

Linda: 'Some people were positive towards the new roles. I would celebrate someone moving on and trying new things. That's my personality and it's been a surprise to me that that hasn't happened. Particularly with professional peer groups. That hasn't been the case with social work. Social workers have seen the partnership potential of the programme, they've seen the advantage, they've seen the positive working with families in Sure Start. The services we can offer. That sort of professional divide hasn't been there. The respect stayed with social work but in the health field it hasn't.'

Challenges to the vision

Jo: 'Shall we go on then to the worst moments. Do you want to give me some worse moments?'

Linda: 'Yes, ... actually I came up with a list ... *The loss of [one of our centres]* in April 2002 was a really bad moment for us. We'd only been in there 18 months. We'd just got the place absolutely buzzing and then for it to be on the council's demolition list, was an absolute shock. Also we'd invested an awful lot of money in it's refurbishment. So that was a very difficult thing to manage and to handle. It also meant that I had to find spaces for 8 or 9 staff at that time and I hadn't got anywhere to place them ... So it meant that the whole of the family centre had to be re-organized. And we were quite literally, and still are to this day, sharing offices. It caused a lot of pressure and a lot of stress. Even more importantly it caused a lot of friction with the parents on Foxhill. Even though we have a nursery on Foxhill, Foxhill parents don't see that they have a centre on Foxhill. I've never got past that to this day and I still pick up the pieces from that. That was a really, really terrible time for us.

The second thing I'd probably say is *loss of* key *staff*. I've only just started to suffer this. It's only been really in the last six months but a classic was just before Christmas this year where I lost qualified nursery staff, just before Christmas and just before OFSTED. Quite literally four weeks before. That was very hard.

And the loss of the home visiting family support workers at a critical time when we'd just got that team sorted. But they've all gone on to better opportunities. They've gone really to a competitor that I can't compete with, which is statutory services. So they've got secure jobs, longer contracts and in some cases more money as well, for doing what we were asking of them here. So no blame to those workers, absolutely great, but when you've trained them up, got them there, got them qualified, it's very hard on the programme. So we're starting again and that's maybe one of the key challenges, starting again.'

Jo: 'When you start again do you start from a new base though?'

Linda: 'We do start from a new base because we've learned, and we start from a new job description quite often. Then there's a dilemma for us because the rest of that team might be still wanting to work to their old job description but life's changed. So through the performance management system that we have, we sit down in supervision and appraisal and look for the changes to bring the team to where we want them to be. It's not an easy process, but at least it's there.

Another area I would say was the worse moment for me as programme manager was when I realized that a vital staff team (the outreach home visiting team) couldn't work as a team because of personalities. I just couldn't build the team, no matter what strategy, what support, no matter what I did. For me that was a really big disappointment, because still to this day, I believe there is an enormous amount of value in the preventative, very early home visiting work with babies they were to undertake. But I couldn't sell the idea to them, even though the workers had applied for those jobs: So the actual dissolving of that team was a worst moment.'

Jo: 'Sure, so that's not being able to match your vision with what actually happened?'

Linda: 'I haven't been able to replace the team to match the vision. If you're two or three years into your programme, you're not actually starting are you? You're half way through a vision.'

Jo: 'Yes, that's right, and you have to modify it in the light of real experience, don't you?'

Linda: 'Yes, and that's what we've done. I think another worst moment was when we **lost the coordinator's post** [of the Sure Start programme] when I became programme manager and … I've not had the funding or the structure to put that coordinator post back in place. I personally think it's a vital post. As the pressures on me as a programme manager have increased, my ability to coordinate the activities and keep abreast of activities and keep the staff team, communities and statutory workers informed has diminished. That was quite a loss to the programme.'

Limits to the programmes' control

Linda: 'Another worst moment for me was receiving **the health visitor report** (see Chapter 8). I found that very hard. When it's written in black and white, to realize those tensions were out there, three years into the programme I felt personally very disappointed. As you know things have turned around tremendously since then. But it was a low point.'

Jo: 'Presumably particularly because that's your background as a health visitor, is that right? Wanting to have that support from your peers?'

Linda: 'Yes ... The report didn't blame the health visitors, it didn't blame my staff it was a 50-50. That was clear. I think what was the worst moment was the realization how helpless I was within it. I can work with my own staff team, but I don't manage the health visitors. I think the worst thing was the realization that this was ... nearly 100 per cent out of my control and I couldn't influence it. So that was quite a realization because I naively expected when I started, that everyone would go with us. I think that when I realized that not everybody would go with us, including my own staff team, it was not a good time.

Another worst moment was when we received a letter, about two years ago saying that we were **not allowed to have basic information and data about families locally**. We expected to have access to basic data and then that was not possible because of data protection, which is obviously understandable. It was a really bad moment and it's caused enormous problems within the programme. I've got are shared targets with the city but unless things change, we weren't able to meet them. This was completely out of my control. So that was a really bad moment, we were all pretty shocked by that. I've had to find ways around it, which we have, but it's just been very, very hard work.'

Jo: 'You've had to think creatively because you've been asked to do these things then the tools you need to do them with have been withdrawn?'

Linda: 'Yes, and that came from having different employers. It was a different health employer when we started who said it was OK. Then a different health employer who said it wasn't OK. And that's fine and I understand that. Obviously we've now resolved that issue but it's taken two years to resolve it. That's a slog by anybody's standards. We felt very isolated and left uncertain about how we were going to progress.'

Jo: 'And shifting goal posts, moving targets ... the structure in which you're working is changing all the time?'

Linda: 'So if anybody could tell me how I could reach 100 per cent antenatal women without knowing who they are, then they're a better person than I am. Remarkably we found 86 per cent ourselves.

Another worst moment for me was I think when we realized ... they're all things I think that are completely out of our control here, was this realization that there was no consistent approach in the city to any data collection and we were to be measured against baselines. That was really difficult and the data that was there, there was a whole question mark over whether it was accurate and who owned the data ... That's been very hard and was a definite worst moment.

Those have been real struggles for us and still continue to this day.'

Jo: 'They are really challenging, all the things that you describe.'

Linda: 'You know we've got past them. I'm reflecting back, obviously we've got past them now. It's so much now that the city has eight Sure Starts. Complex as it is for the city, it's has raised the profile of local programmes enormously. Agreements are now in place. We've worked very positively together on those things.'

Jo: 'I think it's important to put it in that sort of context because we could just sell this as a great success story without seeing all the real work that goes on underneath and that's what you want to unpack and show what it needs and what are the topics that really need addressing.'

Achievements that stand out

Linda: 'So shall we go on [to the most rewarding times?]'

Jo: 'Yes.'

Linda: 'There are a few areas really. One of the most rewarding times was
when we got our *second three year funding* from 2003 to 2006. It
came very late in the day and staff didn't know whether to apply for
other jobs and I was saying, "No". I was reassuring, holding, holding
and eventually on our Awayday we eventually got the fax to tell us
we were getting the funding. We were highly, highly relieved. That
gave us a further three years.

I think another rewarding thing really rather than time, we have
definitely *achieved a core committed workforce* here. I do have a
really committed core staff team. There are one or two exceptions to
that and they are very difficult to manage, but in general that's a
credit to the programme.

I think as well what's enormously rewarding is that I think we
have achieved some fantastic things. I've made a list here. *Two Sure
Start nurseries*. All of those child care places, a *flexible* crèche *team*.

Acquiring a new building was an enormously rewarding thing to
do and quite a weight off our minds. We were really struggling at the
Family Centre with a staff team of over 30 sharing four tiny offices.

I think the antenatal work has been extremely rewarding. They've
achieved their own successes in their own way. They're nationally
recognized and I'm delighted with that.

We had an excellent *Sure Start risk assessment*, we were the first
in Yorkshire and Humberside to get a zero. We had an excellent
OFSTED [inspection] (by government department responsible for
inspection of schools in England) and I think we've *created a lovely
centre for the community*, it's a beautiful centre. It's not by any
means posh or clinical but it's a real family centre and it has a lovely
family feel to it and it's a welcoming centre. So I'm really proud of
that, it's really rewarding to see.

I think another reward to counteract the worst moments was
getting the *consent from the Health Trust to* receive *basic information*. It's only just happened, in the last few months. That shows
what a struggle that's been for a trailblazer programme, but it's there
now. I have to thank my health colleagues for getting that through.
That's brilliant. That's my most rewarding bits I think.'

Jo: 'A couple of things. One was just whether you could say more about the *antenatal success*. If you have something in particular in your mind about that?'

Linda: 'It's a very diverse team. It has local parents, it has professionals. It has para-professionals (a term that nobody likes). They've had to change. They had initial targets around low birth weight and breast-feeding and hygiene. Having to achieve 100 per cent contact and a target that changed towards smoke cessation. So out of all the teams I think they've had a lot of change to get their heads around. We employ breastfeeding peer support workers and then our target is smoke cessation. So that takes quite a bit of managing. I'm particularly delighted because they've worked very, very hard to get their baseline data. They had to do it themselves. The evaluations of the work showed fantastic increase in breastfeeding rates (see Chapter 7) as well to date they've had over 50 women through the La Léche accredited breastfeeding training. The team have also achieved exceptional outcomes regarding their first years' work in antenatal smoke cessation with a 17 per cent reduction achieved. These are really key outcomes.'

Jo: 'That was the other thing I was going to ask you about successes. What about *relationships with local people, with the community*?'

Linda: 'Yes, it's hit and miss. They either love or hate us. There are tensions because we have a geographical boundary. *There are tensions because we have an age limit.*

I understand that there's a good feel in the community about Sure Start, and we don't get refused access and *we are implementing the plan that was shared very much in the beginning with the community*. I think that's really successful.

I think the tensions are around ... , *it's very difficult to keep the community informed.* Even when newsletters and things like that that get posted out, people don't know what's going on off in what area and in what way. I depend very heavily on local professionals to do that for me. Where it does happen, it happens, where it doesn't, it doesn't. But I think in general engaging with the community is as improving, the parental involvement team do awesome work... I think they've been the key to that success. They're not frightened of coming in and saying this committee is fed up about this or that, and you're not supporting that group very well. So it's a challenge in it's own right. You can't do everything with everybody.'

Dilemmas

Jo: 'Are you ready to move on to the next bit? Dilemmas?'

Linda: 'I think the dilemmas are around *local agenda versus national agenda*. The *community* set their own plan and it was mostly around *building self-esteem and confidence and developing opportunities, good childcare, and having a range of facilities.*

Making sure that all the partner agencies in the community held a contract so that we could secure some local specialist work and keeping the whole community and the working community locally engaged with Sure Start through that process is one thing. But the national agenda is changing and has changed and some of the things that the community want we can't give, we can't do it all. We need key partners to share the work with us.

I think a dilemma is funding around some of those things because there is funding in the programme, Sure Start parents might be excluded from applying for external funding, so if there's a group for instance … we wouldn't have the funding for a new group, … but maybe they're women who've come through Sure Start. They might apply for funding, but they would have it refused because they would be seen as a Sure Start group and we should be funding it. So those are just local dilemmas that we have.

I think we've done pretty well meeting national targets. Some of the targets that we have are shared targets with local professionals. So I don't think locally there's a problem there but *I don't think the targets we have are particularly shared with the local community*.

Smoke cessation would be one. Nobody when we wrote our plan, at any of the community meetings said they wanted to achieve smoke cessation or tackle low birth weight. They were much more into getting support at the point of need, a different level of support for different levels of need. Having good childcare is essential when families are stressed. *The community have always been pretty clear about 'this is what we need to prevent a need for that'.* And some of that ties in, but the whole programme has to meet other targets as well.

One of the dilemmas I've had as a programme manager is *re-selling new targets to the team*. It takes a long time to develop a workforce, get them focused, get them working in one way. Sure Start and the team feel that and they're almost waiting for yet another target and at some point the team will turn round and say, 'enough's enough', won't they? … And although the new targets have a component of the old targets, they are new targets by which we need to report against. Anyway, that's quite a dilemma for us.

I talked a little bit earlier about a dilemma is this changing of the focus of the main aim of the teams. I'm selling it, this is where I want you to go, this is what I want you to do. I get them trained, get them upbeat, get them doing it, then within months I can be asking them to take a slightly different direction. That's hard.

I think there are current **dilemmas around data sharing and con-fidentiality**. I think the interface between ourselves and statutory services, particularly around maybe family support work is an area that we just have to work together on every day. Mostly we'll get it right and occasionally we will get that wrong ... I'm continually reminded that when people live locally, they know a lot about some local people and that's a real **confidentiality issue** for us. So I have to drive that home a lot within the programme. It's different for people like me that live 10 miles away, but I wouldn't talk about it anyway, I wouldn't talk about a family. That's a dilemma for some of the staff who live locally where they've had people knocking on the doors and things like that. Exactly what can we share and exactly what can we tell somebody else. I've just spoken to them as a friend because they came at six o'clock at night ... They're dilemmas that I don't think other people particularly face.

I [also] think **motivation** I would have to put as a dilemma. I know I'm very highly motivated and a very positive person. If I dip, my team dips. That's a pressure and I know that, if I'm struggling, they'll struggle. You get a sort of wave. I'm up more than I'm down but ... you almost have to be 100 per cent positive and motivated all the time for this job and nobody's capable of that! ... I don't have a problem with self-motivation but continually motivating others ... It takes a lot of energy.'

Jo: 'That's the thing about breaking new ground isn't it?'

Linda: 'Quite a dilemma isn't it? I have to keep my street credibility within this programme and I use a lot of my personality to do that and sell it in that way. The key to that is being really honest. I don't hold anything back unless it's something confidential that I really can't share. So **being as honest as you can and continually selling the message to your team** is vital.

A real dilemma for us is having a finite budget for a fully fledged, fully running Sure Start with increasing demands on it. A two and a half per cent [increase] from the government in real terms is a five per cent cut in my budget. The increase picks up the cost of living but it doesn't pick up pay increases, and last year we had a one per cent National Insurance increase as well. So last year was even harder for us. If you're managing a budget over a million pounds, that's a lot of money. This is the second year where I've been looking at *job losses* within the programme. That's a real dilemma because all the jobs are needed. They've been really hard decisions to take and it has affected staff morale. It will be exactly the same next year.

I think that's probably more to do with trailblazers. We were up very quickly, up to capacity within a few years ... I know a lot of programmes don't use their full budget. But we do. That's a dilemma for me and a dilemma for the partnership board.'

What makes a programme manager?

Jo: 'Shall we move on to your professional development?'

Linda: 'I've thought about this and wasn't too sure about what in my professional development prepared me for this role. Probably a lot in my own life prepared me for this role rather than the professional route that I've taken. I think if you've needed to be tough in your own life, you've needed to face a lot of things then you know it shapes your personality. Personality is important and it's not particularly centred around a professional pathway.

But what I did think around my professional pathway was I worked locally as a health visitor. Had a really good knowledge of families' needs. I could visually see the impact of poverty and hopelessness every day of my working life. I had a real drive to want to change that, to try and make things better. I started with fairly small things that are still here, thank goodness, to this day. Like Women Supporting Mothers, the teenage mums' group and a few other things like that. I did a piece of work around engaging the community in health services and I learned a lot doing that. Only a three-month piece of work but *I learned such a lot about the anger in this community, but also its commitment to improve itself.* Often when I went along to tenants and residents to ask, 'how about getting engaged with health services and a strategic direction and making some decisions', ... actually what I ended up sorting out was the fact that that person's mother needed a tree chopping down in their front garden because no light was coming in and therefore she couldn't see. So what I learned was that there was a whole tier to be dealt with before you could get anybody to deal with strategic stuff. That's the lesson I've brought with me.'

Jo: 'That's really interesting. Who funded that work then?'

Linda: 'It was funded by … a group of general practitioners working with
        the health authority … I engaged with the community in a very dif-
        ferent way to how I had done as a health worker. I learned that I
        went in with one agenda and in actual fact there was an awful lot of
        things that needed to be put in place first. The community were very
        clear, if Health wanted them to get engaged this is what would have
        to be done. But even at the end of it Health were unable to progress
        the work because it cost money they didn't have … it wasn't the will
        that was missing, they didn't actually have the resources to do it at
        the end. I learned about that.

        Previous project management [of three local projects] … stood me
        in really good stead, because I knew lots of people. I think some of
        the professional development I brought with me was from project
        management and knowledge of local needs.

        The route followed *joint working with NCH* [voluntary agency
        which sponsored the programme], I had a really good relationship
        with [the manager of the family centre]. We've been very much a
        team and I've learned a lot from her. A lot of my professional devel-
        opment has come from having a role model.

        Just before this Sure Start I was awarded a *travel scholarship* to
        Seattle which enabled me to go and have a look at an educational
        experimental unit as they call it. It was a really fantastic nursery for
        children who are living with adversity and in poverty, the scholar-
        ship enabled me to learn a little about Headstart and to have a look
        at some parenting programmes. Four of us went, I learned a lot. It's
        shaped a lot of the vision here. Once I saw some things, I saw the
        gaps here. It's been about not doing it in exactly the same way, but
        learning the good things from that and bringing those back here.'

Jo: 'And seeing potential in that way of *working*?'

Linda: 'Seeing a completely different way *of* working, particularly with chil-
        dren. So that was a very influential part of my professional develop-
        ment.

        I don't think there's a lot more … I *suppose* my health visiting …
        but I don't think it's a special thing that prepared me for this job. I
        think had I been a social worker, had I been a teacher and I'd had the
        same experience I've been lucky enough to have, I think it would
        have prepared me in the same way. So I don't think it's the profes-
        sional qualification that's prepared me for this role.

        Again I am a pretty *motivated person*, quite a good planner. I can
        often find my way through fog and I can find the sunshine at the

end of it. I think that's been pretty important in this. But whether that's come through my professional career or just ... my own personal journey I don't know.'

Jo: 'What holds you there? What *keeps* you there?'

Linda: 'Well there is another key ingredient then and I think it's 30 years in nursing. It's been mopping up. *I've seen what happens to babies when their mothers have been unhealthy.* Once you've seen something like that, to get the chance to *work in a preventative way* is like a gift. That's really what I've always wanted to do. I think that's my absolute driver. Because I've seen it and wanted to prevent it happening.'

Jo: 'I guess this has given you an *opportunity* to do that and to shape things?'

Linda: 'The reason I went into health visiting was because it was preventative work, so I think that probably has prepared me quite well, on reflection.'

Key aspects of the vision guiding the work

Jo: 'That leads to this final *point*. I don't know what more you have to say about it, about the *vision*?'

Linda: 'I don't think anybody *can* be equipped for this job and I think it's a *continual learning* for us all. But there are some things that I wanted ... that I was not professionally prepared for.
        One is around *staff management and human resources management*. I've learned such a lot. As you know we have a leading accountable body who are NCH. I've had to learn about a whole new organization as well as having a whole new organization with Sure Start. I have to work within NCH policies and there are high standards and expectations of NCH managers. Quite often it's like a double job. I've needed to learn how to manage that and at times I haven't been able to do it all. NCH have been supportive and fantastic and understand that we need time to grow. I would say it's taken me ... in fact, I'm still not there. I've only been two years as programme manager, but maybe in four years I will be able to manage both.

Two business plans, two lots of monitoring. That's a lot to have learned. I've had to learn about capital. I've had to learn about managing premises. I've had to learn about health and safety and *risk* assessment, I'd never dreamt of. I've had to use a lot of *common sense* and I've had to learn how to *make a lot of decisions and live with them*. I've had to learn a lot about *finance* and different kinds of *budgets* and I've also needed to learn about *budget projection* and *forecasting*.

Another learning for me has been politics – local, city wide, nationally. I've had to understand the *influence* of politics, politicians and the role of politicians. I've had to learn all about that. How the council works and how national politicians work ... Just managing local politics as well, as you please one area you're certainly going to upset another. So there's been a lot of politics to manage at local level.

I wanted to just say as well, some of the persistent tensions are around staff. Unlike statutory workers, Sure Start staff are on *short-term contracts with short-term funding*. It's really, really tough. So you'd expect the people who come to you either need to be either really, really up for it or they've come for a different reason. That is very, very hard and we cannot compete with statutory agencies who have long-term, mainstream, sustained funding. It's not a job for life here for anybody. So there's a continual tension within the programme. Take externally funded programmes like the peer support breastfeeding. That finishes at end of March. It's proved all it's outcomes, done the cost-effectiveness report, fantastic. But there's nobody to pick that up. It's a real tension.

I think the lack of *space* to work is a continuing tension. I still haven't got enough space for everybody to work. I've still got half a desk in quarter of an office I share with someone else.

I think change, after change, after change really. Managing change. I've learned so much about managing change.

The vision. I was thinking about this and I've come at it from a programme manager's angle rather than the vision that was set for us by Sure Start. Our vision here, and I'm one of a number of key people [who developed it, is] about *creating a multi-skilled workforce locally that works well with the local workers and professionals and the community, meeting families' needs at the point of request*.

We've always had that *vision*. It's an enormously challenging vision I now know. I think we've gone a long way towards it but in some areas we've a long way to go. I've learned that personalities matter and I've learned an individual can make such a difference either very positively or in a sabotaging negative way and often this is out of my control.

My vision was around having a preventative programme, firmly focused from antenatal to four years. It is an *improvement agenda* and I guess there have been some tensions early on because everybody wants you to spend all your time with the children and the families who are most in need. We've needed to meet those needs in partnership with others, but we still have the needs of another 90 per cent of children in the community to meet.

It's the whole community, this, and I think our vision has always been firmly focused on that. Sure Start provides a targeted approach but within a universal service, in a defined geographical boundary.

Our vision was around having *an opportunity to try things out and learn the lessons from them* early on. That was always our vision. That's always been mine as a programme manager. I'm *firmly* committed to this approach. If there's something in the community that we're not meeting, I can check it out, ask questions. Is there a preventative element to it? Is it somebody else's responsibility? Is it Sure Start business? I can check out half a dozen questions and if the answer is 'yes', it's about re-shaping and meeting that need.

A classic would be a *letter from* the hospital about a child with special needs maybe $3^1/_2$ years old. Maybe going into nursery but travelling, and the mother and the child need some extra help but they can only do it at certain times. So I have to then work with my team to say this child fits all the criteria you want to work with. The fact that this child needs the service at five o'clock at night is *our problem, not the child's problem. We've got to find a way of meeting that need.* Rather than having this, I go home at five o'clock and that's somebody else's problem and letting the child fall by the wayside. And that's been hard because people want to go home and work normal office hours. So getting individual needs met is sometimes a challenge to us as well as meeting the needs of the whole community.'

Jo: 'I think what comes *across* most strongly is that clarity and the way in which you express that vision. It is very clear. The other thing that comes across is the honesty with which you look at these things and are able to unpack them and make sense of them. That's really helpful. It's helpful for the programme but in terms of this book it's really helpful in terms of what we can offer to other people about what this is really about.'

19 Looking to the future
Peter Hannon, Caroline Pickstone, Jo Weinberger and Linda Fox

Introduction

The theme of this book has been learning from Sure Start. For us the learn-ing goes on but we want in this concluding chapter to try to draw together some of the specific lessons learned from previous chapters. In doing so we need to point out that evaluation cannot cover everything that has been done and we acknowledge valuable aspects of the programme that we have not been able to investigate. This chapter is also an opportunity for us to reflect on what we have learned about the process of undertaking evalua-tion and research in a local programme. We then venture beyond our own documented research and evaluation to explore general lessons about the programme. Finally, we identify some key issues and questions in need of research and evaluation and share our own hopes and vision for the future of Sure Start. This chapter differs from earlier chapters in that some views expressed are less directly linked to specific findings. We are sharing views rather than reporting findings. However, as we have been observers of the programme over several years, we hope that our considered reflections may be of interest to others who share our concern to learn from Sure Start.

Specific lessons learned about the programme

In Chapter 1 we explained that, at the beginning of the programme:

> No-one could be certain that a programme could be devised, implemented, managed and sustained over a period of years. No-one could be certain what would work and what would not. Yet there was a shared determination that if it did work, that story should be told; if it did not work, lessons needed to be learned.

We are now in a position to share some of the story of what has worked and also lessons about what did not work out as we hoped.

Whatever the initial uncertainties, one finding now that is quite clear is that this Sure Start programme was actually devised, implemented, managed and sustained over a period of years. Appendix 1 shows that it includes a considerable amount of activity and it is now entering its fifth year. The story of what it has involved, through the eyes of the programme manager, is told in the previous chapter, 'Bringing it all together'. There have been many challenges to be overcome but local energies, coupled with national funding and support, did make things happen.

Also clear is that there are services in the programme that have worked well, in some cases dramatically so. For example, Sue Battersby's evaluation of peer support for breastfeeding (Chapter 7) indicates that it succeeded in more than doubling the breastfeeding rate in the area and that the scheme had additional benefits for the women who acted as the peer supporters. Margaret Drake's evaluation of Connecting with our Kids (Chapter 4) shows that the Webster-Stratton parenting education course was successfully transferred out of its original clinical context to a community-wide service; and that parents valued the course when they completed it (and in later years). Jo Weinberger's evaluation of the Family Support Service (Chapter 3) shows that it succeeded in being flexible, responsive and able to help the families referred to it in ways that other agencies would have been unlikely to achieve. The account by Simon Martinez (in Chapter 10) of the work of the Early Years Team showed that its input into community play settings raised the quality of play and learning, an improvement detected by independent quantitative measures. The work of the programme's community teacher (evaluated by Jackie Marsh and Jan Forde in Chapter 11) showed how valuable her role was, even though it involved extreme demands in relation to the available time resource. The Young Families' Advice Service (evaluated by Imogen Hale in Chapter 16) succeeded in being accessible to families with young children and had a substantial effect on their lives in terms of increased housing security and reduced child poverty by bringing financial benefits to families entitled to them. The evaluation by Robin Carlisle of the early stages of the Home Safety Scheme (Chapter 9) shows that the scheme was reaching families and that they appreciated the service. The account of community involvement by Helen Lomas and Peter Hannon (Chapter 15) shows that there was community input into the programme, and, for a significant number of parents, the programme created a ladder of development opportunities.

Yet some of the research highlighted areas where services met more challenges. Our original view of evaluation – encapsulated in the maxim, 'No mistakes, no learning' – stressed the importance of identifying those aspects of the programme that did not work (or were problematic) so that appropriate action could be taken. There are instances of this in previous chapters. Anne Morgan's evaluation of dialogic reading (Chapter 14) showed that, despite very strong – apparently evidence-based – claims from the United States about its effectiveness, there was little impact on Sure Start children's oral language (although there appeared to be some benefits for their literacy development). Consequently that approach has not been pursued. The evaluation of how health visitors from the statutory service linked with the programme (Ann Rowe's report in Chapter 8) revealed problems beyond the power of those professionals or of the programme to solve (although these have now been addressed at a higher organizational and policy level). The evaluation of Connecting with our Kids (Chapter 4) showed that efforts to involve fathers directly were unsuccessful and that different approaches were required (thus leading to more use being made of mothers to involve their partners and later to the appointment of a men's project worker to operate across the entire programme). Another issue where research has forced rethinking concerned the difficulties of reaching families through home visits. In the 2-to-3 years age period, for example, this meant that, despite considerable efforts, no more than half the children in the area could be contacted and assessed for language development (see Caroline Pickstone's report in Chapter 12). The evaluation of some services revealed tensions in that maintaining a focus on the Sure Start area seemed to require turning away out-of-area families (even when they lived only a few yards outside the area and were requesting support). In the end, this problem was overcome by accepting that maintaining the integrity of services for within-area families could only be achieved by accepting the necessity of working with some families who were out-of-area.

Four chapters in the book report studies (all survey-based) undertaken to inform, rather than evaluate, the programme, or undertaken to provide a baseline for future evaluations. From the first baseline cohort of the community survey (reported by Jo Weinberger in Chapter 2) we learned that, while parents clearly expressed some unmet needs (which the survey enabled us to identify), Sure Start had begun to make an impact on individuals and families. Caroline Pickstone's research (in Chapter 12) found that trained support workers could identify children with very delayed language skill who needed referral for specialist assessment. Jackie Marsh's survey of the Sure Start children's media experiences (Chapter 13) has highlighted an area where there might be scope for intervention building on, rather than disregarding, families' current practices. Deborah Crofts' survey of support received by teenage mothers (Chapter 5) shows the relatively small amount of support provided by statutory services (in comparison with the girls' own mothers) and, again, provides a baseline against which future Sure Start provision can be assessed.

In summary, specific lessons have been learned about some aspects of the programme that appear to have been successful and some that have required rethinking. Also, we have learned about the current views and experiences of families in the community as a baseline for future work.

Aspects of the programme that we have not evaluated

Like trying to read a newspaper by the light of a torch beam, evaluation can only illuminate a portion of a programme at any one time. Constraints of time and other resources mean it is not possible to evaluate all services.

Appendix 1 lists services in the programme at the time of writing, from which it can be seen that not all feature in this book. The selection of services for evaluation reflect priorities of the programme's Research and Evaluation Advisory Committee and concerns of key programme staff. Evaluations of some important services (for example smoking cessation) are in progress; others await further study. In the community impact studies, it is still too early to report findings (since they depend upon comparing data from forthcoming surveys to data from pre-programme baseline surveys such as those described in Chapters 2 and 5). We have not been able to find space in this book for all the studies that have been undertaken, such as the evaluation of a service for new-to-area families. Reports are available via the NESS website, www.ness.bbk.ac.uk. Also, it must be recognized that the programme and its services are dynamic. All this is a reminder that learning from Sure Start needs to be a continuous process. Our hope, nevertheless, is that the work represented in this book ranges sufficiently widely, and touches upon enough fundamental issues, to be of interest to other Sure Start programmes, to comparable initiatives, including children's centres, and to policymakers.

Lessons learned about the process of local evaluation and research

Before considering some of the wider lessons about the programme, it is worth reflecting briefly on the process of research and evaluation within the programme that has led to the writing of this book. Our work began with the hopes expressed in Chapter 1. To what extent have these been realized? To answer this question, the four authors of this chapter, in consultation with other contributors to the book, have reflected upon their experiences since the programme was established.

Our first reflection is that it has actually proved possible to secure widespread support for, and participation in, research and evaluation. We cannot claim that all members of staff, and all members of the community associated with programme, are dedicated to research and evaluation, but it can be seen from the contents of this book that several have been sufficiently enthusiastic and committed to carry out and write up studies. Also, despite the anxieties that any of us would have when faced with the prospect of having our work evaluated, we do not believe that there has ever been any serious objection or obstacles placed in the way of evaluation activity. The culture within the programme, viewing research and evaluation as an integral component of service delivery, has been open to developing and changing on the basis of evidence.

Another noteworthy feature of the research and evaluation activity has been its trans-disciplinarity. Just as professionals from different backgrounds have been brought together in developing and running a Sure Start programme, so research into that programme has brought together researchers from different disciplines, in our case principally from the health, family support and education fields. Each has learned from the other. Educational researchers, for example, have learned from health colleagues' ways of thinking about public health, service audit and medical ethics, while health researchers have learned from education colleagues' approach to child assessment and social research. We have all expanded our horizons and research perspective beyond our initial disciplines and learned how other disciplines share a concern with fundamental issues such as equality of access, reach and community participation.

We have, however, encountered difficulties. One is that, despite the readiness of programme staff to be involved in evaluation, inevitably there were periods when service responsibilities had to take priority, thus slowing the progress of some studies.

The involvement of members of the community as interviewers for the parent survey was, in many ways, a success (as can be seen from Chapter 17), but the work was difficult, especially when it was hard to contact families for interviews. Their success in the work, paradoxically, created other difficulties. The opportunity, training and support that enabled women to work as interviewers also gave some of them the experience and confidence to return to, or seek, fuller employment. Those who gained other jobs had no time to continue as interviewers. Also, the nature of the employment – short term and irregular hours – combined with the demands of family life with young children, often made the data collection a slow process. The University team had continually to train new interviewers, and while this enhanced capacity in the community, it made it difficult to complete surveys on time.

Obtaining and managing basic data posed another challenge. In the early years of the programme, obtaining the names and addresses of children aged 0–4 in the area was never easy. Difficulties were exacerbated by the programme being outside the statutory health system so that data protection considerations meant agencies were reluctant to pass on data relating, for example, to names and addresses of new births. It was not until the third year, when there were many other Sure Start programmes operating throughout England, that access to data improved. Even when basic data were obtained, there were challenges in managing it efficiently to meet the needs both of the programme and of research and evaluation. A typical Sure

Start programme needed to know details of up to 250 antenatals and 1,000 children and their families at any one time, as well as manage daily changes such as transfers of 0–4s in and out of the area. The database needed to respond quickly and accurately to answer queries about take-up of services, and for the completion of monitoring forms. Another important requirement of the database was to provide families' contact details for staff wanting to communicate with them or make visits. Today there is commercially available software for this purpose. When our programme began, it took considerable time and effort – from a senior member of the programme staff with research expertise – to design appropriate, linked databases and to devise reliable inputting procedures. As we intended to use the data for research purposes we also had to devise ethically sound ways of transferring anonymized records into datasets for statistical analysis.

A final difficulty concerns sharing research and evaluation findings with the community. In some ways this has been easy in that it is built into the programme design. For example, the programme management board (which includes parents and other members of the community) has always been interested in the progress of research and evaluation and ready to discuss issues arising from it. Also, there have been well-received presentations of research and evaluation work at community update meetings, workshops and conferences. All parents participating in the interview survey were sent a summary of findings. The problem is that there have not been enough of these occasions and, in effect, much of the volume and detail of research and evaluation has been out of sight of the community. A further problem has arisen in communicating particular findings. For example, while the programme has been concerned to reduce the proportion of low birth weight babies in the area, sensitivity has been needed in discussing this with mothers who may have had low birth weight babies themselves or who may believe it is better to give birth to smaller babies. These are all issues that continue to be addressed.

General lessons about the programme

In this section we want to move beyond the evidence base provided by the other chapters in the book to consider broader lessons learned by contributors in the course of their involvement with the programme and its evaluation. We have – as a group – reflected on what our experience has taught us. What we have learned relates to five key issues: (i) the innovatory character of the programme; (ii) whether the programme as a whole is more than the sum of its parts; (iii) the impact on families; (iv) the area focus; and (v) the emergence of a new workforce.

(i) The innovatory character of the programme

It is clear that Sure Start *has* provided a context for innovation and that the programme *has* done new things. This is evident from Appendix 1, which details the full range of programme activities. That the range is so wide is perhaps a result of a 'no blame' programme culture that has empowered staff to try new ideas to meet diverse needs in the community. Also, because funding decisions could be made quickly by the programme itself, it was possible to support good ideas without having to follow lengthy bureaucratic procedures, thus releasing everyone's creativity. Many services were individually new in never before being accessible to families in the area; they were certainly new in being offered together as part of a comprehensive package. Staff were able to go out in the community with what the programme manager referred to as a 'shopping basket' of opportunities from which they could help families pick what they needed for their circumstances. Families have had the opportunity to take up numerous activities, some rarely heard of until recently (such as the Webster-Stratton parent education course, baby massage, the Community Health and Development course) as well as some that are familiar but had hitherto been limited (such as childcare, benefits advice for young families). Also, for some parents, there have been opportunities to develop personally through their involvement in the programme.

(ii) Whether the programme as a whole is more than the sum of its parts

There is some evidence that offering a combination of services within one programme has added to the value of all the services. There have been links between them. Parents using one service can be referred on to, or encouraged to take up, other services, for example, from the breastfeeding support scheme to baby massage or, for a parent with a sensory disability, from a language check to support to attend a mother and toddler group. If parents have a positive experience of one service, they are more likely to take up another if it is in the same familiar setting or obviously part of the same programme. It has been noticed that, as the programme has become more established, families who take up one service usually go on to more. It would have been very difficult to establish some services if others were not already established. Examples of this are the way in which a bereavement group grew out of the family support service, a teenage mothers' group developed out of the antenatal service, and a 'Play and Say' language scheme in toddler groups developed out of the 'talking check' service. Crèche provision has supported other services by freeing parents to participate. Services can share the same reception and secretarial infrastructure, database, and publicity. Every service has the potential to support every other service.

(iii) The impact on families

Previous chapters have described the impact of specific services on families, particularly on parents. What about the overall impact? Although research cannot yet tell us exactly how much impact there has been, with how many families, it is reasonable to conclude from studies in this book that to some degree children born in the Sure Start area are now less likely to have a mother smoking in pregnancy, less likely to be born below weight, less likely to be in poverty, less likely to be evicted, less likely to have an accident in the home, more likely to have been breastfed, more likely to experience good-quality out-of-home play and learning opportunities, more likely to have language delay identified and addressed, and more likely to have warmer and non-confrontational early relationships with their parents. Over and above this, staff who have worked with parents are convinced that many have gained enormously in self-esteem and confidence and that they have higher aspirations for their children as a result of engagement with the programme.

(iv) The area focus

An essential characteristic of the programme, in line with Sure Start policy, has been its focus on a clearly defined area. This has sometimes created difficulties, such as those discussed earlier in relation to out-of-area families wanting to use services. It has also been difficult on occasions to link with other agencies in primary care, social work and education whose own boundaries do not neatly map on to the programme area. It has been important to remember that families even in small geographical areas are heterogeneous and do not all have the same needs. On the other hand, within the programme there is strong support for the area focus. It is felt that the credibility of the programme in the eyes of the community, local loyalty to it, and even local pride in what has been accomplished individually and collectively depend upon the programme's association with a small locality. Also, from a practical point of view, having services within pram-pushing distances of families is very desirable. One member of staff commented, 'The message from people is that they want services that are local and accessible'. The area focus is welcomed by staff too. One said that it was good to be told, 'This is your patch'. Finally, it should be noted that for research and evaluation purposes it is very helpful to be able to define the population for a programme in geographical terms. Overall, we feel the advantages of having an area focus outweigh the disadvantages.

(v) The emergence of a new workforce

One of the most striking features of Sure Start is the way that workers from different agencies and professional backgrounds have been brought together to work towards a common aim. In addition, opportunities for pid work and volunteers, have been created. This has not been without difficulties. At first, the programme was not able to offer permanent employment contracts to staff (although it can now do so, subject to funding). Another issue relates particularly to the health professionals working for the programme. At the beginning they reported feeling isolated and marginalized by their peers, even if on secondment. The midwife in the programme could not be seconded; being employed to work in the programme meant that she lost her health employment status and was subsequently classified as a 'radical and independent' practitioner, no longer able to remain a member of the Royal College of Midwifery. The community teacher's commitment to the programme and to the community distanced her from normal educational support services and promotion opportunities within the local education authority. One has to ask whether Sure Start is a professional opportunity or a professional cul de sac. An additional pressure on Sure Start professionals is that they feel they need continually to prove the worth of their work, unlike their counterparts in statutory agencies whose activities are not scrutinized in the same way. The only good thing that can be said about these difficulties is that they have had a bonding effect on programme staff.

Despite insecurities relating to employment, programme staff find the new Sure Start way of working rewarding. Different professional skills have been respected while, at the same time, professional boundaries have been broken down. For example, a social worker and a midwife have been able to work together with a group of teenage mothers before and after the birth of their babies; a teacher and a social worker have collaborated in parent education courses. Such collaborations would be difficult to sustain within statutory services. Professionals have had more opportunity to extend their work beyond the boundaries of their conventional roles and to respond flexibly to families' needs, for example a teacher working with parent groups, a midwife working on smoke cessation and breastfeeding, a social worker supporting families before children need the protection of outside agencies. This could have been difficult within statutory services. There is no doubt that the opportunity to work with families in these ways has kept staff within Sure Start. There is a widely held feeling that 'there's no going back' to the way they worked before.

Key issues and questions for the future

Our experience and reflections about Sure Start have brought some key issues into focus and left us with questions about them.

The most crucial issue for Sure Start concerns its impact on children and families. Everyone – from parents, members of community, workers, to civil servants and politicians – wants to know what difference it makes. Although we concluded earlier from findings reported in this book that children in the programme are more likely to have certain beneficial experiences and less likely to have adverse ones, this is not enough. We need to know *how much* more likely are the beneficial experiences and what is their cumulative effect, at school entry as well as later in life. Integral to this is the issue of *reach*. Programmes can only have an impact on communities in so far as they reach the families for whom they are intended. Some early childhood programmes achieve a high level of reach; some do not (Weinberger et al., 1986; Hirst and Hannon, 1990; Duggan et al., 2004; Nutbrown, Hannon and Morgan, 2005). A low level of reach means that a programme, however excellent its design, is unlikely to impact at the community level. There is a need – hopefully to be met by the National Evaluation of Sure Start – for controlled studies of impact on child and family outcomes. They might include comparisons with conventional services. Local evaluations might be able to make a small contribution – perhaps more to the issue of reach than to the issue of impact where they will find it difficult to identify appropriate controls. The concept of 'reach' is a complicated one (requiring distinctions between different kinds of reach, at different times, for different kinds of families) that might be usefully explored within a single case study.

A second issue, closely related to impact, is *cost-effectiveness*. There is an understandable desire on the part of policymakers to know what it costs to achieve certain impacts. Sometimes this question is asked about Sure Start in general, sometimes about particular programmes, sometimes about services within programmes. It is a very difficult question to answer, particularly in relation to specific services within a programme because of the inter-connections between services, and the probability of the whole of a programme being more than the sum of its parts. Even at the level of the programme, there are difficulties. Programme effects can be varied and sometimes immeasurable. For example, parents' self-esteem, confidence and aspirations for their children are valuable effects, but they are not easily measured and may only emerge after years, decades or generations have passed. Sure Start is showing that social benefits – enhancing the social capital of a community – must be considered alongside more easily measurable health and education outcomes.

A third issue concerns the viability of Sure Start programmes as organizations. When one considers the difficulties experienced by the workforce (such as insecurity and professional isolation) and the difficulties faced by the programme manager (recounted in Chapter 18), it is surprising that so much has been achieved against the odds. How to reduce those odds – without reducing programmes' cutting-edge quality – is a policy challenge. It is helpful, here, to distinguish between the concept of Sure Start programmes – the integration of a wide range of community-focused services – from the organizations that deliver them. The concept appears to be robust; the organizations less so.

A vision for the future

Sure Start as we have known it in the four years of the Foxhill and Parson Cross programme is about to change. This will be the effect of new national policies (Department for Education and Skills, 2003) that envisage families with young children in disadvantaged communities being served by a system of children's centres. The future is not clear, but programmes may well become less autonomous, less community-driven and less closely linked to specific areas. On the other hand, the work may become more financially secured, more standardized, and some workers may have more security and career development opportunities. Whatever happens, we would hope that the commitment and achievements of thousands of workers and parents across the country, including those in Foxhill and Parson Cross, will not be forgotten. The lessons from this remarkable, adventurous episode in the history of early child health, care and education in England can be a basis for future developments.

Our own vision for the future is that services will be focused on areas similar in size to current Sure Start areas, that services will be provided through sustainable organizations in which there is genuine community input, that there is an integrated, secure, well-trained and well-supported workforce, that there is a balance between top-down and bottom-up influences on service development and that services reach all the families – children, mothers, and fathers too – that they are intended to benefit. Whether or not this happens will depend upon the extent of public and political commitment to families with young children and the continued readiness of workers in the field to take on new challenges. It also depends on continued learning from research and evaluation.

References

Department for Education and Skills (2003) *Every Child Matters*. Cm 5860. London: The Stationery Office.

Duggan, A.K., McFarlane, E., Fuddy, L., Burrell, L., Higman, S.M., Windham, A. and Sia, C. (2004) Randomized trial of a statewide home visiting program: impact in preventing abuse and neglect. *Child Abuse and Neglect*, 28: 597–622.

Hirst, K. and Hannon, P. (1990) An evaluation of a preschool home teaching project. *Educational Research*, 32(1): 33–9.

Nutbrown, C., Hannon, P. and Morgan, A. (2005) *Early Literacy Work with Families: Policy, Practice and Research*. London: Sage.

Weinberger, J., Jackson, A. and Hannon, P. (1986) Variation in take-up of a project to involve parents in the teaching of reading. *Educational Studies*, 12(2): 159–74.

Appendices

1 List of Sure Start services

2 Interview schedule for survey of parents of 4-year-olds, condensed version

Appendix 1
List of Sure Start services

To give an indication of the range of activities in the programme, here is a list of the services up to the time of writing. All relate to more than one objective or target, and there are many links between services. While it has not been feasible to cover the entire range of services in the chapters of this book, they all make an important contribution to the working of the programme as a whole.

The following is an alphabetical list of the main services with brief descriptions where not self-evident from the name of the service:

Antenatal workshops and educational sessions including telephone support and 'drop-in' services

Antenatal home visiting

Antenatal and breastfeeding support (see Chapter 7)

Antenatal and postnatal support groups, e.g. Babies to First Steps group and baby massage

Baby groups

Baby and infant massage

Bereavement group, a support group for parents whose baby has died.

Breast-feeding peer support and training with nationally recognized certificate from the La Léche League, a non-profit, non-sectarian organization dedicated to providing education, information, support and encouragement to women who want to breastfeed (see Chapter 7)

Children and the media – media literacy study (see Chapter 13)

Community teacher (see Chapter 11)

Connecting with our kids (see Chapter 4), groups that offer advice and help to parents who need support to manage their children

Cook and eat sessions and **Cooking on a budget**. The dietician provides advice and support on feeding problems, and supports healthy eating activities and groups.

Courses for parents e.g. Introduction to Community Development and Health, and help with accessing other courses

Crèche provision to enable parents to access meetings, activities and training

Dialogic reading (see Chapter 14)

Domestic Abuse Forum, extra help for family members who live with violence

Exercise for babies

Family support, one to one and groups (see Chapter 3). The team provides 'crisis intervention' and extra support for families who are experiencing significant difficulties. They work with families on issues such as children's behaviour problems, housing difficulties, education, benefits and so on.

Home safety service and accident prevention (see Chapter 9). The worker delivers and fits home safety equipment and offers testing of small electrical appliances and makes and fits garden fencing.

Home visiting

Lone parent group

Make It Clean Support Group, support group for families with drug or alcohol problems

Music and arts activities

'New to Area' programme, peer volunteer befriending scheme providing support for families new to the area

Newsletter for parents

Parent and toddler groups

Parent involvement in the programme. The team support and encourage families to get involved in Sure Start at varying levels, including management and development of the programme. Parents are helped to access education, training, employment and volunteering opportunities (see Chapter 15).

Parents' art group

Parents-to-be sessions

Peer support to antenatal and postnatal mothers

Pilates exercise group

Play and learning opportunities (see Chapter 10)

Pregnant teenager group

Sensory room for children with special needs

Shoppers' crèche

Sleep Clinic

Smoke cessation, work in the home and in groups

Talking Checks at 20–24 and 31–35 months (see Chapter 12)

Speech and language (play and say) playgroups with emphasis on promoting language development

Story Sacks

Teenage mothers' support group

Teenage parents' support (see Chapter 5)

Weaning your baby (Weaning Workshop)

Weight loss group

Wider Opportunities for Women (previously Women Supporting Mothers), peer volunteer befriending service to isolated women in the area

Wrap-around care, extended day care

Young Families' Advice Service, community settings offering advice around housing, debt and money management, claiming tax credits and other benefits (see Chapter 16)

In addition:

Three **family centres** – meeting place where families can come for help, advice and support

Two **community nursery and early years centres**

Support and information for all expectant parents

Support, advice and encouragement to parents wanting to return to work and practical help for parents applying for jobs

Extra services and support for families with children who have **special needs**

Extra support and activities for children with **speech and language difficulties**

Extra support for **parents experiencing problems with their children's behaviour**

Extra support in the home for all families with **a new baby** from health visitors and Sure Start workers

Appendix 2
Sure Start Fox Hill and Parson Cross/Sheffield University School of Education interview survey of parents of 4-year-olds in the Sure Start area

First of all, I wondered whether you have ever heard of Sure Start?

A About the child and family

A1   Does _____ have any older brothers or sisters?

Ages_____ Do they live at home?

A2   Does she/he have any younger brothers or sisters at home?

Ages_____

A3   Who else is there at home? [*e.g. partner/spouse*]

B Play and learning

B1   Has your child ever attended any of the following:?

	Yes	No	If yes, how often?
– a **baby group** – If yes, which one?	☐	☐	regularly/occasionally
– a **parent & toddler group** – If yes, which one?	☐	☐	regularly/occasionally
– a **playgroup** – If yes, which one?	☐	☐	regularly/occasionally
– a **nursery** – If yes, which one?	☐	☐	regularly/occasionally

– **a crèche** [If yes, supporting what
activity/activities] ☐ ☐ regularly/occasionally

– **a childminder's** ☐ ☐ regularly/occasionally

B2 Has anyone ever spent time talking with you about your child's **play
and learning**?
If yes, who was it? Can you tell me a bit about what was said?
Did it make a difference to what you did with [child]?

C   Parenting support and information:

C1 Have you ever had any problems or concerns about your child's
talking or listening?
If yes, what did you do, who did you speak to, did it help?

Was ____ referred to a speech therapist?
If yes, what happened?

C2 Have you ever had any problems or concerns about your child's
behaviour?
If yes, what did you do, who did you speak to, did it help?

C3 Have you ever had any problems or concerns about what your child
eats?
If yes, what did you do, who did you speak to, did it help?

C4 Have you ever had any problems or concerns about how your child
plays with others?
If yes, what did you do, who did you speak to, did it help?

C5 Have you had any other problems or concerns **as a parent** that we
haven't talked about yet?
If yes, what did you do, who did you speak to, did it help?

C6 Have you been to any **groups about parenting**?
(e.g. a parenting programme) *If yes*, what was it?/what were they?
Where did it take place?/Where did they take place? Was it helpful?/
Were they helpful?
Did it make a difference to what you did with [child]?

C7 Going back in time, do you remember if you went to any **antenatal groups** or **workshops**?
If yes, can you remember which ones? (e.g. breastfeeding workshops, aqua-natal, stopping smoking, one to one support, others ...)

C8 Have you been to any **other groups** at all since [child] was born that we haven't mentioned yet?
If yes, can you tell me which one/s? Do you still go? What were/are they like?
What would you say you have gained from being part of this/these group(s)?

C9 When [child] was a baby, was she/he fed on **breast** or **formula milk** (or other e.g. soya)?
If breast fed, do you remember how long for? [e.g. up to 6 weeks, 4 months, other]
Did you (or partner) have any support in breastfeeding? (e.g. visits, phone calls) *If yes*, who gave it to you? Was it helpful?
Do you remember how old [child] was when you introduced other food and drink? (Age in months).

C10 Can I ask, did you **smoke** before you knew you were pregnant with [child]?
Did you smoke while you were pregnant with [child]?
If yes, did you give up smoking at all while you were pregnant, until after __ was born? [by 6 months? by 9 months? other]
Did you start smoking again after [child] was born?
Did you or anyone else at home smoke when _____ was under 2?

C11 A lot of mothers suffer from **depression** after having a baby. Did this happen to you (your partner)?
If yes, did you (your partner) get any help?
Who gave it to you? Was it helpful?

C12 Has anyone ever got you any **safety equipment** that you needed for your child [e.g cot, highchair, fireguard, pram, safety gate, smoke alarm, car seat, other]
If yes, who gave it to you?

C13 Not everyone is clear about their entitlements. Have you had any help or advice about **benefits** or **money matters**?
If yes, who gave it to you?
Did they tell you about benefits that you were entitled to that you didn't know about before?

C14   Have you had any other **help or advice** about **looking after [child]** since she/he was born, that we haven't mentioned yet? (e.g. baby massage, young mum's group, family support). *If yes*, what was it?

C15   Have you had any other **help or advice** we haven't mentioned yet. *If yes*, what was it?

D   Parent and child together

D1   Do you ever get the chance to spend time **playing** with your child? *If yes*, can you give me an idea of how often that happens? (never, rarely, weekly, several times a week, daily, more than once a day).

D2   Do you ever sit down and **read together** with _____? *If yes*, can you give me an idea of how often that happens?

D3   Do you ever **write** with [child] or ever help her/him with writing? *If yes*, what kind of help do you give? Can you give me an idea of how often that happens? (never, rarely, weekly, several times a week, daily, more than once a day).

D4   Since leaving school have you had problems with your own **reading**, **writing** or **spelling**? *If yes*, have you had any help with this?

D5   Does your child ever **borrow toys** from anywhere? *If yes*, from where? e.g. toy library, nursery, story sacks … How often? (once a week or more / between once a week and once a month/less than once a month).

D6   Are you a member of the **library**? *If yes*, which one? Is _____ a member of the **library**? *If yes*, which one? Did you collect a Bookstart bag and books when your child was younger?

D7   Does your child ever **borrow books**? *If yes*, from where? e.g the library, nursery, story sacks, other … How often? (once a week or more/between once a week and once a month / less than once a month).

D8   Roughly **how many books** would you say ___ had of his/her own, just a guess?

D9   Has she/he had **favourite books**, or a favourite?

D10   Does your child know any nursery **rhymes** or other rhymes off by heart?

D11   How many hours would you say _____ watches **TV** or **video** a day? (less than an hour, 0–2 hours, 2–4 hours, 4+ hours).

D12   Do you ever sit with him/her and **watch TV** or **videos together**?

E   Your family's health

E1   Would you say your **child's health** has on the whole been:

good   fairly good   not good

E2   Has she/he had lots of **illnesses** or had particular health problems? *If yes*, what?

E3   Has she/he ever had been admitted to **hospital** as an emergency? *If yes*, what was this for? [gastro-enteritis, respiratory infection, severe injury, other]. How old was [child] at the time?

E4   Is your child registered at a **dentist**? If yes, does _____ attend appointments?

F   Parents' satisfaction in parenting

F1   Taking all things together, how do you feel about being a parent? Would you say it is generally:

great   mostly OK   difficult?

F2   What would you say were the best things about being a parent?

F3   What would you say were the most difficult things about being a parent?

F4 *(If applicable)* How do you think your **relationship with your partner** affects your children?

F5 *(only when interviewing parent without another adult present)* When in your home, do you ever feel concerned about your own safety, or your child's safety? *If yes*, in what way?

G Parents' background

G1 How long have you lived in this area? How do you feel about it?

G2 This is a question about local services for young children. Would you say you were very satisfied, satisfied, dissatisfied or very dissatisfied with local services for young children?

G3 Have you noticed any improvements in what's on offer to young children and their families in the time that you've lived here?

G4 Can you tell me how old you were when you left school?

G5 Did you get any qualifications (exam passes) at school?

G6 What's the highest level qualification you've got so far?

G7 Are you involved in any education or training courses at the moment?
If yes, which one(s)? Where? How did you hear about it/them?

G8 Do you think you're likely to do any education or training courses in the future?
If yes, which course(s)? How have you heard about courses?

G9 Would you mind telling me if you are receiving benefits at the moment? *If yes*, which ones?

G10 Are you involved in any community activity or voluntary work at all? *If yes*, what kind?

G11 Are you in paid employment at the moment?

G12 What is your current job or your last main job?

Ask only if a partner/spouse was mentioned earlier in interview as living at home.
G13 Can you tell me whether your [partner/spouse] is employed at the moment?

G14 Can you tell me what is your [partner/spouse's] current or last main job?

Ask <u>only</u> if the parents are unemployed <u>and</u> there is another adult at home.
G15 Is anyone else in the household employed at the moment?

H Final questions

H1 Finally, in a sentence, could you tell me what, if anything, Sure Start means to you?

I2 Is there anything you want to ask, or anything you want to add to what you have said?

Subject Index

Author index